TWENTY-ONE BOXES

Robin's Story

and

The Tragedy of the Edenton Seven

Betsy Hester
with Robin Couto

First published in the United States by IngramSpark

TWENTY-ONE BOXES: Robin's Story and the Tragedy of the Edenton Seven
Copyright © 2024 by Betsy Hester
All rights reserved.
Printed in the United States of America.

Design by Diana Wade
Original Cover design by Jim Adams, Brackonteur.com

Library of Congress Cataloging-in-Publication Data available upon request

ISBN: 979-8-9897150-1-5

First Edition: 2024
author.betsy.hester@gmail.com

To

Bryson and Charlie

and to

Haydin, Addie, Miller, and Sammy,

*our precious grandchildren, who are the same ages as
the Little Rascals children.*

*Their giggles are contagious. They see the world with
imagination and wonder.*

They don't always tell the truth.

They love to talk silly about body functions and body parts.

*They love wild and bizarre tales of flying dragons, witches,
sharks, and hot air balloons.*

They believe everything we tell them.

— Betsy Hester and Robin Couto

How can I live without my name?
I have given you my soul, leave me my name!
—Arthur Miller, *The Crucible*

Parental fears over the safety of their children spiked in the 1970s and 1980s. Those anxieties soon morphed from suspicions of strangers to fear of their children's caregivers. In 1983, a California woman accused her son's preschool of sodomy, which resulted in charges against the owner of the McMartin Preschool and six other people for heinous sexual abuse crimes against more than four hundred little children who had attended the preschool. With no verifiable physical evidence or eyewitnesses, the case eventually ended in a mistrial. The societal impacts, however, were significant. The McMartin case gave rise to a flood of startlingly similar accusations against day cares and caregivers across the country. Eventually, the hysteria made its way to Edenton, North Carolina, home of the Little Rascals Day Care, forever changing the town and the lives of the seven innocent people charged.

In the research for *Twenty-One Boxes*, I conducted nearly two dozen interviews with defendants and their court-appointed attorneys, doctors, parents, and some of the children connected to the case. Some individuals who were part of the trial are now deceased, notably both judges who sat on the bench for the first trial. Therefore, much of this investigation relied heavily on primary sources from the trials: personal letters, journals, letters from the defense attorneys, court documents, and hundreds of artifacts stored at the Duke Law Library. The items preserved at the J. Michael Goodson Law Library were the most important primary sources, including significant court documents (mainly from Robert Kelly's trial): indictment information, evidence from the trials, lists with names of the children referred to as the "indictment children," notes from police interviews, therapists' notes, summaries of parent journals, and thousands of pages of trial transcripts from Kelly's criminal trial. I also consulted regularly with experienced and respected legal minds to present a fair, critical analysis of the case.

I read and referenced numerous books and journals by leading experts, such as Maggie Bruck, Peter Ornstein, and Elizabeth Loftus, on related subjects like the reliability of memory, child witnesses, and constructed memories, as well as the research into the "satanic" sexual abuse hysteria, child molestation, the role of the media, the Salem witch trials, and investigations into the case itself and flaws in the prosecution. As much as possible, given that more than three decades have passed since this case was tried, I used trial artifacts as evidence regarding the argument that this case was a miscarriage of justice. Much of this was possible because of Lew Powell's passion for this cause. I took great care to ensure that there was evidence to support statements or assertions in this book.

In some cases, it was necessary to paraphrase some information in documents, but in most examples, the quotes are taken directly from resources, including the trial transcripts. Sources are cited in the Notes at the back of the book in the order of appearance in each respective chapter. Because of the sheer volume of pages of trial transcripts, it was impossible to include more testimonies than are here in this book. I did what I could to protect the children, so their names and some parents' names were withheld. In the case of some individuals involved, it was impossible to protect their identities and still be able to tell the truth.

The most important interview was with Robin Boles Byrum (who now goes by the name Robin Couto), the youngest defendant charged. She is the centerpiece of this book, and ten chapters are told through her voice as "Robin's Story." But her story is deeply intertwined with her co-defendants, the Edenton Seven, so this book is also a moral, ethical, and legal examination of the day care child sexual abuse case that erupted in 1988 in Edenton, North Carolina, and nearly destroyed their lives. Readers may find some of the chapters difficult, particularly regarding the testimonies from the children, parents, and university doctors. At times, those testimonies contain graphic details that some readers may find disturbing. I agree. They were disturbing. However, the truth is not always pleasant, and these details are necessary to understand how the prosecution achieved a guilty verdict.

This book is not about whether child sexual abuse is real. It is.

Instead, this book reveals how in this particular case, the evidence of sexual abuse simply was not there.

CONTENTS

FOREWORD

Betsy Hester, a celebrated English teacher, used *The Crucible* to teach literary analysis, writing, and critical thinking to generations of high school students. In *The Crucible*, Arthur Miller explored the dark social forces that were at play in the 1690s in the witchcraft trials in Salem, Massachusetts, in which more than twenty members of the community were accused, convicted, and executed, largely on the basis of children's accusations.

At one point in the play, Judge Thomas Danforth articulates the fundamental assumption of the prosecutors, namely that children's "innocence" gives them a unique ability to see the truth. Addressing John Proctor, one of the accused, he states:

"Do you know, Mr. Proctor, that the entire contention of the state in these trials is that the voice of Heaven is speaking through the children?"

As such, the prosecutors argued that accusations made by child witnesses were to be accepted, no matter how preposterous they might appear.

Fast forward to the early 1990s, when prosecutors in North Carolina operated from a similar belief system as they brought charges of sexual abuse against seven individuals associated with the Little Rascals Day Care Center in Edenton. Once again, children's reports were central, and without invoking the voice of Heaven, the argument was that these statements—even those that seemed inconceivable—must be seen as truthful accounts of what had been experienced or witnessed. So strong was this point of view that "Believe the Children" became a mantra that appeared on bumper stickers around North Carolina.

Betsy followed the Little Rascals case from the time of the initial accusations, noting the parallels between the events in Edenton and those in Salem three hundred years earlier. First, in both locales, charges were brought based on children's statements, without regard for the ways in which they might have been obtained. Second, in both places, the prosecutors failed to test alternative hypotheses and single-mindedly pursued evidence that was consistent with their beliefs. And third, fear stalked the streets of both towns because residents were being "named" by children and some of those named were threatened and pursued aggressively.

Given these and other parallels, Betsy began to think seriously about writing a book about the Little Rascals case, using Miller's play as an organizing device for exploring its complexities. As the case evolved, she became increasingly concerned about the Salem-like social hysteria that gripped Edenton and ensnared anyone associated with the day care center. But even though she became an expert on all aspects of the case—including the human costs of a modern-day witch hunt—the book remained on Betsy's to-do list for years. All of this changed when unexpectedly she came to meet one of those who had been ensnared: Robin Boles Couto.

Robin Couto was a very young preschool teacher when she joined the staff of the day care center in 1988. She taught at Little Rascals for just a few months before the allegations of abuse led to its closing, and she was the last defendant to be charged. Now, thirty years after the dismissal of charges against her, Robin was ready to revisit those very difficult years. Not only was she willing to talk with Betsy, but she was eager to join forces to ensure that the long- contemplated book became a reality. The result is *Twenty-One Boxes*, a very impressive analysis of the Little Rascals case written by Betsy, but with several unique chapters authored by Robin.

Those years of teaching *The Crucible* certainly paid off for Betsy as she organized the book. Reflecting on the miscarriage of justice in Salem, she was in a good position to raise a series of critical questions about the events in Edenton. How, for example, could so many people—including parents, attorneys, and law-enforcement officials—abandon common sense? How did a concern about one inappropriate disciplinary action get transformed into charges of sexual abuse that were eventually leveled against seven individuals? What combination of social forces and legal threats contributed to the wildfire that was consuming Edenton? These— and many other—excellent questions provide the foundation of this book. To address these questions, Betsy spent countless hours in research in various archives, in consultation with experts in law, psychology, and medicine, and in meetings with anyone associated with the case who would agree to talk with her.

The net result of these efforts is a very important contribution to our understanding, both of this case and of others in which the principles of logic are suspended and social pressure results in conformity. Betsy skill-fully places the Little Rascals case in the context of a wave of similar cases that swept the nation in the 1980s, noting prevailing—but baseless— claims of satanic ritual abuse. She focuses extensively on the ways in which parents came to believe that their children must have been abused, even though there was no physical evidence and the spatial layout of the center made it essentially impossible for the claimed abuse to have taken place. As she compellingly tells the story, both police and prosecutors played an active role in spreading these devastating but false beliefs.

Betsy then very effectively lays out the ways in which the young children—who initially denied that anything untoward had happened— were "interviewed" repeatedly over many months by police, attorneys, therapists, and parents, all of whom believed that the defendants were guilty of unspeakable crimes. And she documents how months of therapy—with therapists selected and funded by the prosecutors— resulted in the children eventually coming to indicate that their teachers were guilty. Similarly, she details the countless conversations between children and their parents that focused on getting children to confirm their parents' fears and beliefs. Importantly, once the children did just that, the authorities indicated that it was important to believe the children. Note, however, that "Believe the Children" only seemed to hold when children stated what the prosecutors and parents wanted them to say, as early denials were dismissed, as were others that did not fit with the storyline being promulgated.

In addition, looking back on the chain of events that propelled the Little Rascals case forward, Betsy shines a necessary light on the misconduct of professionals associated with its development and prosecution. As she points out, not only did the therapists approach the children with clear beliefs in the guilt of the accused, but their sessions with the children were also designed to yield evidence that was consistent with these beliefs—no matter how long it took to do so. She also directs attention to the misbehavior of the prosecutors who failed to disclose boxes of important evidence for the defense team, as required, and to the pro-prosecution bias of the judge in the trials that often left the truly heroic defense attorneys fighting as though they had one hand tied behind their backs.

One other example of misconduct is highlighted in Twenty-One Boxes, and this takes us to the unique contribution that Robin Couto makes to this book. As the newest teacher at Little Rascals, Robin watched as her colleagues—one by one—were charged and arrested. She then found herself under extraordinary pressure, as investigators pushed her relentlessly to turn on the others. When she failed to do so, indicating truthfully that she saw no evidence of abuse at the day care center, she was pressured further by being told that some children had named her as one of the abusers. Then, when she still would not provide evidence against the others, she was charged, too, with unspeakable crimes. Robin ended up spending a year in jail because of the extraordinarily high bail that was set, and during that time she was pressured to accept plea deals in exchange for turning on her colleagues. In a remarkable show of moral courage, she never did so, as she felt that she could not admit to a lie, even if doing so would enable her to save herself.

Little Rascals was the longest running and most costly case in North Carolina history, and Betsy has done us a remarkable service with this much needed and insightful book. As she amply documents, many aspects of the case were seriously flawed, but its most problematic feature—from an evidentiary standpoint—was the way in which "evidence" was obtained from the children over a period of more than two years from the presumed abuse through the trials. What can be said about the accuracy of children's statements after such an extensive period of interaction with police, parents, therapists, and attorneys? Can they be taken as accurate expressions of what had (or had not) been experienced or witnessed? Betsy argues that the children's statements were seriously tainted, and their ideas of abuse likely came from the adults with whom they interacted.

In concluding that the children's statements are essentially worthless, Betsy is backed up by more than thirty years of research in developmental and cognitive psychology on the abilities of children to accurately remember events that they have experienced or witnessed and to resist suggestions regarding events that did not take place. We know that the way children are questioned is critical for accurate reporting and that interviewers with preconceived notions pose questions in a biased manner. We also know that both repeated and suggestive questioning, as well as simple conversations with an ill-informed adult, can easily distort a young child's report and lead to the construction of a seemingly real, but nonetheless false report. And we also know that within relatively short delay intervals, young children can accurately report the details of events if they are questioned appropriately, but they do not do as well after long intervals, or when questioned suggestively. They most certainly do not do well when they have been exposed to suggestive questions and conversations over an extended period of time, and yet these are exactly the conditions that were operative in this case.

In short, as Betsy indicates in this much needed book, there was no reason whatsoever to Believe the Children who attended the Little Rascals Day Care in Edenton.

> —Peter A. Ornstein, Ph.D.
> F. Stuart Chapin Distinguished Professor, Emeritus
> Department of Psychology and Neuroscience
> University of North Carolina at Chapel Hill
> January 2024

PART I
THE DELUSION

Chapter 1

A Mutual Fate

And the cacophony rises . . . "I saw Sarah Goode . . . I
saw Goody Osborne . . . I saw Bridget Bishop . . . George
Jacobs . . . Goody Howe . . . Rebecca Nurse . . . Elizabeth
Proctor . . . Giles Corey . . . John Proctor . . . Mary Easty."
—Arthur Miller, *The Crucible*

In 1988, my husband and I were busy raising a family when news stories broke across the country of ritual child sex abuse scandals and satanic cults. In what seemed to be a hysteria reminiscent of the Salem witch trials of 1692, parents were terrified their children were in danger at the hands of trusted caregivers. As stories intensified, the naming of supposed perpetrators began. Children named adults and other children, and then it spread like wildfire, consuming everyone in its path. The delirium spread from state to state, wrapped in whispers and accusations, irretrievably damaging lives.

Without warning, a toxic poison erupted from the murky depths of the Albemarle Sound, and the past and present converged. As a result, some say, the soul of the quiet, rustic town called Edenton, North Carolina, was destroyed. The child abuse hysteria seeped into the life of Eastern North Carolina, poisoning everything it touched and shattering much of what people believed about Southern decency, truth, and goodness. By the time the stories took hold in Edenton, it was alleged that more than ninety children, the same ages as my own at that time, had been sexually abused behind the doors and windows of an established and honored day care owned by the Kellys, who were Edenton natives and friends with almost everyone in town. People were horrified and filled with fear and questions. "Who are these monsters? How could this happen?"

Like many, my husband and I followed the story from the original accusations made in early 1989 and through the subsequent trials, reading everything available. The media was our only source for what was happening in the sleepy little town less than two hours from our home. We recognized names from the news. The parent-accusers became celebrities of sorts. My attorney husband, Joe, knew many of the defense lawyers, prosecutors, and judges, whose names would forever be linked in history through their roles on both sides. It was the "Little Rascals Day Care Case," and the world would come to know the accused as the "Edenton Seven": Bob Kelly, Betsy Kelly, Dawn Wilson, Scott Privott, Shelley Stone, Darlene Harris, and Robin Byrum.

The case was filled with uncertainties. We had seen something similar only a few years earlier, when the media circulated disturbing accusations from a California case in which hundreds of children were allegedly abused. More cases alleged abuse in Massachusetts, New Jersey, New York, Tennessee, Texas, Florida, Minnesota, and Ohio—all with eerily similar accusations repeated, as if someone had hit replay. Intellectually, we struggled to accept that the allegations could have happened. The accusations of brutal rapes, sodomy, drinking blood, eating feces, oral sex with children, and even animal and human sacrifices were impossible to believe. How could such monstrous violations have happened, and in every case, no one had seen anything? No one had ever reported missing animals or a missing baby?

Months turned into years, and long after the Little Rascals trials ended, the cases were overturned on appeal. Though the charges were dismissed, my husband and I continued to talk about Little Rascals Day Care. Of the seven defendants, not one admitted guilt or turned state's evidence against the others. All seven refused to cooperate with the state in exchange for freedom or lesser sentences. Why? Who would not do that to save themselves?

This book is about nineteen-year-old Robin Boles Byrum, (now Couto), the youngest of the defendants, who was charged with twenty-three counts of sex offenses against little children. As a result of the charges and an exceedingly high bond that she could not pay, she lingered in jail awaiting trial, separated from her infant son for nearly a year. Even so, she refused the state's relentless pressure to confess to the charges. What nineteen-year-old girl with a baby at home would refuse to "tell the truth" . . . unless she *did* tell the truth—which was that nothing had happened?

Dozens of experts and researchers began to study the phenomenon, delving into the ritual abuse cases, examining the roots of the child sexual abuse hysteria, and exploring the dangers of believing charges of abuse without physical evidence or adult eyewitness accounts. Ofra Bikel's documentary, which aired on PBS on *Frontline*, brought the defendants, accusers, and trials into viewers' homes from the first charges, and Bikel's team continued covering the proceedings for over six years through the trials, verdicts, pleas, and dismissals.

Afterward, as the Little Rascals story receded from public view, it never did for us. Joe and I were convinced that nothing had happened. The pictures in the news of young Robin Byrum sitting in the courtroom, thin and pale, haunted us. We knew about the excessive bond that kept her locked up and away from her baby. We celebrated from afar when the charges were finally dropped, but as years became decades, we wondered what had happened to Robin and the others. Was she okay? Were the children involved okay? As adults, did they ever question if any of the stories were really true?

Fast-forward to April 2022. I walked into my husband's office to say "hello," which was something I rarely did. He was finishing a meeting with a female client seeking advice on a minor legal issue regarding a neighbor. Joe had no idea who she was when she came into his office. After hearing about the neighborhood conflict, he realized his partner had already talked with someone else in this case, which presented a conflict of interest, so he couldn't help her. But then she smiled and said, "That's okay. Someone told me you want to talk with me?" He was perplexed and asked, "About what?" And then she introduced herself.

When Joe saw me, he nearly fell backward, pulling me down the hall. "You have to meet someone! You have to meet this lady." Standing just outside his office was a lovely woman, smiling as if she knew me.

"Bets, you'll never guess who this is." Joe said. I couldn't, but it was obvious from his animation that she was a need-to-know. And then he said to me, "This is Robin. Robin Byrum . . . the nineteen-year-old from the Little Rascals Day Care case!" That's how much we talked about that case. Everyone knew we followed it. And everyone knew Joe. The word had gotten back to Robin, and there she was. I felt as if I was in the presence of a legend.

My husband and I had just had one of our recurring conversations about Little Rascals a few days earlier as we were planning an upcoming trip to Edenton, North Carolina, located two hours east of Raleigh and two hours southwest of Norfolk, Virginia. The town proudly boasts of a rich history. It was the birthplace of former slave and abolitionist Harriet Jacobs and an original signer of the Declaration of Independence. It has changed very little since it was founded in the early 1700s, and some of the homes located in the historic downtown date back to those early families, with some still owned by their descendants. Edenton is small, quiet, and charming.

Each spring, we rode in a coastal cycling event sponsored by Cycle North Carolina, and in 2022 Edenton would be the host city. On those weekends, we spent three days spinning around the coastal towns, along the Albemarle Sound, and through Chowan County. The coastal ride always reminded us of the Little Rascals scandal, and each year as we cycled, my husband would say to me, "Write that book."

If I have learned anything in life, it is that chance plays a part in everything that happens to us—something that proved true that day in April

2022. A long series of serendipitous events brought Robin Byrum into my life and me into hers. More than three decades since the accusations, Robin lives in quiet obscurity, many miles away from Edenton and her past. She built a new life, but the tragedy of Little Rascals Day Care never went silent for her.

Something extraordinary happened in that chance meeting at my husband's office that we both have since tried to understand and explain. Robin said she "felt as though this was meant to be . . . and somehow, I was placed there" for her. She made the intuitive observation that even the simple reason she came to seek my husband's advice on an unrelated matter was part of this moment. We embraced our mutual fate and formed a bond that freed both of us, for her to talk about her story, and for me to write this book at last.

After this meeting, Robin decided it was time to make a painful, long-avoided journey into her past. She climbed into her attic, thick with stagnant air and memories. There sat a box, containing hundreds of pages of court documents, letters, and affidavits, many of which she had never wanted to read. It was all staring back at her as she recalled the fall of 1988 and a decision that would be the darkest coincidence of all.

The emotion she locked away long ago finally caught up with her and consumed her. She began to cry the long-held tears of a damaged young mother trapped in a dangerous web that nearly cost her everything. Through all those years, no one ever told Robin's story, not even Robin. She knew she now deserved the healing that would come from purging the memories. She admitted that she still hides her experience from others, fearing they will judge her. Robin's beloved mother desperately wanted her fully vindicated but did not live to see that happen. Sadly, even now, we question, *Will Robin live to see it?* Robin's criminal record still reflects twenty-three charges related to conspiracy and child sexual abuse as "dismissed by DA," citing "no previous prison time" served. Did that year she spent in jail waiting to be bonded out simply disappear? You could argue she has been serving a life sentence ever since.

This book was a journey, like the restoration of an old house when one tears out a cabinet or rips out a wall. Underneath lies another layer, or a discovery of something else. The deeper I went into the case of the Little Rascals, the more I learned. It was like scraping away layers of generations-old paint, and all of it was necessary to understand what truly happened. For me, each discovery led to another revelation, another connection, another shared experience.

Months after Robin and I began this project, she came across a second box buried deep in the recesses of her attic. This box was filled with dozens of fading, musty letters written by her, her mother, her friends, and her supporters. Sitting amongst those letters, Robin again felt her pain rising to the surface. She relived her past, letter by letter, but it also brought more healing. Afterward, she posted to her social media about finding *"one more box of letters (the holy grail) . . . from over 30 years ago,"* and I posted a heart. She understood that I knew why this was significant.

That simple heart emoji drew Lew Powell, a retired newspaper reporter, to me, and so began our shared connection to this project. We talked regularly by phone and email, though a five-hour drive separated our homes. Lew learned about the case in 1990, and his moral outrage was exceeded only by his passion to see justice served. His website, littlerascalsdaycarecase.org, explains that he learned about the case as it spilled into the news, much like my husband and I did. But it was Ofra Bikel's *Frontline* documentary, "Innocence Lost," that bound him to the tragedy. He was deeply troubled by the inconsistencies in the case, the bizarre nature of the accusations, and the striking similarities to dozens of other cases across the country. He amassed a collection of artifacts that preserved the Little Rascals case for eternity, and his efforts are an invaluable resource for anyone interested in the truth. His passion for this case ran deep, and he wanted me to write this book. He suggested I reach out to Nancy Smith, who is the sister of Betsy Kelly—the day care owner who was one of the seven defendants. After she connected me with Betsy, and because of Lew and my own absolute persistence,

I connected with some of the children, now adults, who had made the allegations, and who'd had three decades to reflect on the event that also shaped their lives.

As this book delves into "Robin's Story," the Edenton Seven, and the Little Rascals Day Care case, the purpose is not simply to retell the events, but rather to serve as a vessel to give Robin her voice about how she was charged with unimaginable crimes against the little children in her care. Like many who have written about the cultural phenomenon surrounding the day care child sex abuse cases of the 1980s, this book attempts to understand how reasonable, intelligent, and educated people became consumed by suspicion and innuendo in Edenton. Was this a twentieth-century witch hunt?

After twenty-five years of teaching Arthur Miller's *The Crucible* to high school students, I found the connection between Edenton in the 1980s and Salem, Massachusetts, in 1692 to be haunting. Miller's play condemned two of the most significant persecutions in American history: the Salem witch trials and Joseph McCarthy's communist hunts in 1950. In both cases, the conspiracy of lies was undeniable. Sadly, collective hysteria didn't stop there or with the Little Rascals case. It proved we do not learn from our past, and Robin became my John Proctor (*The Crucible's* protagonist) in the classroom. Her story was a living, breathing example of what happens when we abandon rational thinking. There truly is a powerful link between literature and life. Hopefully, the lessons for my students were to reason critically, question deeply, and seek the truth above all else.

In John Proctor's words in *The Crucible*, as he realizes the world has gone mad: "We are what we always were . . . but now the crazy children are jangling the keys to the kingdom, and common vengeance writes the law."

CHAPTER 2

ROBIN'S STORY—THE BOX OF MEMORIES

You own everything that happened to you. Tell your
stories. If people wanted you to write warmly about
them, they would have behaved better.
—Anne Lamott

This book has been thirty-five years in the making; but then, I haven't been in a hurry. The fog of 1989 had to lift before I could see sunshine on the horizon. My memories were just that . . . a thick, consuming fog that, at times, threatened to swallow me whole. My momma, an enduring ray of hope through it all, told me "to suck it up, be strong, and most of all bloom where I was planted." I tried hard to live by her powerful words, but life happened to me, like a slow-motion, head-on collision, and it wasn't always easy to bloom or even accept the life dealt to me.

Growing up, I was mostly alone and learned how to fend for myself, not in a bad sort of way, but in a way that meant knowing how to make decisions and choices on my own. Before I knew it, three decades crawled past me. I was fifty years old and a grandmother, yet I still carried a mountain of painful experiences behind me, like a ball and chain. In 2021, I lost my mother, but truthfully, I'd lost her a few years before that when she began suffering from dementia, a disease that slowly robs its victims of their "self," their identity, their memories, and eventually, their life. What irony. I would have given anything to lose the memories of that earlier time in my own life—but that's for later.

My mother and I had grown much closer over the years since Little

9

Rascals Day Care stole time from us. Maybe this was in part because, as an adult, I knew the facts. I knew what I was charged with. I knew the date my charges were dropped. But mostly, it was possible because I knew what Momma and others who loved and supported me had sacrificed for me. December 13, 1996, the day the charges were dropped, was the day my mother finally had some peace. She consistently encouraged me to remember how much she loved me, to keep my spirits up, and not to let life make me bitter. She believed, in time, that I would be able to move on. Those words were compelling. I knew Momma never wanted me to dwell on my painful past. Neither did I. So, to defend myself against the ravages of the memories, I kept them all locked away in a box in my attic for more than three decades.

Then more pain came along. Within eighteen months, I lost my mother, one brother was diagnosed with inoperable cancer, and the other committed suicide. Sadly, I hadn't even known those two brothers existed until I was an adult. I learned about one in 1991, just as the day care scandal reached its peak, and the other became known to me much later in my life. Now, I worried I would lose him as well. All of that crashed down on me and finally broke me. Unfortunately, my family didn't fully understand, and I felt utterly alone and helpless in my grief. My husband was working extremely long hours, and my sons, now adults, didn't know the complete story because I had protected them as much as I could from my story. They knew basic facts, but they didn't know what they didn't know—the agonizing details that still caused me so much pain.

Meeting Betsy Hester that day in her husband's office was one of many events in my life that I couldn't explain, but it moved me to a place I hadn't been to in a long time. After we agreed to work together, I called my dear Aunt Penny. She, Uncle Scotty, and Aunt Sue were the village that helped raise me. I told her, "Finally, I am going to tell my story." They were so excited and made me promise to hurry it up!

It struck me when I sat down with that box of artifacts, the one I had long refused to open, that I had never looked at the paper from all those years ago that declared the charges against me. I feared that bin was my Pandora's box. I didn't want to open it because it would release the furies and drag me back to the shadows of 1989. I feared any contact with the contents, or anyone associated with it, as if Little Rascals would ooze back into my life, one malignant memory by one malignant memory. I wasn't sure how this story would evolve, or if that even mattered. I could pretend Little Rascals didn't happen. But no matter how hard I tried, I couldn't hide from the ghosts of my past.

I decided I was tired of being held hostage to the memories, and with Betsy Hester's help, I was finally going to put my story down on paper.

Lurking in the dark was that blue-gray tub, a container full of every-thing my family and I endured because of the Little Rascals allegations. Once or twice, I peeked inside at the curled newspaper clippings, folded magazine articles, and dozens of manila envelopes full of court motions and judicial orders. Mixed together were "Thinking of You" cards, crumpled notes of encouragement, fading letters from lawyers, notes by prosecutors, rulings by judges, articles from newspapers and magazines. Alongside all of that were the letters from my grandfather, who faith-fully wrote several times a month to encourage me. I wanted those letters separated, fearing the rest would contaminate them. His words were too pure to be boxed with the bad, and I cherished every word he put on each piece of paper. His letters were long, sweet, rambling pages filled with words of much-needed love and hope during my darkest moments. Even decades later, I could hardly get through them without tears flooding back, recalling our shared agony.

Inside that box was my past, those lost years. I hadn't read any of the letters from family and friends since each one arrived through the prison mail system way back when. Like my emotions, I'd buried those artifacts where the world would not find them.

Though I probably should have, I never sought help in the form of therapy to deal with any of it. Long ago, Aunt Penny worked as a head nurse at the VA Hospital in Lexington, Kentucky. For years, she helped veterans with PTSD, and she believed that I suffered from it too. I'm sure she was right, but I couldn't talk about that trauma.

As part of my bond release during the trial, I was ordered to "stay away from Edenton," a line I never crossed and never wanted to cross. Honestly, I wanted to forget everything about Edenton and the Little Rascals case. I wanted to move on. I especially refused to cry. But I knew I needed to. I needed to cry deeply with the bone-crushing cry, a weeping that rocks a body to the core, so intense, so profound that it reaches into the soul. How could I?

Until that chance meeting in a lawyer's office, I'd run from my story. I absorbed myself in raising a family and very deliberately saturating my time with busyness. Why? Because I feared the quiet, the nighttime when memories might seep back into my life, and I simply couldn't bear that feeling again.

Everyone around me watched me immerse myself in one project after another. I was forever painting a room in my house for the umpteenth time, and starting and restarting a garden in my yard, staying occupied with anything that allowed me to lose myself and keep the memories away. I was afraid, really afraid, to stay idle too long. It wasn't so much that I had excess energy to release; instead, I didn't want the flashbacks to penetrate the wall I had built around myself.

I'm unquestionably not over it. Perhaps, after so many years, I should be. Still, the lies that were told, the accusations that were made, and the weeks that turned to months didn't just rob me of nearly eight years of my youth. They robbed me of my baby, my mother, and my grandparents. How could I ever forgive the people who did this to me? I didn't do any of the dreadful things they accused me of. Yet I was thrown into prison and deprived of my freedom and my family, constantly tormented by a fear that they might come back and take me away again.

It was finally time. I took out a legal pad and unpacked my past for the first time since it all happened. Once I began, the floodgates ruptured, and I couldn't stop. I journaled for days and weeks in a feverish attempt to release the demons. As the memories poured out, I realized I needed to remember. And then it happened. The inevitable seismic wave of Little Rascals Day Care finally crashed in on me.

CHAPTER 3

ROBIN'S STORY—MERE HAPPENSTANCE

Being a mother is the biggest gamble in the world . . .
and an act of infinite optimism.
—Gilda Radner

Much of my life's story is the one my mother told me, and that story was built by her life decisions and the moves that we made together right up to 1988. But to understand how the pages of my life's story fit together and how I ended up at Little Rascals Day Care, I must go back . . . way back . . . to my beginning.

My very first chance meeting was the day I was born. There I was, coming into the world at a strange crossroad in the universe, a sort of blur of time and chance. Growing up, Momma loved telling me the story of how I came to be her baby. It was back in 1970 when she was working at a hospital in Orlando that specialized in labor and delivery. This hospital was known for helping women put up their babies for adoption. One day a young woman came in, already in labor and ready to deliver me. When she got there, she told the staff that she already had one child, a two-year-old boy, a brother I would not learn about for many years. My birth father did not want me, so he gave her $100 to abort me. Instead, she took off for Florida, and I was born right there in that hospital that day.

When the doctor delivered me and then placed me into the hands of the person who would be my new momma, the doc said, "Lou, we have a baby girl. You want her?" Momma was married to a nice man, and she wanted a baby. But she knew adopting me would change things, and it was likely she would be raising me by herself. But honestly, I think that was okay with her because she was fiercely independent, and maybe that's why she was working at the hospital to start with. Had those first decisions by my birth mother or the woman who would become my Momma been altered slightly one way or another, my life would have been very different . . . or I would not have lived at all.

After three days, the hospital let Momma take me home, but she certainly wasn't ready for that; after all, it wasn't like she'd been pregnant and had nine months to plan. It is an understatement to say she was unprepared for me. To complicate things, I was born with foot and leg problems and had to be in a cast for months, plus a brace for several more months before anything else could fall into place. Now, it wasn't part of her plan to stay married, but she needed help. As a single mother, she knew she would need her Kentucky family. She made plans with my grandparents, who would help orchestrate our move to Kentucky. My Pap-pa stopped everything he was doing and drove from Kentucky to Florida to pack up the truck. Then Momma and I headed home to our new life and to where the next chapter of my life's book would begin.

Once in Kentucky, we moved in with Aunt Penny and Uncle Scotty, whom I would grow to love very much. In no time at all, Momma found a job at the University of Kentucky. After about a year, we saved enough money for a place to rent. After nearly two years, we had enough money to buy our own home. That's when Pap-pa and Mam-ma moved close to Momma and me because she worked long hours at the hospital, and I needed someone to be there for me.

Momma had a small army to look after me. We had good neighbors who pitched in, as well as my grandparents who helped on nights and weekends when Momma was on call, and the nice lady next door who helped the most. She was a single mother, too, and she took me to Girl Scouts and Bible school—all the things Momma didn't have time to do. For a while, another neighbor was there for me when I got off the bus . . .

until something happened with one of her boys. I was only seven years old and can't remember what that boy did to me, but Momma never talked about it again. All I knew was that was the end of that, whatever *that* was, and I never stayed with that family again.

From then on, Momma decided I was old enough to have a key to the house to let myself in, get my own snack, and wait until she got home from work. I was what everyone called a "latchkey" kid, and there were plenty of us in the 1970s. But she believed she could trust me. I was a good girl, and I always did what she told me to do. Frequently, my grandparents would call and check on me, and sometimes my Aunt Penny or my grandparents would come to sit with me until Momma got home. I was always happy when they came to be with me because I didn't like to be alone in the house.

When I was nine, my grandparents and Momma had the idea that we should all move to a farm in the country where we would live together, along with Momma's brother and his family. It was far from the city and all my friends, and I was lonely except for my baby cousin to keep me company. It was no surprise that I became especially close to him. He was a real sweet spot in my life, and this was the first time I realized just how much little kids would mean to me. I loved the responsibility of taking care of him with my grandmother by my side.

Unfortunately, the situation didn't work out so well, and things were about to change again. An old house on the property suddenly burned down, and everyone said my uncle did it for the insurance money. Things got ugly after that, with lots of yelling, screaming, and threats. All of that was enough to shake up my mother, and she realized she didn't want to build our house, our world, in the middle of that farm. When my grandparents grasped the reality that we were leaving, they tried to convince Momma to stay, but she was stubborn and refused to live next door to her brother. That ended my grandparents' dream of all of us being together. They adored me, and that separation proved to be hard on all of us, since they were my constant while Momma worked long hours.

Momma's decision, in a few short years, would rewrite my future and change our lives more than we could imagine.

Once Momma made up her mind to do something, she didn't stop. She saw a job posted in a medical magazine, applied for it, got an interview, and off we went. Momma, Aunt Sue, and I drove all the way across North Carolina to a peculiar little town called Edenton. The obvious problem with moving to Edenton was that we would be so far away from our support system. But Momma said, "We are starting fresh," and I knew she wasn't afraid to live away from family, considering she had done that since she was eighteen years old. She had been the only one in her family courageous enough to venture out of Kentucky. In fact, after graduation, she went straight into the Army, which took her across the country from Denver to Texas. She then moved to Florida . . . to me . . . to Kentucky . . . to Edenton . . . and to my destiny.

Momma and Aunt Sue promised our trip would be an event—an adventure! And it was. In 1982, we took old Highway 64, a two-lane road that traveled through dozens of small towns. Most of them were not unlike Edenton. These towns were spread out all along the way, and any one of them could have been a new place for us to build a life. But no, we were headed to Edenton.

The drive took us four or five days to get there and back. When we arrived in Edenton, I was surprised there was only one tiny hotel, the Coach House Inn, where we stayed for two days, one day for the interview and one day to recover before making our way back to Kentucky. It was no surprise that Momma got the job, and in the summer of 1982, she and I moved to Edenton. Eventually, Momma was promoted to the head of the anesthesia department at Chowan Hospital, which was unheard of for a nurse, but it was a small rural hospital with no anesthesiologist on staff. That meant more money for us, so we bought a house, but it also meant more responsibilities for her with more work, longer hours, and way too much time alone for me. I was a very lonely eleven-year-old. But time did what time does, and it moved on.

Eventually, Edenton came to feel like home to both Momma and me. We shopped at all the local stores, got to know folks, and made a life for ourselves. When Momma had a night off, one of our favorite pastimes was to visit the local video store to rent one of the newest movies on VCR tape. We lived in fear that one of those tapes would get stuck in our video player, and we'd have to pay for a new tape because the man who owned the store always charged more to replace it than it would cost to buy it anywhere else in town.

Before I knew it, I was a teenager. I made friends easily, and honestly, life for me was mostly normal and happy. Eventually, I even had boyfriends. The first one was at fourteen, ending with the painful breakup that happens in young love, and the next one was at seventeen. He was the one who would become a central player in the next chapter of my life's book. Sadly, Momma still worked all the time, meaning she wasn't around to help me work through the breakups or to help me make adult-like decisions I wasn't ready to make. I just had to take control and figure things out on my own.

One way I took control was by working. I liked being busy, and I liked making my own money, so I found jobs tutoring kids, working at a tanning and beauty salon, hostessing at a local restaurant, and even typing for a local author. I mostly loved working with kids, so I babysat often. One family in particular liked and trusted me a lot, so I sat for them regularly. They trusted me so much they even took me on their family vacations and paid me really well.

But I knew I didn't want to babysit for the rest of my life. My real dream after high school was to be an airline stewardess. Graduation was in June, so Momma and I met with someone from a potential school in Florida. Afterward, they left papers for Momma and me to sign. I wouldn't turn eighteen until December, so she had to sign for me. Yes, indeed—I had a plan. But, as it turned out, my story was about to take a different twist.

At the time, my boyfriend Kevin was a constant in my life. Although

I wasn't old enough to sign a legal document, I was old enough to fall in love. Or so I thought. Kevin was cute. He made me smile. He filled a lonely spot in my life and made me feel needed. But more, he needed me. At seventeen, how could I know whether he was good for me? It wasn't long before we were doing what young kids in love sometimes do. We thought we were so smart. We knew where we could be alone, and we'd sneak to his grandmother's apartment to fool around . . . always careful not to risk me getting pregnant.

I graduated in June but was suddenly unsure about my future if it meant leaving Kevin. That summer, my best friend, Wendy, told me about an opening at a local day care center called Little Rascals. She said her future sister-in-law, Betty Ann, had worked there for a couple of years and really liked it. Betty Ann's little boy was there, too, and he also loved it. Wendy thought it might be a good fit for me because of my experience with kids. Since all my friends were headed off to college, and I had Kevin in my life to complicate things, I wasn't so sure about working for an airline anymore. Besides, I loved kids. Maybe this was a perfect fit.

That summer changed everything for both of us. We were young and naive, and we weren't careful. We didn't really think about what was ahead of us. In hindsight, I realize he didn't want me to go to stewardess school or have a future without him. If I was pregnant, I would be tied to him for life. And suddenly, we were going to be parents. Were we ready? Was I ready? No. But it didn't matter. Looking back, it all seems like a terrible collision with fate. We would soon have a baby coming, but he wouldn't arrive until after my world had turned upside down.

CHAPTER 4

STRANGE BEHAVIOR AND INVISIBLE CRIMES

No account of the dreadful tragedy [is] more accurate
or truthful than Governor Hutcheson's narrative . . . his
theory was . . . that it was wholly the result of fraud and
deception on the part of the afflicted children.
—*The Witchcraft Delusion of 1692*

Many have studied and written about the ritual child abuse scandals of the 1970s and 1980s. But the one that mattered to Robin Byrum in 1989 was the witch hunt that started in Edenton and centered around parents' fears and suspicions of their toddlers' strange behaviors—bedwetting, tantrums, soiling pants, baby talk, and waking from bad dreams. For Robin and others who lived through the Little Rascals case, a disturbing interconnection across time takes us back to early colonial America. However, the residents of those early American colonies did not invent the diabolical conspiracy. It has been around since the dawn of time. Thousands, perhaps millions, have been charged with compacting with the devil and practicing witchcraft across the centuries.

The malevolent similarities between Edenton and Salem and the superstitions that took root in both places were astounding. Both communities were small coastal towns founded long before the Revolutionary War, communal in a sense, deeply religious, and similarly divided economically, politically, and socially between powerful, wealthy families and the laborers who supported their lifestyles. Many superstitious practices connected to witchcraft were linked directly to their slaves and indigenous peoples, both of whom they desperately feared, only to be accepted by willing believers and promoted by unlikely interlocutors. Clearly, social divisions, religious anxiety, and superstition contributed to the hysteria that erupted. The townspeople also suffered from uncontrollable guilt that was fed by religious fanaticism. Mixed with malicious vindictiveness, it was a dangerous combination that made it especially menacing and damning for anyone accused.

Similar to Little Rascals' parents, Salem's colonial villagers feared unexplained and strange behaviors in their children. They readily blamed those doings on "dark magic, witches, the invisible, and the devil."[1] Most dangerous of all was their unholy "preoccupation with the sexual side" of witchcraft, with rampant beliefs that "Satan had sex slaves... and witches frequently engaged in sexual practices"[2] with Lucifer himself.

Communities across colonial North Carolina were no strangers to the belief in the supernatural for evil purposes. One only needs to read *Witchcraft in North Carolina*, which contains multiple accounts of "hags and cats bewitching" neighbors.[3] These beliefs were clearly irresistible, along with the pervasive belief that Satan was (and likely still is) loose in North Carolina.

Much of the fear from the mountains to the coast was fed by outrageous claims of witchcraft. It was not uncommon for villagers and town folk to gather to talk about witches, conjuring, hags, ghosts, compacts with Satan, shapeshifting, and sex with old Beelzebub. And it was known that doctors frequently attributed diseases of unknown origin to "supernatural agencies of the malignant kind." To cure unknown illnesses, they would prescribe things such as "drawing a picture of the witch on a piece of wood and shooting it with a silver bullet." Animals could also be possessed by Satan. "Cattle and hogs supposed to be under the spell of witchcraft" were branded with a hot iron and then "burned to ashes." Women, believed to have compacted with Satan, were tried by "witch swimming."[4] The accused was tied to a chair and dunked in a river or lake. If they floated, they were guilty of witchery. If they sank, they were innocent. One must wonder how many passed that test.

Edenton had its very own celebrity, Dr. John Brickell, who settled in Edenton in the early 1700s, not long after the end of the hangings in Salem. He practiced medicine, but he became most notable for his publication of *A Natural History of North Carolina*, said to be a "grotesque" work that was "largely compiled" through plagiarism. He took nearly word for word from the works of other authors, such as John Lawson, an earlier author of *History of Carolina*, who wrote about "Hobgoblins and Bugbears" who suckled the souls of "white men" through witchcraft.[5]

Though I could not locate a documented case of anyone being hanged in or around Edenton for the practice of witchcraft, there were abundant stories of suspected witches all along the coastal areas expelling "foul objects, pins and needles," or "transformation by witch ointment." Brickell wrote extensively about the "great Inchanters" and their use of "many Charms of Witchcraft." He claimed to know for a fact that their "Conjurations" caused huge "Firestorms" that had the "strong smell of Brimstone." He was well-known for "prescribing remedies of reptilian origin," such as cutting a live toad in half to be placed on the bite of a rabid dog to draw out the poison.[6]

Witchcraft in Salem was well documented. Salem parents were known to seek fortune tellers, experts of the time, in search of explanations for the strange behaviors in their children, especially their daughters. Not lost in this, and not unlike Salem's fortune tellers, the therapists of the Little Rascals case interpreted "normal behaviors" through a sort of checklist that, to them, "suggested abuse." [7]

Both the Salem and Edenton witch hunts began with one individual. In Salem in January 1692, Rev. Samuel Parris, the local minister, possessed an insidious paranoia toward members of his congregation. He believed they were out to get him, and all historical evidence points to him as the instigator for the original calling out or naming of people as witches. He was bent on protecting himself and sought revenge against his perceived enemies. That, combined with his "deep concern with Satan," made him particularly lethal to anyone in his way.[8]

In the meeting house, his small congregation was segregated much the same as the town: supporters of Parris sat in the front, men and women were separated by the center aisle, adults were separated from children, and servants were separated from slaves. He was preaching his weekly sermon full of hellfire, brimstone, sin, and the "drift of the Devil to pull [them] down."[9] Tituba, Parris's slave, watched Parris's niece and another girl whispering during the sermon, something strictly forbidden. But there were whispers in town as well. Over previous weeks, other village parents had noticed their daughters behaving strangely—solemn, sullen, and hysterical. Things went missing. Had the girls been stealing eggs to play fortune-telling? It was a common "vain curiosity" for village women to drop an egg white into a glass of beer and water to look for predictions of a future husband in the way the white curled and moved in the beer.[10]

In his book, *The Devil in Massachusetts*, Marion Starkey traced the trial records of the Salem witch trials and noted that parents were troubled by the continued strange behavior of the girls. They became obsessed with trying home remedies for the "afflictions," before turning to prayer and finally to a local physician, Dr. Griggs, who had a limited "medical vocabulary" to diagnose the girls' afflictions. He eventually ruled out all possibilities but one: "The evil hand is on them." Parents became more desperate for answers as their behaviors grew more concerning. Parris's daughter, Betty, was the first to show signs of "hysteria," and he was compelled to prove there was "no negligence on his part." The villagers learned that Parris's daughter was showing signs of being tortured by spirits, so the "decision was reached . . . that the girls must name their tormentors . . . [so they could] be brought to justice."[11]

The girls used folk magic, strictly forbidden by the church, and when Parris caught them, their fear of punishment drove them into fits of terror. Starkey's research showed it was "the fact that [at that time] the girls craved . . . [sexual] mysteries" and were rebelling "against every restriction placed on them by adult society." At the same time, they were "having a wonderful time" with the "notoriety and attention." Later, a powerful prosecutor for the courts, Rev. John Hale, damningly wrote he feared "the hand of Satan was in them." As he and other powerful ministers asked the girls "who afflicted them," the girls "drew blank [and] fell dumb." They insisted, "No one afflicted us; it just happened." But the court knew "the witches could not be identified without the help of the girls . . . and they must somehow be made to . . . name their tormentors." With each interrogation, the girls' afflictions grew more troubling and bizarre, and the investigators demanded, "Who torments you?" It was then that Parris "found his mind turning to Tituba."[12]

Curiously, while all this was happening, the village mothers continued to seek the help of experts in folk magic. Mary Sibley, a neighbor and parishioner of Parris's, supposedly visited Tituba to ask her to make a "witch-cake . . . using her [daughter's] urine mixed with rye meal, formed into a small cake, baked in hot ashes, and then fed to the [family] dog." They believed this "witch-cake" could be an antidote to someone else's harmful magic and perhaps could even cure the children.[13] Unfortunately, as the relentless mothers sought more and more folk magic, matters worsened. The more they pursued it, the more the girls' "agitation increased." In turn, the children became desperately frightened by suggestions that Satan and witches were coming after them, and their behavior escalated into a frenzy. From the moment Parris discovered what had happened, he relentlessly questioned and violently threatened his daughter, and the "tragic little Betty" sobbed what sounded "like an accusation," whimpering out, "'Tituba . . . she . . . oh Tituba.'" The "other girls, faced with evidence, agreed to charge" their tormentors.[14]

What began with the accusation against Tituba soon turned to Sarah Goode and Sarah Osborne, and all three women were powerless or outliers in this society. The naming evolved over the months into charges against many, and most were common folk at first. Rebecca Nurse, one of the most famous accused, was hanged. One man, Giles Corey, was pressed to death with massive stones for refusing to confess. John Proctor, the protagonist in both the real-life tragedy and Arthur Miller's stage version, *The Crucible*, was hanged in the end for refusing to confess—not even to save himself.

Before long, the naming spiraled out of control, with the girls pointing fingers at more and more people, up to and including the wives of judges and even judges themselves. Before the frenzy ended, dozens were jailed, and twenty were executed by hanging. Henceforth, history would forever remember a group of little girls who turned loose the invisible world and started the Salem witch trials of 1692.

History has taught us very little, and conspiracies continued to spring up over the centuries. Richard Gardner, a child psychiatrist, wrote extensively about child abuse. Though he was highly criticized for his controversial theory called "Parental Alienation Syndrome," he eventually demanded a more scientific approach to investigating child sexual abuse. In 1990, he published *Sex Abuse Hysteria: Salem Witch Trials Revisited*, explicitly about false allegations in the child abuse scandals. In his view, the world was "witnessing the third greatest wave of hysteria ever seen in this country. The first was the Salem witch trials, lasting months; the second was the McCarthy era, which lasted four years; and the third hysteria, the Ritual Child Abuse Scandals, lasted over a decade." [15] In an all too familiar way, the scandal consumed Edenton with a prodigious fear of invisible crimes against the little children. Those little children began naming names, which propelled Edenton into what many refer to as a modern-day witch hunt—one that entangled seven unsuspecting adults working at a simple day care.

CHAPTER 5

Robin's Story—A Quiet Tranquility

If you want to assert a truth, first make sure it is not just
an opinion that you desperately want to be true.
—Neil deGrasse Tyson

It was August 1988, and I was no closer to deciding about my future than I was in June. How could I have known what was to befall me when I made that call to Little Rascals to talk with Betsy Kelly, the owner and operator?

"YES, we are hiring!" she said.

"Could I come down for an interview?" I asked her.

At the time, I thought perhaps if I got this job, it could carry me for a few months until I decided on my next step. I went that same day. She asked me to come during naptime so we would have some quiet time to talk.

When I met her, my instincts told me, *She's nice and kind.* Betsy liked my babysitting background but was a bit concerned about my age. She worried I might be too young to be responsible for a room full of toddlers alone. She also worried that state regulations for operating a day care may not allow it. If Betsy Kelly was anything, she was careful about her kids. But since I was there, she wanted to observe me interacting with the children and to see how the kids reacted to me. I distinctly remember thinking, *It's a crowded house, with sweet little kids lying everywhere at naptime, just little people snoring and dreaming.* I thought they needed more space. She must have sensed my unease because she assured me they were moving to a new building very soon. I stayed for a long time that afternoon, getting to know the kids, taking them to the bathroom, picking up nap mats, and simply playing with them. They were such a happy group of toddlers. I was in heaven.

Betsy Kelly checked my references and, within days, got back to me, telling me I had the job. I was to start as soon as they moved to their new building, if not sooner. She wasn't sure exactly what class I would be in, but she liked me, the kids liked me, and she wanted me on her staff. I accepted the job and started a few weeks later, in mid-September, in the brand-new day care building that was a daytime home and safe place for dozens of giggling, screaming, laughing, and affectionate little kids of all ages.

The new building was spacious enough for our big day care family to move around, play, and learn. There were five classrooms, a dining room, a kitchen, and a large play area in the back. The rooms at the front of the building had huge windows with no curtains or blinds, letting in lots of light and giving it an open feeling. It was cute to see moms often walking by, peeking through as they arrived to pick up their precious cargo. Moms and dads came in at all hours from morning to evening to collect their children, to say "hi" to staff, and sometimes just to drop in and check on their kids during their own lunch hours. Every room also had a red emergency exit that was always locked for safety and led directly to the outside. Otherwise, it was an open, lively space.

At first, I floated from classroom to classroom in the mornings to help out and then supervised the after-school children in their own special space in the front of the building. We were right next to the two- and three-year-old class, and next to them were the four- and five-year-olds. Eventually, Betsy put me in charge of the two- and three-year-olds. It was amazing to have my own room to decorate, plan a schedule, and be responsible for my kids. The class had about ten children, a designated play area outside, and a shared lunchroom.

Everyone at Little Rascals was very close, even the parents of the children. There was a "quiet tranquility," an expression that Lynne Layton, one of the accusing parents, would later claim to Ofra Bikel was "a cover-up for what was really happening in that building."[1] This was also when I became friends with two of my colleagues, Shelley Stone, who taught the four- and five-year-olds, and Dawn Wilson, who prepared all the food for the day care. Though I didn't interact much with the babies or older kids, I also became friends with Betty Ann Phillips because her son was in my room. My kids were happy. Their parents were happy. I never had problems with temper tantrums or behavior issues of any kind. No one ever complained.

By January 1989, I had been working there barely three months. With the bitterness of winter, there was suddenly a cold kind of tension, and trouble was brewing at Little Rascals that extended into Edenton. Whispers were spreading that a mother thought Bob, Betsy's husband, had done something to one of the children. But what? None of us could figure out what he was supposed to have done.

That was when I decided to tell my Momma I was pregnant. No one else knew, and no one could tell I was almost five months pregnant. Telling Momma wasn't going to be easy. I was afraid she might send me away when she found out I was going to have a baby. After all, Momma's rules were Momma's rules. It was her house, and she could be very military-like. When she talked, I listened, and I never interrupted her in any way. With my fear fully loaded, I slowly walked into the room. Momma was lying down in the den watching TV when I asked to speak with her. As I gathered my courage, I begged her not to get mad or to raise her voice. I blurted out my news. "Momma, I'm going to have a baby." She didn't utter a word. There was nothing but a long silence. She hung her head, looking sad, then slowly got up and began talking. She wanted to tell me her own story.

In a quiet and measured voice, Momma began, "When I was in the Army at nineteen, I got pregnant and gave my son up for adoption." I was in absolute shock. At that moment, I forgot about my own dilemma.

She went on, "I went through the entire pregnancy without telling my parents back in Kentucky." At nineteen, Momma was utterly alone in her predicament, so she moved to a group home for unwed mothers in Texas, where she had her baby. This was why she didn't yell at me. Momma wasn't angry with me at all. She understood.

Then Momma did what she did best. She went quickly into fix-it mode and told me what we could do now. First, she suggested I could give up my child for adoption.

Shocked, I shouted, "Absolutely NOT!"

With that, she assured me that she would help me with certain things, but she wanted it clear that she would not be responsible for my child. "You might just have to go on welfare," she said. She also wanted to know about Kevin and his family, declaring, "I do not want them parading through my home when the child comes, so you'd better find a place of your own." My path . . . Momma's path . . . our paths . . . happenstance.

That same day, I told her about the rumors about Bob at the day care. People were saying he had touched some of the kids, and the Department of Social Services people were coming to the day care. Now, they wanted to talk with me, and I was worried. All of us at the day care were stressed. The intensity of the interviews was increasing, and questions were flying. "What happened to the children? Who did what?" By then, rumors about little kids and sexual abuse at the day care were all over town. We were all worried about where this was headed.

After hearing this, Momma thought it was odd they were coming to talk to me and the other workers. She wondered aloud, "Why?" She was justifiably concerned, but in her natural optimism, she assured me I would be fine. She told me, "Go in there and just be honest. Tell the truth, and everything will be okay."

When I was interviewed the first time, I certainly didn't know what to expect. There were plenty of rumors and whispers, but people weren't talking to us. We heard people saying Bob had done something ugly and had touched one of the children. But none of us knew anything or had seen anything because there was absolutely nothing to see. It wasn't true. After all, he was hardly ever there. We all answered the questions the same way. In the first interviews, DSS mostly asked about daily routines at the day care, especially how often Mr. Bob was in the building and what he did while he was there. Then the number of interviews increased.

Sometime shortly after that, Betsy called us together. We had already heard the rumors, but she wanted to tell us why we were being interviewed: there was an allegation against Mr. Bob, and he would no longer be at the day care. At that time, I didn't think any of it concerned me, and neither did my mother. We both trusted and believed that if I told the truth, no matter what was going on, everything would be okay for me.

Over the next several days, some of the parents began pulling their children out of the day care. More rumors circulated. But still, I wasn't worried about being in trouble. I had done nothing wrong. I just worried about not having my job anymore, because I really needed it now with a baby coming. I continued to work at Little Rascals until the doors closed for good in April. Between January and April, half the kids in my class stopped coming. Yet some stayed, despite the rumors. I don't recall how many workers stayed, but there were several of us. I needed to work.

Chapter 6

Robin's Story—A Waiting Game

I will say it, if it is my last time, I am clear of this sin.
—Mary Easty, 1692, in
History of the Salem Witch Trials

While Little Rascals Day Care was collapsing around me, I still felt safe. The kids loved me. I had done nothing wrong. Their parents loved me, or so I believed, but that was about to change.

After her first few meetings at the day care with other employees, the lady from the Edenton Police Department called and asked if I would be willing to come to the station to answer some questions. I was reluctant because I was only eighteen and really didn't know much about the day care. I had only been there a few months. I couldn't imagine what else I could give them information-wise, but I asked my mom if I should go. We talked about it and both decided I should. After all, I didn't know anything, and there was nothing I could tell the woman.

Officer Brenda Toppin was the first investigator to interview me one-on-one in February. She took me into her office, and we were alone in the room. I don't recall Toppin taping the interview, but I don't think she did. She did have a notepad that she occasionally wrote in. The interview took about an hour. She seemed nice enough, but she told me that she knew things had happened at the day care, and that I only needed to tell her what I knew about Bob being there. Specifically, she wanted to know the same things we had all been asked before: how often was Bob Kelly at the day care, and what did he do when he was there?

I told her that at the beginning of the new day care opening, Bob was there a lot, usually in the early mornings, to make sure everything was running smoothly, and he checked on things like electrical stuff, traffic patterns, parking, and playground areas. I also told her Bob had little to do with the kids except to say hello and goodbye to them. He received an occasional hug from his niece, nephew, and daughter, who were all there. But otherwise, he had no physical contact with my kids or anyone else's that I ever saw. If something needed to be fixed or improved, Betsy asked us to make a note of it, and she would give it to Bob. Once the classroom was mine, I realized I needed more built-in cabinets, so Bob added them for me sometime around late October or early November. I wasn't sure about the date. But after the opening, things calmed down, and I may have seen Bob once a week, but no more than that.

I told Officer Toppin all of that, everything I could, everything I knew, but it seemed clear she wasn't satisfied. Before leaving her office, she pressed me by saying "If you remember anything at all, call me immediately and come back to my office."

By the end of April, the rumors took hold, Bob was accused, and the day care was closed. Kevin and I were in the Roses Department Store in Edenton. We were shopping for the baby, and I was very pregnant. We were excited and on a mission for baby boy things that day. While we were there, I saw one of the children from my class. She and her mother, Lynne Layton, were holding hands and walking around the store. I was happy to see them. We spotted each other at the exact moment, and I remember the daughter's reaction when her eyes met mine. We were about forty feet apart, and she let go of her mother's hand and ran to me, shrieking, "Miss Robin! Miss Robin!" Her mother was browsing through items on a rack but seemed startled when she realized it was me, and she frowned as she saw her child run to me. I tried to bend down the best I could at eight months pregnant. She just grabbed me and hugged me around my neck.

Yet it was strange the way Lynne looked at me and then carefully, almost cautiously, made her way toward her daughter and me with a peculiar look in her eyes. She was visibly uncomfortable, and I could tell she wanted nothing to do with me. What she seemed to want was for her daughter to back away. I kept talking to "E" while trying to ignore her mother's anxiety and asking about her day, and then I told her how much I missed her. With that, she had the biggest grin and said, "I miss you too!" By this time, Lynne seemed to be attempting to get away from me and muttered something like, "We need to get going . . . now." I said goodbye to both of them.

That was the last time I would see them until the trials. I knew something was going very wrong for me that day, and my heart broke. It was unmistakable that Lynne Layton was troubled about me, and even though I hadn't done anything, I began to realize people were listening to the lies, and some might be about me.

My sweet little boy was born in June, shortly after that meeting in Roses. It was the happiest day of my life. Kevin and I started planning our wedding for September, and he and I found a cheap single-wide trailer on the outskirts of town. Momma bought it for us and told us once we were married, we could pay her for it on a monthly schedule. She agreed to help us with necessities so we could get on our feet. Kevin also found a job at a local mill, and we were finally starting our life together.

By the time I had my next interview, Bob and Betsy had both been arrested, and all of us at the day care were terrified. It was late in the summer, and this time law enforcement came to my home. Momma was frantic because it included the State Bureau of Investigation. This was the first time I met Agent Kevin McGinnis, and he had one other SBI agent with him who also came to our door. McGinnis insisted that Momma could not be in the same room while they interviewed me, which alarmed Momma. She called a local attorney to see if they could legally interview me alone and was told, "Yes. She is of legal age, and yes, they can."

Unlike the interview with Toppin, the SBI agents turned on a recorder for the interview. They were only there for thirty minutes, but it felt like an eternity. During the interview, the agents informed me that "most of the day care kids were now in therapy," and the children were "implicating lots of people . . . but not you." That pause. It frightened me. He advised me that all I needed to do was tell them what I knew about Bob and Betsy. Seriously? What was I going to say to them? I couldn't tell them anything because I didn't know anything. They were plainly frustrated that I couldn't give them any information other than what I had told Officer Toppin.

"I never saw anything out of the ordinary with Bob or Betsy. I never saw anything with any of the kids, for that matter."

They kept looking at each other and pushing, "Are you certain? We are sure the kids are going to tell everything soon—and you could be next."

Wait. Was that a threat?

At that point, I realized where this was headed. I knew Bob hadn't done the things they were accusing him of doing. Initially, I thought, *How can they arrest Bob without proof? How can they arrest Bob with no witnesses? They must have something, but what is it? It isn't anything I know about.* Well, now I knew. I knew police and therapists were interviewing the little kids, and that's where all this came from. I may have been only eighteen, but I wasn't stupid. I thought the parents were being brainwashed into believing their children had been abused. If it had been true, why didn't they see something was happening? Why didn't they notice their children were hurt when all this abuse was happening?

These thoughts were running through my head in my mother's living room as those SBI agents pressed me for information and became increasingly angry when I didn't give it to them. Finally, they knew they were not getting anywhere with me by threatening that the kids would eventually tell the whole story soon . . . and I might be next. They left my momma's house that day, but they made sure I knew they would be back. I was afraid. I felt like my world was crumbling. I had to figure out how to put this aside because I was getting married soon and had my baby to protect.

On September 22, 1989, I had a second interview with the SBI; this time, there were three agents—McGinnis and two others. I remember this date exactly because it was the day before my wedding. McGinnis called and said he needed to speak with me again. All I could think was, *UGH*! I told him I had already told him everything, that I had a lot going on, and that it was not a good time. He insisted I meet with him. He and the other two agents came back to Momma's house, and once again, we sat in her living room with my baby asleep in the next room. One of the agents, who I wasn't even introduced to, lifted his leg onto the coffee table, brandishing a gun strapped to his ankle. It seemed clear to me that he wanted me to know it was there. The intimidation was terrible at the first interview, but this was much worse. I wasn't necessarily frightened of them, but I was frightened of what could come of all this.

During the interview, they said, "The kids are now saying your name."

I was shocked! I told them emphatically, "They are lying, because I didn't do anything to any child." After months of the children being in therapy, how did my name suddenly pop up?

McGinnis acted like he didn't know what to say at that point. He suddenly sputtered, "I would hate to see you taken away from that baby." We could all hear my baby crying in the next room, where my mother held him. That was the first time I teared up in any of the interviews. I wanted to scream, "How dare you!" I understood that this was meant as another threat. I told them to leave. I was getting married the next day, and I was not having this craziness in my momma's home.

They left, and I didn't hear from McGinnis again—until the day I was arrested.

As planned, Kevin and I got married the next day. Our baby was only three months old, and rumors of the day care were hanging over me. We agreed that I should stay home with him while Kevin worked at the local cotton mill, and this was just fine with me because I loved being a momma so much. Honestly, I didn't know how long I had before I might be the next person arrested. I prayed and prayed and tried not to focus on the day care, but the stories were everywhere.

The rumor ship had sailed, and people everywhere now believed that many kids had been abused. Stories about the day care were all over the news and in the papers. At that point, Darlene Harris, a previous teacher from the day care I didn't even know, was accused too. I thought maybe she worked at another day care or maybe at Little Rascals in the old building. I didn't know Scott Privott either, but he was also charged. I knew he owned the local video store where we rented movies occasionally, but I didn't know him other than to see him at his store. I certainly never saw him at the day care. I couldn't believe people thought that a group of trusted adults and complete strangers like the video store owner could get together and do the things they were claiming we did, yet nobody saw any marks on the children's bodies or heard any child crying or screaming.

At the hospital, Momma was also hearing comments and innuendos about abuse. She would come home from work and just hibernate in her house to get away from it. She couldn't believe the vicious rumor cycle she was trapped in. Some days, she came out to our trailer in the country to see the baby and me, but more just to escape what was happening in Edenton. We were caught in a horrible nightmare, and we all wanted out so badly, but none of us knew how to stop it.

In desperation for peace and an escape, we decided to take a trip to Kentucky, which was good for us to focus on. Only Momma, my baby, and I were going, and it was a much-needed break from Edenton . . . and from Kevin. My Kentucky family couldn't believe everything they were hearing on the news and everything we were telling them. Honestly, they didn't take any of it too seriously. They knew me, and they knew I didn't do anything. So they didn't believe I would be arrested. I think that's how most people who knew me felt. We all believed the justice system would prevail.

Soon the situation around me was amplifying. I wasn't arrested yet, but people were uncomfortable and even suspicious. Most of my friends stopped coming around to see me, and my life was miserable, so I just focused completely on my child. Out of the blue, on a cold, windy day in December, Betty Ann Phillips called to see if she could come over and talk. She wasn't just a coworker; she was also my friend, and her three-year-old had been in my class. The baby and I were alone in the trailer when Betty Ann arrived. She told me she had been following the day care events closely since it closed eight months earlier.

According to Betty Ann, her child was implicated by other children, and the investigators asked her to have him interviewed by Judy Abbott, a state-hired therapist. Betty Ann and her husband were disturbed by the accusations, so they agreed to have him interviewed. They took him to a therapist who told them after only a few visits that she believed their son "was also abused." At first, they were shocked, but more, they were confused. Betty Ann was at the day care every single day. She was right there across the hall from me. Wouldn't she have seen something odd? Wouldn't she have heard something? The more Betty Ann learned about what they said in those interviews, the more she questioned the accusations. She just didn't believe any of it was true.

Betty Ann heard a rumor that I would be next. She felt horrible and wanted to warn me that she'd heard something was about to happen. Was all this because I didn't give the state what it wanted? Is that why they threw me in the mix? I had worked at the day care for three months during the entire time the alleged abuse was supposed to have occurred. Alarmed, I wasn't sure what to do with the information, so I called Momma. It was the first time she believed I needed an attorney and from somewhere other than Edenton. She knew she wasn't going to have a public defender represent me.

I was grateful to Betty Ann because she gave me time to prepare for what was about to happen. It put me in defense mode, a trait I learned from my momma. There was no way I would have them rip me from my baby without a plan in place. It wasn't much of a plan, but at least I knew my child would be safe. My only other concern was my momma. I felt like the state would feed me to the wolves. They weren't concerned about me. I was barely a child myself, and for the next 2,531 days I was like a robot, doing whatever they told me to do—except lie.

CHAPTER 7

THE SLAP

I'll tell you what's walking Salem . . .
Vengeance is walking Salem.
—Arthur Miller, *The Crucible*

Long before September 1988, Betsy Kelly said there were warning signs of potential problems. When she first purchased the day care, the previous owner, Sally Harrison, cautioned her about one mother with whom she'd had some tension. Harrison claimed Jane Mabry was "a mother to fear." Their tension centered around a dispute because Mabry's child didn't get a piece of cake at a class party because he wouldn't wear a bib.[1]

Unfortunately, Betsy Kelly did not heed the warning. When I interviewed Betsy in the summer of 2022, she said, "Mabry was my friend." She remembered Mabry, new to the town, as "relentless in her efforts to be friends" with her, "even showing up at my home and the day care constantly and without invitation." Kelly also reflected that "Mabry did not work, yet her child was at the day care a lot . . . and [Mabry] would randomly just hang out like she sort of belonged there." Kelly's sister, Nancy Smith, then added that she believed "it was a bad omen that Mabry was remembered as someone who had to be the power person . . . had to be in charge . . . and was a troublemaker."[2]

In one of our interviews, Robin and I talked specifically about Mabry. What did she know about her? Robin said she had "only just started working at the day care when everything began and didn't really know Mabry." But she knew who Mabry was because of the "comments around the day care." She had only seen Mabry in passing and never had even a brief conversation or interaction with her. Robin recalls that the staff heard wild stories, like Mabry had sued "Sesame Street because Cookie Monster said something inappropriate," and she sued "Pizza Hut for something" else. She did not know if the accusations about Bob Kelly slapping the child were true, but the staff joked and laughed that Mabry "had a lawyer on retainer for all her futile court proceedings." True or not, Robin had no idea the danger that woman-in-passing posed for her.[3]

As it turns out, what the staff thought about the Mabry child was also true about the other children. According to the Appellant Brief filed in April 1994, many of the parents testified that they had "difficulty keeping their children under control," and particularly their "three- or four-year-old children, [who] were . . . strong-willed, opinionated, headstrong, hyperactive, aggressive, manipulative, controlling, difficult, and willful."[4]

During Bob Kelly's trial, Betsy Kelly stated on the witness stand that Mabry's son "was [too] difficult for anyone but me to handle, and I . . . warned other day care employees and my husband about trying to deal with him."[5] Betsy Kelly remembered Mabry's son being at the day care often, and in her words, he "created trouble everywhere he went, and everything was a confrontation." She said he was "whiney, clingy, and angry, and no one at the day care wanted him around . . . so, he just followed me around."[6]

In September 1988, only a few days after they moved to the new facility, Bob Kelly had an unfortunate interaction with Mabry's son. No one witnessed it, and no one except Bob Kelly knew for sure why it happened. It is an acknowledged fact that Bob slapped the child. Then, according to Mabry, he did not do enough to control the situation. Regardless of what kind of child Mabry's son was or what he did, it was wrong for Bob to strike him.

What followed the slap poured gasoline on a smoldering ember. There are many perspectives on the outlined events, with very little difference between the facts as stated by either the defense attorneys or the witnesses for the prosecution. In the "Statement of Facts" from Robert Kelly's appeal, his attorney specified plainly that Kelly slapped the Mabry child. "After this incident, Ms. Mabry, a long-time friend of the Kellys, [said she] demanded an apology. She was dissatisfied with the Kellys' response. She took her son out of the day care and broke off her relationship with the Kellys. She told her friends that Bob Kelly had assaulted her son." [7]

Was it Mabry's version of events that made this situation so lethal? For perspective, it helps to consider Mabry's own dramatic recounting of the incident. In her interview in the *Frontline* documentary, "Innocence Lost," Mabry said when she picked up her son from day care on the day of the slap, he was "visibly upset." In the interview, she said, "My son declared, 'Please don't make me go back there, Mommy, I was slapped.'" Mabry said that she went home with her son, and he never returned to Little Rascals Day Care. According to Mabry, she later returned to the day care to confront Bob Kelly, demanding an apology. She said he refused to apologize. "Outraged and aggrieved," she again went back to the day care days later, this time to confront Betsy, whom Mabry claimed to be her "best friend," but Betsy refused to apologize. [8]

Factually, questions remain as to whether an apology happened. Regardless, like a slow cooker, Mabry claimed she sat at home for two months and, in her words, "spent a lot of time praying . . . ruminating, thinking something's not right. There was just this gut feeling, there's something not right." She stewed on the perceived injury she and her son had suffered. She told Bikel in the documentary that her husband eventually went to Little Rascals to demand an apology, but Betsy Kelly told him, "The matter was settled." [9]

Later, Mabry insisted, "If Betsy had been different and acted differently that day, and had been more magnanimous and . . . and said, 'Oh, I'm so sorry' and 'We really, really want [him] back.' And I would've . . . I would've bought it. And I'm not so sure I would have been . . . where I was when this whole investigation broke. I could very well have been her advocate [and] at that moment I knew life would never be the same."[10]

It seemed an odd thing for her to say and perhaps even prophetic. Consequently, according to Mabry, an "avalanche of accusations" began; however, it wasn't until "after Thanksgiving, after not getting any [satisfactory] feedback from Bob or Betsy," that Mabry decided she was going to start asking other people "how things were at Little Rascals . . . and that's basically what happened."[11]

So, what did happen?

How were the seeds of suggestions planted all over Edenton? Many blamed Audrey Stever, the mother of one of the children at Little Rascals, as much or more than Jane Mabry, because Stever turned the case of a slap into sexual abuse.

The following timeline is drawn from the "Statement of Facts" from Bob Kelly's appeal that was documented in testimonies and Stever's own journal entries that were withheld from the original defense team. Those resources show that the events after the slap were much more complicated than Mabry's version.

"Sometime in the fall of 1988, [Stever's two-year-old] child began getting confused about which day care he was supposed to attend. He was spending considerable time going between two different day cares and a sitter named Rosa while [his parents] worked long hours." Stever claimed, "I had already toilet trained him . . . [but] he began having accidents. At first, I blamed it on our hectic work schedules . . . because I often worked until eight or nine at night." The Kellys transported the child from another day care to Little Rascals, and sometime that fall, Stever received a phone call from the other day care telling her that her child was "reluctant to go with Mr. Kelly . . . because he did not like Mr. Bob."

By December, Stever had become so concerned about her child that she went to her friend, Officer Brenda Toppin, a dispatcher with the Edenton Police Department. Toppin worked part-time as a dispatcher and part-time doing clerical work because it was a very small police department. The Edenton PD also permitted Officer Toppin to do some investigative work where she developed a particular interest in child abuse cases. When Toppin talked with Stever and her child, she suggested Stever "wait until after Christmas to see if his behavior changed." He enjoyed staying home with his family over the holidays, but in January Stever took him back to day care "so she could run her dance studio." He was unhappy about going back to day care.

On January 13, Mabry visited Stever at her dance studio to tell Stever that Bob Kelly had "slapped her son" and that two other children had been "taken out of the day care." Alarmed by the sudden withdrawal of other children from the day care, Stever was determined "to find out what was wrong" with her son, and she assumed that "whatever was wrong with him was attributable to Bob Kelly." Stever went to Toppin, who advised her to "question [him] why he did not like the day care." And she did. She questioned her child repeatedly about Little Rascals, about Mr. Bob, about times, places, "playing doctor," and nap time. She said she "tried not to ask [him] leading questions."

On January 14, Stever talked two more parents into believing Bob Kelly "had played doctor" with their children and suggested to Mabry that "what happened to [her child] was more than a slap."

By January 17, Stever reported back to Toppin "and decided there was nothing to be concerned about," but Toppin said a "red flag" went up for her as Stever talked about "naptime." Stever suggested to Toppin . . . "this couldn't be sexual; I mean it just couldn't be." But Toppin suggested "that naptime 'is usually when these things happen.'" Stever never took her child back to the day care after that day.

By January 17 or 18, Toppin contacted social services, and on January 19, she told Stever, "You're not going to like this. We think there's something going on, to what extent we're not sure. But [Stever's son] may be one of the victims." And only "six days after the child mentioned Bob Kelly, Toppin determined that there was abuse of several children at

Little Rascals." She had not interviewed any children at this point. Toppin told Stever that it "would be alright for [her] to talk with other parents about this." That same day, Stever went to another parent and "accused Bob Kelly of 'playing doctor'" and suggested she tell yet another parent.

On January 20, at the suggestion of Officer Toppin, Stever took her child to be interviewed by Michelle Zimmerman, one of the four therapists who would go on to interview all the children named in the indictments. Stever began to keep a journal and to pursue her concerns relentlessly, questioning the child repeatedly over the next several days. At the same time, Mabry and Stever continued contacting more parents, spreading more rumors and more fear.

On January 21, Toppin and DSS went to the Stevers' home to conduct the first of many official interviews, and according to Toppin's handwritten notes, she told the not-yet three-year-old to be their "police helper" to figure out "why the children at the day care were sad."[12]

The three adults began questioning the toddler in an unrecorded interview. Toppin later admitted under oath in Kelly's trial to using "the dolls" to demonstrate how Mr. Bob "played doctor," among other things. Toppin decided that "based on [the child's] facial expression and body language that he could not describe what had happened without the use of anatomically correct dolls." She later admitted under oath that she had no training on the dolls, a dangerous tool in the hands of an untrained police dispatcher-turned-investigator. According to her court testimony, "There wasn't a course, per se," but instead, she got her experience "just dealing with [them]."[13] Toppin's interrogation of the Stever toddler lasted more than two hours.

Suddenly, an expanding frenzy entrapped the Edenton Seven much like the web of a black widow spider. It was a messy, tangled, uneven network of rumors that with each new suggestion of sexual abuse ensnared one more victim. Whose child was next? What day care employee? In hindsight, one must wonder how the investigators and prosecutors failed to see where this was headed.

Once Toppin was involved, unsubstantiated rumors rapidly morphed into a full-blown conspiracy. The slap was Edenton's sole physical evidence for what evolved into a true-life witch hunt. The Kellys did not apologize, which fed Mabry's moral outrage. Mabry started making phone calls and visits. Stever, on Toppin's advice, began to share her fears and hysteria with significantly more mothers, suggesting to them that Bob Kelly had been "playing doctor" with their children during naptime. Then another parent decided her three-year-old son's crying and persistent earaches were proof that he, too, had been abused. And as further proof, another parent suggested her child came home from day care "wearing someone else's underwear . . . or without his shoes and socks" [14] because he had also been abused.

Determined to prove her beliefs, Toppin was preoccupied with theories that some evil had occurred, and she continued to conduct interviews and encouraged parents, siblings, and even grandparents to question the children. At the day care, she asked staff to come upstairs to the second floor of the building for the inquiries, the same space where the alleged abuse was said to have occurred. Toppin was looking for anything that confirmed her suspicions. On January 19, Toppin turned over the case to the Chowan County Department of Social Services, but she remained deeply involved in the cases and eventually testified for the state at Bob Kelly's trial.

In time, the child named other children as having been involved, and it would not be long before Toppin interviewed those children as well. After those initial interviews, Toppin made a massive leap from Kelly slapping Mabry's child to accusations of sodomy, rape, molestation, and more. In fact, the Stever child testified two years later that Mr. Bob "stuck a [six-inch] toy knife" in his butt . . . but he didn't cry . . . "because it didn't hurt that much."[15]

The next child interviewed eventually *named* other children . . . and the parents in turn enlisted others . . . and the investigation spread. Soon, many day care employees, including newcomer Robin, were being interviewed by DSS and Toppin. Her interviews focused on the outlandish and heinous accusations of sexual abuse, which had increased from one child to dozens of toddlers, preschoolers, and after-schoolers at the day care center. They interviewed the older children as well, but what did they say? None of them were included in the charges, and no older child testified at the trials. As Toppin pursued allegations, she stated that she believed that even more children had been abused than came forward.

Significant to how this unfolded and before any accusations were made, in the spring of 1988, "the seeds of this case may have been sown" when H. P. Williams, the District Attorney for the first prosecutorial district which includes Chowan County, and Brenda Toppin attended a three-day seminar with numerous "law enforcement and social service workers" in Kill Devil Hills on the coast of North Carolina. They were all there to "learn about the dangers of child molesters operating day-care facilities."[16] This seminar on satanic ritual abuse and identifying the characteristics of ritual sex abuse of children was similar to seminars being offered around the country. Judith Abbott, a social worker, helped lead the seminar, and she was eventually hired by the prosecution. Toppin was the first person to interview children in the Little Rascals case and to advise parents of the abuse. Beyond that seminar, how much formal training did Toppin have, and at what point did the police chief decide she was qualified to investigate the alleged child sexual abuse? And once the SBI was involved, why didn't that agency pursue the investigation more critically?

Testimony was the only evidence, and Toppin's proved to be revealing. It became clear to the defense attorneys that over many weeks, she used intense, leading, and relentless questioning and coaching to convince the children to make disturbing accusations against "Mr. Bob," Robin, and the others. She testified that when one child told her, "Mr. Bob . . . plays doctor . . . and sticks something in your butt," the interview "was not recorded in any way." She testified, "I may have asked certain questions," but she could not remember "exactly what I asked her." She continued to claim under oath, "I was not able to remember just what I said . . . and I can't recall . . . I may have said something but don't remember what," when asked what she'd said to elicit the child's statements. The defense asked her about tape recording the interviews with the children, and she stated under oath, "I never tried to tape little children before," and did not "make it a practice to record them." Nor could she recall what terms the child used to "describe what Mr. Bob did to him." She even went so far as to prepare typewritten notes for her testimony, but then testified that she created them from some "brief notes, handwritten notes" that she "destroyed . . . after the interviews."[17]

Perhaps it was due to Toppin's lack of formal police training, but it was a problem that she did not see it necessary to keep any handwritten notes or audio recordings for any of her meetings with anyone. Later, she admitted to recording and subsequently recording over conversations with the Stever child, as well as other children she interviewed. With no notes or recordings, there was no way for anyone to determine what she actually said to the children or how she questioned them. In other words, there was no verifiable evidence, which seemed to be a recurring pattern in this case.

By the end of February, several more children were involved. The accusations were, in the language of the children, about the same things: "peenies, hynies, ding dongs, butts," and numerous allegations of sexual misconduct. Toppin later admitted under oath that she conducted a "series of meetings with parents and therapists," including at least one meeting with two specific parents and Judy Abbott. During those meetings she testified they "talked about what the [children] had disclosed [to the therapists] . . . in regard to possible indictments."[18] Was she manipulating the children and parents, and were the four state-hired therapists willingly collecting evidence for the state and providing a mechanism for speculation and innuendos?

Though Mabry played a key role in the initial accusations, her child was never named in the indictments, and neither she nor her child testified in the trial. It is not clear when, but at some point, Mabry requested that the prosecution include her child as one of the "indictment children." For whatever reason, the state did not list her son in the Bills of Indictment; however, she remained deeply engaged in the cases and trials, attending every hearing and trial as a cheerleader for the prosecution.

The trio of Jane Mabry, Audrey Stever, and Brenda Toppin turned Bob Kelly's slap into an avalanche of accusations, which became a firestorm that eventually led to the arrests of the seven people. But it didn't just consume the lives of the individuals being accused. It wrecked marriages, destroyed families, bankrupted people, and crippled the community. Worse, many believe it emotionally harmed little children. Worse still, it all could have been prevented before it became a lethal contagion of destruction.

CHAPTER 8

COLLECTIVE HYSTERIA

A false tongue will never make a guilty person.
—Marion Starkey, *The Devil in Massachusetts: A Modern
Enquiry into the Salem Witch Trials*

Edenton is a typical small Southern town. The narrow streets are lined with ancient magnolias, oaks, and cypress trees that weep with Spanish moss, standing guard like silent, tearful observers of a darkness that descended on Edenton and changed lives forever. Barely more than a village with less than five thousand residents in 1988, everyone knew everyone in Edenton, and whispers and gossip readily overflowed from the local grapevine. However, the Little Rascals scandal differed from the usual gossip, and the contagion left no one undamaged. Dozens of parents fell into an unrestrained hysteria with devastating consequences. The stories of secrets and improper touching were told and retold at a fever pitch, traveling from one person to the next, moving too fast to contain.

Like a burning candle, rumor ignites with the strike of a match. It can burn slowly, lingering as a lonely flame in the dark, and eventually, it dies out if there are no lips to whisper it and no willing ear to hear it. But left unmanaged, rumors can become unstable, dangerous, and consuming. It needs only the encouragement of one fiber touching that flame, a willing participant, to set off a firestorm. Did the Little Rascals case begin with such a match strike, as many have suggested? Was it simply an angry, vindictive mother who lit the match?

Similar to the Salem trials and Rev. Parris's accusations of witches, the Little Rascals case began with a single event—the slap by Bob Kelly. But how did that single incident erupt into a full-blown burning mass? Ironically, before the scandal, Little Rascals Day Care was said to be "an exceptional institution" valued by many people as the "best day care" in town.[1] In 1986, Betsy and Bob Kelly took ownership from the previous owner, and soon after, they hired Shelley Stone and Dawn Wilson, both of whom later were charged in the conspiracy. To accommodate their friends and to provide a safe space to care for all those children, the Kellys moved into a newly renovated building on September 26, 1989, with the help of Betsy's father, who designed and bankrolled the new space. It was then that Robin Byrum joined the Little Rascals family.

After the slap, and once the first suggestion of abuse was made, it became a much more complicated situation for the Kellys and the parents. Some of the parents failed to think rationally about the accusations, though that's understandable given that it was their children involved. After all, what responsible parent would turn their back on suggestions that their child had been molested—or worse? Did the alleged scandal explode because the story was embellished and fueled by others who were willing to contribute layers to the inferno? Regardless, as the situation intensified, it spread rapidly, consuming individuals, the town, the state, and the nation.

Each step in the timeline played an important role in moving the events forward. As the weeks dragged on, the casualties of the rumors were mounting, and the day care staff was dragged into chaos, one at a time. Yet they all continued to trust and believe that truth would prevail. Unfortunately, they were entirely at the mercy of the collective hysteria that seemed impossible to calm. Rumors quickly morphed. Ambiguous accusations that something happened turned to dark and sinister charges of sodomy; sexual exploitation; vaginal penetration with penises, knives, and felt pens; anal penetration; rape; oral sex; penetration with scissors; animal sacrifices; baby killings; and more. Meanwhile, law enforcement, interrogators, and prosecutors became deeply fixated on proving true what the parents were told—and what investigators wanted to believe had happened behind closed doors.

At what point and with what person could the firestorm have been contained?

Many experts who later examined this case suggested that Brenda Toppin, an untrained investigator, was the principal architect of the allegations. Did she decide early on that abuse had occurred, and then sought to prove what she believed to be true without looking for physical evidence or eyewitnesses? Her critics believed she relentlessly pushed and prodded the parents and children into believing sexual abuse had taken place. Wouldn't the next step require having trained investigators look critically at the evidence or lack of it? Was the state interested in extinguishing the flame or finding the truth? Eventually, the Department of Social Services and the SBI took over the investigation from Toppin. What were they looking for? Facts? Evidence? Witnesses? And the prosecution—what was their goal? Were they determined to find the truth or push an irrational narrative?

What about the parents? Could any single parent have stopped it?

Some of the day care parents were personal friends of the Kellys. They knew Bob and Betsy well. According to Audrey Stever in an interview in Lisa Sheer's article, "The Demons of Edenton," the town was "a very social town . . . and people wanted to support them." In spite of that, the Kellys' friends quickly accepted and magnified dozens of dangerous accusations. Chris Bean, a local attorney, was a longtime, close friend of Bob Kelly's, and his wife, Grace, was said to be "envied in Edenton society."[2] The social pressure was intense. Could a suggestion by the Beans that everyone take a pause and critically examine what was being suggested have stopped the case? Or what about Dillard Dixon, a regular golfing buddy of Bob Kelly's, and his wife, Scotty, who both turned on the Kellys. Could they have insisted everyone stop and examine the accusations?

And what about others? There was Lisa Baker, whom Bikel referred to as a "chain-smoking and neurotic mother" in the *Frontline* documentary.

She frequently dropped off her child so she could pursue her passion for riding horses. Instead of asking if any of it was possible, she admitted to "grilling sessions at bedtime," asking her young daughter repeatedly what happened and who violated her.[3]

What about Patricia Ashley Kephart Forward, a friend and connected mother, who was an auditor with the State Bureau of Investigation? Instead of questioning if the charges might be fabricated, did she instead use her connections to feed the inferno?

Could Lynne Layton, the mother Robin saw in the department store just after the day care closed, have stopped it? Or did she join in the hysteria at the expense of her young daughter and Robin Byrum, her child's beloved teacher? More than a year after Robin was charged, Layton took the stand as a witness for the state at Robin's bond hearing. Layton testified about that encounter at the store the previous April, but her version directly contradicted Robin's recollection of the event. Layton testified that she "spoke to Robin first as her young daughter hid behind her leg, afraid to speak to Robin." According to her account, she encouraged her daughter by saying, "Say hello to Miss Robin." When the child supposedly refused, she told her again, "Say hello to Miss Robin. Give Miss Robin a hug." The child whispered, "Hello," and that was the extent of it. When cross-examined by the defense if her child had "said anything to her or to anyone about anything that Robin had done?" She replied, "No," but she did tell the court, "Bob had done things to my daughter."[4] Why would she force her toddler to hug someone that she believed had sexually violated her child or any child?

Of all those parents whose children filled that day care center, some part-time and some full-time, how many tried to stop the hysteria? Some said they were riddled with guilt over leaving their children for long periods of time to pursue jobs, hobbies, and fun. Some were simply dragged into the contagion because they were there. Some were thought to be opportunists who perhaps wanted to feel connected or powerful. Regardless, enough parents believed they had put their children in harm's way, and the fear and guilt that took hold of them gave the case momentum.

What about the therapists? Could they have stopped the malignant growth of the allegations?

Accusations flowed freely, and Stephen Ceci, PhD in Psychology at Cornell, and Maggie Bruck, PhD, of McGill University, expert psychologists on child suggestibility, wrote extensively about flawed interview techniques therapists used with the children to extract accusations of sexual abuse. They believe that young children are "more prone to change their answers when asked the same question" repeatedly in an interview… and they will also "change their answers to please the adult . . . or because of interviewer's suggestions." Further, Ceci and Bruck expressed concern about the lack of any "testing for alternative hypotheses ... and the use of coercive techniques." [5] All were true about the Little Rascals case.

It is absolutely possible for a child to be molested without physical evidence of the abuse. In this case, were the alleged perpetrators careful not to leave signs? Considering the nature of the allegations, perhaps no signs of physical injuries were present because no abuse happened. No child went home with a suspicious injury. No child went home terrified, traumatized, or bloodied, and no evidence backed up allegations of penetration, rape, or sodomy. No baby went mysteriously missing from the day care, and no evidence supported accusations that babies were murdered or ritually sacrificed. No hotel employee reported grown men taking toddlers into motel rooms. No marina employee reported a man loading toddlers onto a boat. No hot-air balloons were sighted. Did someone rape the children in the abandoned second floor or in the check-in room? Did the teachers dance naked in the classrooms? Did they have sex with the children on boats floating in the middle of the Albemarle Sound? No.

No specific times or dates for individual or group crimes were given, but all were said to have occurred sometime between September and December 1988.

CHAPTER 9

ACCUSED

At the end of January and following the first formal complaint of sexual abuse leveled against Bob Kelly, the Kellys adamantly denied all accusations. Bob and Betsy Kelly began the difficult task of informing employees and parents that Bob was being investigated for child abuse. The reaction of the staff and most parents was absolute shock and utter disbelief. They knew Bob. They knew Betsy. They had never seen anything out of the ordinary. The Kellys feared where this was headed, so they hired a local defense attorney and friend, Chris Bean, to represent Bob. By February 3, more children were at the center of the investigation, and the SBI had gotten involved. During the interviews with the children, and without the knowledge of the employees, more and more of them were being implicated daily.

On April 14, 1989, the State of North Carolina arrested Robert Fulton Kelly Jr. and formally charged him with hundreds of counts of child molestation. He was placed under a $1.5 million bond guaranteeing he would remain in jail. Eleven days later, on April 25, Kelly and Bean appeared in district court for his scheduled probable cause hearing. Such a hearing is not constitutionally required but is often held for the state to produce sufficient evidence to establish probable cause for the crimes alleged to have been committed. It would give Bean a glimpse into some of the evidence the prosecution would use against Kelly.

However, Kelly's probable cause hearing was never held. According to the Appellant Brief to the North Carolina Court of Appeals, Bean later made public statements and then testified under oath that at this point, he "believed adamantly and completely in Bob Kelly's innocence. And for all those months, until that day had believed in his total innocence."[1]

Yet on that same day, Officer Brenda Toppin and H. P. Williams approached Chris Bean in the courtroom, pulled him aside, and proceeded to inform him that another child had named *Bean's* child. That meant his own son was now listed in the indictment. As it turns out, at the same time Toppin and Williams were warning Chris Bean, Grace Bean was also being warned by another mother that their child had been molested. Everyone was utterly shocked. Bob Kelly was now accused of molesting his own attorney's child. Bean was told that the child's friend suggested to investigators that Mr. Bob was "looking at hineys . . . playing with ding dongs . . . [and sticking] things in [both boys'] butts."[2]

On April 29, 1989, Little Rascals closed permanently. At least two children, later named as victims in the indictments, remained at the day care to the very end. Brenda Ambrose, who was both a parent and an employee at the day care, said it was because she "believed it was all a vendetta" and did not believe any of the accusations at first, until her own parents raised questions about possible abuse.[3] She then put her child in therapy with Betty Robertson in early June, where he remained for nearly two years. Another mother, Carla Bateman, who testified for the state at Bob Kelly's trial, kept her child at Little Rascals because neither she nor her husband believed the accusations. Eventually, the other parents wore her down. She called Toppin "with an uneasy feeling," put her child in therapy, kept a daily journal, and later, under oath, claimed her child had been severely abused.[4]

Within a few days of the revelation to Bean in the courtroom, the Beans also put their son in therapy with Robertson. They claimed at first that they "did not want to get involved." However, the Appellant Brief reveals that the "social pressure for Bean to stop defending Bob Kelly" was intense. The more children and families who were implicated, the more pressure was applied to the Beans to become part of the "in-group."[5] Though their son denied the allegations for weeks, he remained in therapy with Robertson. After more than six weeks, Robertson reported her certainty that the Beans' child had been abused. It was even more weeks before he made bizarre claims against Kelly, saying that he had touched his "number one . . . and number two with his hand" and put a burning candle and a burning flower stem in his "number two." He also said he had been on a tugboat with Bob Kelly. Furthermore, he accused Kelly of shutting him up in a refrigerator, trying to shoot an apple off another child's head, and hanging him and another child in a bag in a tree.[6] After Bean withdrew from the case, he went on to say he fully believed the charges against Kelly were true.

Only ten days later, the grand jury handed down shocking indictments against Bob Kelly. The indictments had exploded to one hundred felony counts listing charges that supposedly occurred between September and December 1988: indecent liberties; first-degree rape; fellatio; digital, anal, and vaginal penetration; intercourse and oral sex with Dawn Wilson, Betsy Kelly, and Robin Byrum; crimes against nature; and conspiracy to commit indecent liberties. However, the accusations morphed into more than touching children's genitals and sodomy. In therapy and later on the witness stand, the children told stories of killing babies, cooking children in a microwave, "peeing" and "pooing" on the children, throwing them overboard into a shark-filled river, and inserting sharp objects such as scissors into their rectums. They also told bizarre stories of ritual killing of animals, flying witches, flying children into outer space, taking them up in hot-air balloons, taking them out into alligator-filled waters, and many more charges.

With Bean out, Kelly needed a new attorney. Late one night in September 1989, Judge Frank Brown of Tarboro telephoned W. Michael

"Mike" Spivey to represent Kelly. It was going to be a difficult case, and Judge Brown warned him it would likely take some significant amount of time. That would prove to be an understatement, but Spivey didn't hesitate to accept the case.

On September 1, 1989, Betsy Kelly was arrested on charges similar to her husband's and was placed under a $1.8 million bond. That same day, Scott Privott, a video store owner and friend of Bob Kelly's, was also arrested and placed under a $1 million bond. Privott consistently asserted that he had never stepped one foot into the day care, and there was no eyewitness or evidence from anyone that he had ever been inside. His video store did have an adult section, which was common in the 1980s, and the parents, SBI, and prosecutors attempted to find evidence of child pornography, specifically any having to do with the children at the day care. All their efforts produced nothing. Teachers Shelley Stone and Dawn Wilson were also soon arrested, and the grand jury continued adding more indictments.

Robin and every other employee not already implicated were on edge. Who would be next? Robin would soon learn that after many months of Toppin's intense interrogation of the children, they alleged that Robin "kicked the children . . . hurt [them] and put scissors into [their] privates . . . touched [them]" and "had sex with Bob in front of the children," among many other charges.[7]

CHAPTER 10

ROBIN'S STORY—CHARGED!

The conditions of the prison were appalling . . . the jail
keepers used shackles to hold the condemned—the
young, old, and ill included. . . Once convicted, it was
usually only a matter of days before they were executed.
—Exhibit at the Salem Witch Museum

Things were closing in around me. I knew what was getting ready to happen, and I needed to take control of my life and the situation around me. I was tired of waiting around, and I wanted to make sure they didn't arrest me while I was alone with my baby. I knew Agent McGinnis was going to arrest me, and it was likely my last night with my little baby. How could I even prepare myself to be separated from the only thing in the world that was mine? I loved him with all my heart. That night, I fell asleep with him in my arms, snuggling him so I could kiss him as if it would be the last time. It was a long, painful, sleepless night.

Kevin and my mother-in-law worked at the same cotton mill, and it was getting ready to shut down, which was common in those days. That meant they would be laid off for some extended period of time. I had to wonder if this was another coincidence, or just good timing, if there was such a thing in this situation. Yes, good timing. That mattered.

Consequently, I arranged for Kevin to take our baby to his mother's, and I went to my momma's house to make a phone call to McGinnis at the SBI. I knew once I made the call, I probably wouldn't be able to stop the inevitable results. It was Monday, January 9, 1990. Momma didn't go to work that morning so she could be by my side. Momma and I thought we planned this fateful day very carefully and believed we were driving this train. We could not have been more wrong.

Two years after I first walked into Little Rascals, six months after Bob Kelly's arrest, and four months after Betsy Kelly's arrest, it happened. Two police cars pulled up in front of Momma's house. She was so proud and so private, and I knew this was destroying her. Agent McGinnis and two other suited men from the SBI got out of their cars and came into my mother's house, which was so frightening. They told me they needed to talk with me at the police station. Momma and I went with them, yet instead of just "booking" me on something, McGinnis took me into a small office in the back of the police station. It was just the two of us in a tiny room with two chairs and a desk. He escorted me to a lone chair in the corner. He then planted himself behind the desk and, like a predator, slowly, ominously, wheeled his chair right up to me. Fear grabbed me by the throat. This interview was already different from the first time we talked. The attack began.

McGinnis started talking, but I was crying—not a sobbing kind of crying, but a silent tears-flooding-down-my-face crying—and I was finding it hard to listen to him. I felt trapped, and though I didn't want to listen to him, he kept pushing me to give him affirmation that SOMETHING happened at the day care. By this time, he reminded me that not only had Bob and Betsy been arrested, but also Dawn Wilson and Scott Privott, with all of them under huge bonds and awaiting trial. If I gave him what he wanted, the case against the others would be complete, and I could go home. He pushed for that. He pushed hard. He wanted me to confess and to turn state's evidence. I continued to assert that I didn't see or hear anything suspicious at the day care, and there was nothing I could give him. It was the same thing I'd said in all the previous interviews, and it was clear McGinnis was losing patience with me. Ironically, thinking back on that moment, I don't believe he wanted to arrest me, but I believe he thought he could break me. But there was nothing to break . . . except my heart.

"You have one last chance," McGinnis said. "I'm going to ask you one more time. Did you see Bob or Betsy touch or harm any of the kids?" After a long, silent pause, he sneered, "I would really hate to see you go to jail trying to protect them."

Stunned, I didn't answer him. I couldn't. All I could think was that I had already given him the truth, but I would soon learn that wasn't what he wanted. I was still refusing to look at him, which seemed to make him angry. He propelled out of his chair, yelling at me like a crazed monster. In a rage, and I believed to elicit absolute fear in me, he hoisted his entire leg, kicked the desk, and knocked it completely across the room! It worked. I was paralyzed.

His anger boiled over and he said, "Your name has been brought up during therapy sessions."

I said nothing. Then, out of frustration, McGinnis finally had some officers haul me off to arrest and charge me. Fortunately, Kevin came with me, and his mother had the baby. Sheriff Fred Spruill was assigned the task of escorting me to a town nearby that housed females because the Chowan County Jail was for males only. In what I think was a show of sympathy, he allowed Kevin to ride with me in the police car. I know I caught Chief Spruill glancing sympathetically at us in his rearview mirror. He was probably thinking that we were just two kids—still teenagers— going through this nightmare. Anyway, I'm pretty sure even now that Sheriff Spruill was only doing his job. His eyes revealed his compassion for me and my situation.

McGinnis said some child had "named me," but what exactly was I charged with? Why did they arrest me? Because some little child said that I did something? Because I wouldn't tell the officers something I didn't know? Because I wouldn't tell them lies? I was completely disoriented.

As it turns out, the indictment against me had been handed down on January 9, 1990, the same day I was arrested. The charges against all seven of us had exploded to include ninety-two children, twenty-nine of whom would be named in the indictments, with more than 375 charges, ranging from conspiracy to rape. Eventually, I was moved to the Beaufort County Jail and placed under a $500,000 bond.

The charges against me were unimaginable: one count of conspiracy, eight counts of first-degree sex offense, eleven counts of indecent liberties with a child, one count of crime against nature—twenty-one counts in all. Twenty-one counts of sexually abusing, kicking, punching, and sodomizing two- and three-year-olds at Little Rascals . . . all sometime between the end of September and the end of December. I had loved those little children so much. How did this happen? Did anyone really think I did these things? Did people really believe any of us did this? I was trapped in a nightmare from which I couldn't wake up.

As soon as she could, my mother went to see Jeff Miller, an attorney in Greenville, North Carolina, who was referred to her by friends at work. She told him my story, and he agreed to represent me. In a letter to my mother and me, he promised he would do all in his power to keep his legal fees reasonable and said that he deeply believed in my innocence. Soon after, Miller wrote to Judge Bradford Tillery, who was the pretrial judge presiding over my case. In the letter, Miller requested a bond reduction hearing, stating the bond was "excessive" under the circumstances. He then came to see me for the first time while I was still in the county jail. I was very confused about all that was going on, but he assured me that he and Rachel, his wife and paralegal, would stay in touch and keep me informed. And they did. He assured me that they would take care of Momma too. He also told me that the SBI had arrested Darlene Harris, another day care employee. That made seven of us accused of these awful crimes.

Once in jail, the officers first searched me and reported I only had ten dollars cash in personal property in my possession. That was it—ten dollars to my name. I was in shock those first few days. It was a cold building with white cinder-block walls and automatic cell doors. They put me in a cell with three other women, four bunks, and one toilet. There was a sort of television screen outside the cells connected to a camera that let the officers check on us as they walked by. Though I knew it was inevitable that the news would reach the other inmates, I was thankful to arrive after supper, because I was so afraid that I would have a rough time with them. There I was in a cell with no pillow, no sheets, and only a hard bunk with a thin pad for a mattress. The guards gave me an orange jumpsuit to wear, the colorful symbol marking me as an inmate. Jeff Miller quickly arranged for me to have necessities, and Momma funded a special jail account that allowed me to purchase other things from the county that I needed for subsistence.

Time was frozen still that first week in jail, and I was in complete and utter despair. I was heartbroken, the reality of my plight consuming the entirety of my body and mind. I stopped eating. I stopped sleeping. Writing and receiving letters and talking to God were all I had, and I did all three constantly. Yet, I had to wonder, *What have I done to deserve this?* The pain of missing my baby was so deep it was more than I could bear.

And I was also worried about Momma. On the surface, she was the strongest woman I had ever known, but I was afraid this would break her. It certainly was breaking me. In one letter, she wrote to me about simple things like "playing cards" and "going to work," and about trying to keep things normal, but I knew it was all crushing her. The rumors in Edenton were spinning fast, and there she was, trapped in the middle of the cyclone of lies. She even had to work with some of the day care parents at the hospital, enduring their stares and whispers. Her friends were scarce, and the few she had were constantly questioning her about what I knew. Nevertheless, Momma tried to assure me in her letters that she focused only on work, and she was doing whatever she could to get me back home.

Friends matter in life, and sitting in prison, my girlfriends helped save me. Wendy, Karen, Diana, Susan, and LaDonna all wrote to me, and each said similar things: *"How are you doing? Are you eating? I can't believe this happened to you. We're praying for you. I know this is hard on you. We love you. I saw the baby."* It was clear they really didn't know what to say, so mostly they just made small talk, talk to make me feel better, talk to reassure me, talk to ease my worries about my baby. Like a dagger to my heart, the comment about seeing the baby hurt the most. They could see him, but I couldn't. They all promised to be in court for my probable cause hearing on January 22, and they didn't disappoint me.

The truth appeared in a few letters in ways that stood out to me. Teresa, Kevin's sister, shockingly wrote her expressed outrage that she *"hoped those parents who signed the indictments would ROT IN HELL."* Others saw it for what it was. LaDonna, my momma's neighbor, shamed the *"entire thing as a witch hunt and that the only mistake I made was going to work there in the first place."* She also wrote that a lot of other people were doubting the other arrests. There were no truer words, or so I hoped.

Accepting that job at Little Rascals Day Care in September 1988 had changed everything for me. I kept thinking, *If only I hadn't done that. If I had made that one decision differently.* The reality was that I had been in the wrong place at the wrong time, and now I was in danger of paying for that decision with my freedom—with my life.

Somehow, Jeff Miller was able to arrange for my grandparents to see me in jail. I don't remember much about the visit except the small window we talked through, and my Pap-pa's blue eyes staring at me through his tears. Before the visit, Momma tried to keep the Kentucky family informed about the interviews and how everyone was being implicated, including me. Pap-pa was a big teaser and joker, and I was his favorite victim. On the last visit home, before I was arrested, he'd teased me about the day care, never really believing that I would be arrested. Because my name was Robin, he jokingly called me "jailbird." When he visited the jail that day, he apologized profusely for having teased me. It weighed on him so much that all he could do was stand there, beg for my forgiveness, and cry. I had only seen him cry one other time in my life, and I was heartsick then. But this time was different. It crushed me because his tears were about me. But I refused to cry. I couldn't. I had to show him I was strong. I had to show him I was going to be okay. Other family members were there that day, too, but I only remember him. All my life, Pap-pa had been my foundation, my rock. He adored me, and I adored him. I had to believe I was going to make it through this, no matter what.

The next few days came and went. I continued to try to console myself by reading my letters and my Bible and by trying to ignore the horrible comments other inmates were making about me. Momma's letters came daily and were especially comforting. In them, she reminded me how much she loved me, begging me not to *"become embittered and cynical."* She knew this place, this experience, was going to change me, but she didn't want me to *"become tough"* like the other women around me. In one letter, she wrote, *"I'd never heard you say 'damn' so much as you did in your first letters to me."* If she only knew what I was hearing . . . and saying.

In this threatening place, the swearing wasn't all Momma had to worry about. Caution was my only friend, and Momma warned me about the people around me and told me *"not to talk about anything to anyone except your lawyer . . . not to anyone . . . the SBI, the DA, not anyone . . . without Jeff Miller there."* She feared that someone would be *"nice to me"* and act like my friend only to get information. They weren't my friends. Not one person in jail was my friend.

Then one day, out of the blue, Tracy Pittman, a woman I knew from town, was brought in and placed in my cell. My radar went off. Why was she in this jail, in this cell, at the same time as me? I found it odd the way she quickly latched onto me. I thought about Momma's letter warning me to *"trust no one."* Suddenly and without notice, my attorney scheduled another quick meeting with me at the jail, and it was then I learned the reason she was there. He believed the Pittman girl was a setup. Just like Momma feared, the state was trying to get information from me and hoped they could do it through Tracy. Well, that didn't work out too well. There was nothing to get, and I was especially quiet and kept to myself in my own space.

CHAPTER 11

CONSPIRACY AND PANIC

Extraordinary claims require extraordinary evidence.
—Carl Sagan

In Salem, Massachusetts, the children were frequently either the source or reason for the naming of witches. There was a profound trust and belief in the children's testimony and their accusations against individuals. Investigators, who were church officials, would use leading questions to elicit desired responses. In time, they got what they sought through coercion and fear. Many months after the hunt for witches had begun, Salem magistrates of the court were demanding of the children that they tell, "'Who afflicts thee?' . . . and now were asking with . . . special urgency." On Friday, March 11, 1692, Ann Putnam professed that her "eyes were opened . . . I saw and named another witch . . . a local woman, not a tramp or a slave, [but rather] a member of the congregation in good standing . . . Martha Corey." Only eight days later, Corey was arrested, accused of "sending her incorporeal essence, her Shape, among the children."[1]

In 1692, for an accused witch, the presence of a "devil's mark," a simple mole or mark, was proof enough that Lucifer had entered the person and taken over their soul, and proof that the defendant had sent their "shape" on one of the children.[2] Nathan Dorn, historian on witchcraft, wrote, "On May 2, 1692, Susannah Martin—accused of flying through bedroom windows and performing sexual acts on sleeping victims—underwent a penetrating and humiliating examination by Judges Hathorne and Corwin, searching for the witch's teat believed used to feed their familiars . . . and despite a lack of evidence, she was found guilty." In her examination, the interrogators were "searching for the devil's mark . . . stripping her naked . . . and examining her body minutely, running pins through any abnormality they found." What they discovered was a "sort of 'proof against which there is no disproof.'" Martin was executed for witchcraft two months later, on July 19, 1692.[3]

In 1989, the "proof" that the devil had suckled on Edenton's soul was the slap by Bob Kelly, compounded by cries from mobilized parents, untrained investigators, anatomically correct dolls, unqualified therapists, and the political ambitions of prosecutors. As in Salem, everything about the charges against Robin and the others depended on proof against which there was no disproof, the testimony of young children. Many believed the accusations were coerced from them over months by adults, people with authority, who were determined to get the answers they sought. And in the opinion of the authors of the April 2021 *New York Times* article, "It's Time to Revisit the Satanic Panic," those inquiries "could and . . . did lead to false accusations."[4]

Questioning was the crucial tactic used in those interrogations, and it yielded the same results from all the children, every one of them. The children consistently denied, denied, and denied the abuse. . . and then admitted it. . . and subsequently named other children they claimed had also been abused. The newly named children were then dragged into the investigation, incessantly questioned by parents and experts only to deny, deny, deny—and then admit. This climate was clearly what the appellant attorneys referred to as "a reflection of deep-seated cultural anxieties" characterized by volatile, irrational, and pervasive fear among parents that their children would go missing or suffer horrendous sexual crimes by satanic cults, particularly where they were the most vulnerable, in their day care.[5] In the Little Rascals case, the uproar from parents and the public alike was deafening to "believe the children," even if those children were denying the allegations or making fantastical, improbable, and impossible accusations against the defendants about whom there were no witnesses and no verifiable physical evidence. The authors of that *New York Times* article interviewed Nancy Lamb, the prosecutor, who bemoaned, "We can't explain all of these things, why some of it is so bizarre. We don't know what [Kelly] told them. He's turning their world upside down."[6]

But children *never* lie. Right? That is, these children weren't lying unless they denied that something happened. If they denied it, according to the therapists, *then* they were lying. In Gretchen Passantino's article, "Innocence Lost in Landmark Child Abuse Case," she suggested that one way this "nightmare developed . . . was the false assumption that . . .therapists can always discover the truth in child abuse cases."[7] The therapists attempted to wake up children's memories of sexual abuse that supposedly only those interrogators could awaken so the children could recall them through intense therapy, coercive questions, dolls with exaggerated and erect penises, oversized vaginal and anal openings, and overtly graphic images that introduced ideas into the children's heads. In other words, they pushed until they got their desired results.

The Chowan County district attorney's office created a list of four recommended therapists: Judith Abbott, Brenda Robertson, Michele Zimmerman, and Susan Childers. All of them were within driving distance of Edenton, and those four therapists went on to interview nearly all of the children involved. Like the Salem witch hunt "inquisitors," did those mental health experts repeatedly ask child after child specific questions that piloted them to the desired answers? Did those answers confirm the therapists' beliefs? What about the children whose parents sought experts who were not named in the indictments? Why were those children not on the state's list? Was it because they denied anything had happened? Also, some of the children who were initially identified were never included in the indictments. Why? And what about the older children who were interviewed? What did they say? The state's final list was limited to twelve "indictment children," all under the age of five. Did they testify the way the state wanted them to testify? Did Edenton's little children eventually make dangerous, dark, malevolent accusations against the seven individuals from Little Rascals Day Care because that's what they believed adults expected them to say?

How was it so easy to convince parents that something happened behind the doors of Little Rascals Day Care? Like Rev. Parris of Salem, investigators and therapists were unshakable in their beliefs that something evil had occurred. Elizabeth Loftus is an expert on the "malleability of memory" who has been recognized by the American Psychological Association as one of the one hundred most eminent psychologists in the twentieth century. She is well known for her work in the field of reliability of memory in the face of hostility. Writing about the Little Rascals case, she concluded, "Parents were seduced into believing that the phantasmic accusations were true" through what she called "a leap of faith."[8]

Brenda Ambrose, an unindicted employee of the day care—and one whose child was named in the indictments—told *Frontline* that her daughter was in Robin's room, located directly across from Betty Ann Phillips's classroom. Ambrose maintained that her child was somehow sexually abused by Robin and others inside Robin's room. However, she was not sure how it happened. She did not hear or see anything, nor did she see a behavior that would indicate anything had happened to her child, or to any other child. She even testified that she would "periodically . . . peek in on [her daughter] . . . when she was asleep during naptime . . . and had no reason to believe anything was going on." [9] Like the others, she put her child in the hands of therapist Brenda Robertson in early June 1989, and after a period of months, her child made disturbing accusations of sexual abuse. She remained in therapy with Robertson for more than a year.

Parent Lisa Baker was also interviewed by Bikel for *Frontline's* "Innocence Lost" series. In the documentary, she said, "I pushed and pushed my little one . . . especially in bedtime," begging and pleading with her three-year-old night after night to "tell Mommy what happened. You have to tell me."[10] It appeared that she wanted her child to admit that something had happened to her at the day care. When she didn't get an admission, she subsequently put her child in therapy with the same therapists as the other parents, where the child remained for ten months before ultimately giving the adults the answers they wanted.

Parent Lynne Layton revealed a disturbing moment of transparency in her interview in the *Frontline* series, during which she swore that "there is not one hair on my body that even has a doubt." She was "completely positive they did this." Later, when Bikel pushed her to question if it was possible that Robin was not part of it, Layton insisted, "No, Robin was in it . . . my child told me so." She said, "I never coaxed information from my child," but then paused. "I did ask . . . Cut this. Wait a minute. I don't want to incriminate myself here." Another pause. "My child has incriminated Robin . . . very seriously."[11]

Child abuse, and specifically child sexual abuse, is real. Tragically, it happens, and society cannot and must not ignore claims of abuse. In turn, how authorities investigate those claims is essential in the pursuit of the truth. The power of suggestion is real, and after many months of therapists relentlessly suggesting to vulnerable children that they were molested, experts maintain the children from the day care scandals were led to believe that the implanted memories were true. That said, this made it much more difficult to dismiss the possibility that something bad happened. It also made achieving a fair trial for the accused nearly impossible.

In *New York Times* article about the "satanic panic" related to day cares, the reporters attempted once and for all to lay to rest the "baseless conspiracy theories . . . of mass child abuse" that haunted parents and day cares in the 1970s, '80s, and into the '90s.[12] The day care panic was especially troubling as seemingly ordinary parents, healthcare professionals, and others embraced the frenzy and found themselves willing participants in believing stories about the existence of massive satanic cults, child exploitation rings, and ritual sexual abuse that existed at the hands of their daytime custodians. At least in part, it is suggested that their willingness to believe such things could have been driven by deep parental guilt as working mothers placed more and more children in the hands of caregivers and day care centers and created an increasing number of latchkey children.

Evangelicals, religious leaders like Pat Robertson, and conservative political pundits did not miss the opportunity to join in on the moral crisis. Driven by ideals founded in the zealous Puritanism of 1692, they launched a culture war against divorce, abortion, feminism, gay rights, and pornography, all based on that conservative ideology. They feared "a decline in religiosity" as the root cause of the "decline of the [nuclear] family."[13] They seized on every opportunity to exploit the crisis and join in the moral panic, arguing that the rise in child sexual abuse was because mothers were no longer in the home, which in turn caused the nuclear family's collapse.

According to experts, accusations came from the parents themselves, who were credible-seeming people. Their fears were further fueled by television talk show hosts like Larry King, respected and renowned news programs like *20/20*, reporters like Geraldo Rivera, and celebrities like Oprah Winfrey, all airing segments amplifying the phenomenon.

Michelle Remembers, a troubling book co-authored by Michelle Smith (a pseudonym) and Lawrence Pazder, her psychiatrist-turned-lover-turned-husband, seemed the likely source for the initial hysteria in the day care panic. The book was an immediate bestseller, published in 1980 by a company that specifically distributed works that focused on the occult, demons, and hell. As much as a decade later, Smith appeared on Oprah Winfrey's talk show to promote her book, awakening public interest and inciting fear. The allegedly "true story" was about Michelle retrieving lost memories of herself as a four- or five-year-old child, held captive and tortured for a year by her mother and a "fiendish assemblage of satanists."[14]

Pazder treated Michelle [Smith] Proby over a period of about seven years, during which time they left their spouses to marry each other, documenting all their "forbidden doctor/patient relationship in the pages of the book." According to Pazder, his initial interest in her was to help her deal with a troubled, unhappy childhood and the trauma of a recent miscarriage. That therapy soon evolved as he openly showed her tenderness, comforted her physically, sat close to her, and held her while he hypnotized her repeatedly to help her find those "recovered memories."[15]

While under hypnosis, Michelle supposedly began to reclaim bizarre, grotesque, and unbelievable memories. In the sessions, she visualized sex with "a dark man named Malachi." She claimed Satan grabbed her around her neck, "surgically implanted horns and a tail" on her body, and forced her to "eat body parts of corpses." She was supposed to have participated in bloody rituals where he sacrificed a baby and made her lie in the blood. His helpers "ripped live kittens apart with their teeth" and dismembered bodies of fetuses and rubbed them on her. Her mother forced her to "eat her own feces," to "urinate and defecate on the Bible," and more.[16]

Richard Beck, an investigative journalist, published *We Believe the Children: A Moral Panic in the 1980s.* In it, he criticized Pazder and Smith, noting that they made nearly a half-million dollars on the sale of their book and that Pazder went on to speak as an "expert on recovered memories," coining the phrase "ritual abuse." In defense of their book and against mounting criticism that Michelle's story was false, Pazder once told a reporter that "if she made things up . . . it would be the most incredible hoax ever." As in the dozens of ritual sexual abuse cases that followed, investigators found no corroborating evidence of any of the incidents she explicated in alarming detail in her book: no missing babies, no blood, nothing. The book was eventually completely debunked as fiction when authorities could find nothing to support her claims. Investigators even discovered that Smith was actually photographed for her school yearbook during the time she was alleged to have been kidnapped. Pazder said afterward, "It was not our desire to cause a witch hunt," but it did. According to Beck, what it also did was cause "the public to [wrongly] confront sexual abuse . . . as a [full blown] moral panic."[17]

In 1983, as the abuse fever took hold, dozens of other individual and day care scandals erupted from California to Canada to North Carolina. The "Hamilton Case" in Ontario, Canada, was yet another example of the power of this contagion. In 1983, two young sisters, five and seven, accused their mother and her boyfriend of horrifying acts of cannibalism, serving plates of human flesh, sacrifices, bestiality, gruesome satanic sex orgies, and more. All the accusations originated from the persistent quizzing by a hyper-religious, overzealous foster care mother, who then reported the abuse to law enforcement. The mother and boyfriend were charged and imprisoned. They were eventually exonerated, but not until their lives had been destroyed.

By 1989, as Edenton was giving energy to the Little Rascals case, works like *The Courage to Heal: A Guide for Women Survivors of Child Sexual Abuse* by Ellen Bass and Laura Davis, and Judith Herman's book, *Trauma and Recovery*, were flooding the market and grabbed society's "collective awareness." Suddenly, well-intentioned mental health professionals moved from the idea of "suspicion to confirmation."[18] These first-generation mental health experts believed the brain was capable of and even hard-wired to suppress painful sexual trauma memories, and patients were rewriting personal histories under the coaching of therapists who convinced them, often after months and years of therapy and under hypnosis, that terrible things had happened to them, destroying lives, families, and communities.

As a result, "the battle cry that children don't lie" was heard, and the mental health industry promoted "a misadventure." In a *New York Times* opinion essay, "The Forgotten Lessons of the Recovered Memory Movement," Richard McNally, a Harvard psychology professor, condemned the idea that memories could somehow be retrieved and said "the disastrous results" of that movement were "the worst catastrophe to befall the mental health field since the lobotomy era."[19] Like the four therapists who interviewed the children in the Little Rascals case, the market was flooded with mental health experts who promoted themselves as "healers," determined to help the young and old retrieve memories of sexual abuse locked away in their subconscious. That movement of "therapists who described themselves as clever detectives searching patients' lives for unexplained emotional responses . . . to repressed abuse scenes" also believed they were the "key . . . to exposing a hidden evil across society."[20] They began writing books and offering seminars, workshops, and training sessions designed to educate the public, social service workers, law enforcement, and prosecutors on identifying visible and invisible signs of satanic ritual trauma, sexual abuse, molestation, victimization, and repressed memories.

In a presentation to the University of North Carolina School of Law in April 1993, Jeff Miller and Mike Spivey, who were appointed to represent Bob Kelly in his trial, warned that in child abuse cases, the "experts who examine the children on behalf of the state become allies of the prosecutor. They assist in collecting statements and allegations in support of the prosecution, and frequently assist in the formulation of strategies and evidence." In the case of the Edenton Seven, they said, therapists were chosen from an "approved list" and used methods that were "severely criticized by scientific and professional literature" and later by the courts.[21]

According to Miller and Spivey, it was common for therapists to ignore that children live in a world that "borders between fact and fantasy," where fantasy can be "grossly manipulated" into fact by questions that "implant a desired result." Did the Little Rascals therapists use methods bordering on interrogations? Was it possible that they used questions that were not only unethical but dangerous? Was it possible they believed that they would guarantee justice was served? Did they use what Miller and Spivey referred to as "techniques designed to help, even prod, the children into revealing [there had been some] past sexual abuse?" Unfortunately for the defendants, there appeared to be no clear-cut guidelines about what was legally and ethically appropriate for therapists to ask while investigating the abuse.[22]

To counter the contagion, authors like Martyn Kendrick, who wrote *Anatomy of a Nightmare,* raised important questions about how these cases happened when a thorough investigation failed to turn up a single piece of evidence to support the claims. He wrote that in nearly all the cases, after interviews and "generous use of anatomically correct dolls," social workers, police, and judges collectively agreed "the children had been abused," even if the children denied it happened or eventually admitted they made it all up.[23]

Lee Coleman, a renowned medical doctor/psychiatrist, and Patrick Clancy, an attorney, studied this phenomenon from two sides: mental health and the courts. In 1997, they coauthored an extensive guide called *Has a Child Been Molested?,* intended to help all involved understand and appropriately handle sexual abuse allegations and cases. As experts, they had previously testified for both prosecution and defense teams. They acknowledged that they could not ignore "the undeniable fact that molested children might not readily reveal what happened to them." After all, molestation does not necessarily leave bruises and broken bones.[24]

Troubled by the hysteria, Coleman and Clancy believed that the mental health professionals who saw the children "persuaded police and child protection agencies that children would never say untrue things about sex, no matter how they were interviewed . . . and that children never fabricate the kinds of explicit sexual manipulations they divulge in complaints or interrogations."[25]

In a 1983 article titled "The Child Sexual Abuse Accommodation Syndrome," published by the National Library of Medicine, psychiatrist Roland Summit, a leading figure and spokesperson in the child sexual abuse crusade, wrote he believed that "once a child claimed abuse, vigorous investigation was no longer necessary to determine whether or not it had actually occurred." Summit is credited with the theory that "when children say that they have been abused, we can be certain that they have been—period." Further, that theory was based on "disclosures" he insisted were "made during my work with incestuous families."[26] As a result, his theory that children don't lie became the pervasive school of thought, which in turn became the rule for conducting the investigation in the Little Rascals case. Further, Summit benefited professionally from diagnosed sexually abused children that were seen by therapists in criminal cases in which authorities "found no positive evidence" of abuse, yet described the examinations "as consistent with a history of abuse." According to Richard Beck, rather than asking for more clarity and proof, Summit simply "validated" therapist's findings.[27] Several states have since prohibited testimonies using Summit's theories because they are not generally accepted by scientists, and furthermore, his theories are widely criticized for misuse by law enforcement and prosecutors.

In Coleman and Clancy's extensive study of the McMartin Preschool case, they found that the "use of techniques like 'anatomically correct dolls' . . . now recognized by experts as 'contaminators'" was especially dangerous when "combined with leading and suggestive questioning." Their study confirmed what other experts were also seeing: "The child is *believed* if the accusation is made, but *not* believed if the abuse is denied," and this thinking brought "glorious simplicity to the difficult task of investigating such a charge." Even more troubling to them, judicial programs such as Parents United in California trained "police officers as . . . treatment facilitators . . . and therapists as key [players] in abuse investigations," and suddenly a system evolved where "investigators . . . sought to corroborate charges rather than evaluate them."[28]

Before long, the federal government seized on the madness, driving more panic and creating "a bizarre and volatile political atmosphere."[29] They formed task forces and commissions, passed legislation, and even established an entire division within the FBI called the Behavioral Science

Unit located at FBI headquarters in Quantico, Virginia. Agent and profiler Kenneth Lanning was a subject matter expert on sexual victimization of children, satanic ritual child abuse, recovered and repressed memory, the suggestibility of children, and the ramification of confirmation bias. He consulted on thousands of cases during his twenty-year career and became the nation's leading expert in his field. At the time, he was assigned to investigate the rampant rumors about the underground network of satanists.

In a 2019 podcast interview with Jerri Williams, also a retired FBI agent, Lanning talked about the phenomenon of large numbers of individuals who "believed something happened that [facts proved] did not." It was his research on ritual and satanic abuse and sexual exploitation of children that inspired his own book, *Love, Bombs, and Molesters: An FBI Agent's Journey*. In it, Lanning wrote that he found "people do not rely on facts" and "regardless of intelligence and education, and often despite common sense and evidence to the contrary, adults will believe what they want to believe based on their need to believe."[30]

Lanning studied sexual deviant behavior for over forty-five years. In 1983, he was consulted on his first case of repressed memory and sexual exploitation. Subsequently, over the next weeks and months, he received a "deluge" of calls from more alleged victims of bizarre activity from their childhood, hysterical parents who believed their children were victims at the hands of caregivers, and the therapists and investigators who were pursuing those accusations. Lanning said he could not justify the "idea that a group could torture and kill large numbers of [children] and then keep it a secret." In an interview with the *New York Times*, he admitted that "anything was possible," but he also made it clear that through all his investigations, he never found any physical evidence to corroborate any of the charges.[31]

Lanning worried that the hysteria could mute the concern and necessary attention to "less-sensational but far more likely instances of child sexual abuse." The main argument he heard was that "we must believe the children" because they could not possibly invent the charges and claims. He eventually began to doubt the concept of "repressed memory" at the center of the child sexual abuse scandals, and he came to believe that the moral panic of the seventies and eighties was perhaps the result of centuries of denial about the sexual abuse of children and a belief that children do not lie about these things.[32]

Along with overzealous, leading questioning and imprecise medical tests, the accusations became a self-fulfilling prophecy, and interestingly, Lanning discovered that often the very same group of psychologists was identified in nearly all the alleged ritual abuse cases. He later reflected that these incidents "just didn't happen" and that extremism by "those who believed wholeheartedly in the child ritual abuse [in the absence of physical evidence] were indeed members of a 'witch hunt.'" Lanning also offered a warning as verdicts were delivered in case after case. He believed that the people who pursued the convictions and said they "sincerely believe in ritual child abuse" must be willing to accept "responsibility for the damage they do with these cases."[33]

Beck's 2015 book detailed "a decade-long outbreak of collective hysteria" and "climate of fear" that took over the country beginning with the 1983 McMartin Preschool child abuse case. As with Little Rascals, the owners and workers were accused of "mutilation, killing animals, sexual abuse," and more. After seven employees and the sixty-seven-year-old grandmother were arrested and charged, one mother told the interviewer, "There is no doubt in my mind that my son has been abused." She said, "You cannot—he cannot—have made any of this up. There is no way."[34]

The parallels between the McMartin case and the Little Rascals case were substantial. In the interview for "Innocence Lost," Chris and Grace Bean made a similar claim that their child could not have made up the abuse. They believed little children simply do not have that kind of *knowledge* to make up those stories. The mother who made the original charge of molestation in the McMartin case was relentless, just as Mabry and Stever were in the Little Rascals case. Even though her child initially denied any abuse, the mother pursued it, contacting other parents and, ultimately, law enforcement in search of support for her "suspicions."

According to Beck, in the McMartin case, the police agreed to mail a letter to two hundred current and past families of the day care seeking information from any child who may have been a "witness to any crime" or who may have experienced "oral sex, fondling of genitals, buttock or chest area, and sodomy." They were asked to "complete an enclosed information form and return it as soon as possible." The fear was established and the seed was planted that sexual abuse was possible. Parents believed the suggestions in the letter, and before long, the affair became a full-blown witch hunt. In response to the hysteria, Lanning said there were actually "mental-health professionals out there . . . looking for tunnels where children were alleged to have been abused."[35]

The charges against the McMartin Preschool defendants were bizarre and dubious at best, again disturbingly similar to those levied against the Edenton Seven. Sociologist Mary DeYoung studied the phenomenon and wrote, "The unifying factor . . . was unquestionable that in cases with such grisly allegations, it would be imperative to support the victimized children at all costs—this translated into believing them without any regard for other factors that might be at play in the case." In other words, without any verifiable physical evidence. The media contributed significantly to spreading the hysteria, and the "widely publicized McMartin case . . . left the public . . . primed to believe the allegations" against Robin and the others, regardless of the untrustworthy and improbable nature of the accusations.[36]

Kee MacFarlane, an unlicensed clinical social worker who became director of Children's Institute International (CII), which works against child abuse in Los Angeles, was best known as the creator of the anatomically correct doll. She was eventually hired to interview the McMartin children. MacFarlane was well known by the law enforcement community, who considered her to be a "'specialist' in child sexual abuse."

In fact, she trained "thousands of [other] medical health professionals, law enforcement and child protection [officers] on the use" of the dolls.[37] Were any of the therapist-social workers in the Little Rascals case among the thousands trained by MacFarlane?

In his booklet about molestation, Coleman observed that MacFarlane's true talent was "manipulating the children in claiming abuse with no apparent concern for the truth." She used "untested efforts 'to try to combine' therapeutic and forensic interviews," filling interview rooms with "questionable toys: a 'detective dog' that could find 'yucky secrets' and child-sized and adult anatomically correct dolls with erect penises, vaginas, breasts, and pubic hair." In her techniques, she used the dolls to encourage the children to "demonstrate how their abuse had taken place." When interviewed, if the children responded "no" when questioned, MacFarlane insisted they would have said "yes" had they not been afraid of their teachers. She pursued what she believed to be true, ultimately interviewing four hundred McMartin Preschool children from as far back as ten years and claiming 100 percent of them had been abused. Eventually, most of MacFarlane's techniques were ruled "inappropriate."[38]

In the meantime, MacFarlane added even more alarming practices to her interviews. In studying the videotapes of her interviews with the children, Coleman and Clancy said she was single-minded, and they found her "techniques of play therapy, machines to tell secrets into, talking puppets, and leading and suggestive questioning" highly disturbing. They added that law enforcement trusted her completely and never viewed even the first videotaped interview in the McMartin case—[39]or subsequent ones. And if the interview practices were "highly disturbing" in the hands of someone like MacFarlane, imagine the suggestive nature of the interviews by Officer Brenda Toppin with little or no education or training in the use of those dolls with the Little Rascals children. Since no recordings of those sessions survived except part of one, and only scant notes were taken (in Toppin's own words), it is impossible to know what actually happened. When Coleman and Clancy reviewed the interviewing methods in the McMartin case and the minimal records in the Little Rascals case, they concluded, "It was quite obvious the cases were complete fabrications."[40]

Similar to the Edenton case, the McMartin case featured a lack of any physical evidence or eyewitnesses. MacFarlane needed proof and quickly found willing doctors who would join the case. She convinced Bruce Woodling, a forensic physician specializing in finding "subtle signs of abuse," to join her team. He was known for making sweeping diagnoses confirming abuse using a colposcopy. He trained MacFarlane to conduct forensic examinations on the children using the colposcope, a microscopic instrument that takes a highly magnetized photograph of the "anal and genital region." And then, according to Coleman, that photograph "gave a false impression" of normal variations, but because they were enlarged, those variations "implied an injury had occurred." MacFarlane then hired Dr. Astrid Heger, a pediatrician, to conduct the examinations of the 360 children in the McMartin case. Using those techniques, Heger asserted that more than 80 percent of the children she examined showed signs of sexual abuse. Besides McFarlane and Heger's questionable examinations, no other physical evidence was ever found.[41] Like in the Little Rascals case, the McMartin children repeatedly denied they had been abused—until after months of intense therapy when forty-one children finally admitted it. Coleman and Clancy later expressed that those examiners claimed to find "subtle indicators . . . [that completely] lacked [any] scientific evidence" to support the diagnoses of abuse. It also concerned them that they did not photograph "hymens or anuses of normal, non-abused boys and girls" so that they could be compared scientifically.[42]

After the McMartin case ended with not guilty verdicts on fifty-two counts and mistrials on the remaining thirteen charges, and despite the fact that Peggy McMartin Buckey and her son, Raymond Buckey, sued the district attorney and MacFarlane for "malicious prosecution" and won, all three medical experts in the case rose to prominence in their fields among the child sexual abuse network of healthcare followers. MacFarlane's many critics charged that her relentless, repetitive, and leading questioning led the children to create false or implanted memories. Did Officer Toppin and the therapists ruthlessly apply those same techniques in the Little Rascals investigation? Many medical experts have refuted Heger and Woodling's medical claims about what constitutes proof of abuse. It is interesting—even puzzling—that they became the reliable source for the state's medical experts in the Little Rascals case.

Chapter 12

Constructed Memories

Our memories are reconstructive. It's a little like a
Wikipedia page—you can change it, but so can other
people.
—Elizabeth Loftus

In the Little Rascals case, one cannot ignore the impact of the power of suggestion over the children—what they remembered versus what actually occurred. According to researchers Maria Zaragoza, Robert Belli, and Kristie Payment, "Children will remember misleading suggestions" and have a "tendency to conform or comply with suggestions provided by an adult authority figure." Only through careful assessment can evaluators—for example, properly trained mental health experts, law enforcement, and attorneys—adequately determine the level to which the memory is a result of one or the other. Zaragoza et al. concluded that young preschoolers are particularly susceptible, and that repeated exposure "to suggestion increased the incidence of false memories."[1] And the more repetition, the more the children remembered seeing things they never saw.

In October 2019, Elizabeth Loftus, an expert in memory malleability, appeared as a guest on the podcast *Speaking of Psychology*. Kaitlin Luna, who interviewed Loftus regarding her research, asked, "How can human memories be manipulated?" Loftus explained, "[Memories] can be manipulated when people talk to each other after . . . let's say some crime is over that they may have both witnessed. They can be manipulated when they are interrogated by an investigator who maybe has an agenda or has a hypothesis about what probably happened, and communicates that to the witness, even inadvertently. People can be manipulated when they see media coverage about an event, let's say it's a high-publicity event that is talked about a lot on television or in newspapers. In all of these cases, the opportunity is there for new information, not necessarily accurate information, to contaminate a person's memory."[2]

Certainly, the Little Rascals case was all over the news, and the town of Edenton was on fire with conversations about it. Parents were feverishly pursuing the truth from their children at home and through the state's therapists. In response to other cases like the McMartin Preschool and Little Rascals, one attorney warned about the "cottage industry of poorly trained and politically inspired sex abuse therapists" that had sprung up.[3] Were there opportunities for any of this to contaminate the children's memories or to implant false memories? Many believe so.

In *Child Eyewitness Testimony in Sexual Abuse Investigations*, Bruce E. Mapes, who holds a PhD and is a forensic and clinical psychologist, examined many studies on the reliability of child testimony based on age. He referenced studies by leading experts on memory and recall in child witnesses who were three-year-olds, the same age as many of the children in the Little Rascals case. They found that a "memory decreases significantly after a delay of one to three weeks," and memories for a child that age are "likely to be [little more than] repetitions of parental renditions."[4]

Further, Judith Adams, PhD, a licensed psychologist in clinical and forensic practice, researched scientific evidence in child abuse cases and determined that "poor interview procedures can lead to false allegations" and grave consequences from "inadequate training and biased inter-viewing procedures." She noted that the "most problematic are those in which there is no physical evidence."[5] Mapes also expressed concern about the "timing of interviews . . . because the legal process [was] dragged out across months or years."[6]

In 1994, Loftus and her colleague, Katherine Ketcham, published *The Myth of Repressed Memory* about the connection between repressed memory and sexual abuse. Loftus and her team "conducted hundreds of interviews with accusers and accused, therapists, lawyers, psychologists, psychiatrists, sociologists, criminologists, and law enforcement," one of whom was Agent Kenneth Lanning of the FBI. Loftus wrote that altering or creating memory is much like how we "mold and form clay." As an expert who regularly testified at criminal trials, she was concerned when an individual's fate was dependent on memory and, therefore, frequently cautioned courts that "memories are flexible and superimposable . . . a panoramic blackboard with endless supplies of chalk and erasers." Loftus further explained that the mind should be thought of "as a bowl filled with clear water. Now imagine each memory as a teaspoon of milk stirred into the water. Every adult mind holds thousands of these murky memories . . . who among us would dare to disentangle the water from the milk?"[7]

Loftus conducted research and interviews with numerous individuals who claimed to be victims of molestation. Most were interviewed following hours and months of therapy, including hypnosis. She found that "psychologists forcefully and repeatedly emphasized the emotional story-truth of repressed memories rather than their historical happening-truth." In other words, the individuals often were coached by well-meaning therapists into believing a "colorized version" created through suggestion, imagination, and a desire to "battle demons," as opposed to the "happening-truth," the black-and-white "indisputable reality" of what really happened with physical evidence to support it.[8]

Clearly, a critical component in the explosion of the moral panic began with the parents. Energized into action by therapists' and other parents' inflammable suggestions, they pushed and pushed unsubstantiated accusations without verifiable physical evidence, and the world followed. According to Lanning, the allegations were initially parents' interpretations of things their children did or said. Then parents began to "network with each other," and it suddenly became a "contagion."[9] This was certainly true in both the McMartin and Little Rascals cases. And the parents and the public continued to be more than willing to push the charges against individuals and day cares.

Lanning reported that the FBI investigated many hundreds of sexual abuse allegations in dozens of cases, with nearly two hundred people charged and almost one hundred convicted. They were all charged with similar satanic abuse based on bizarre, improbable stories and unsubstantiated charges. Lanning wrote that they all were defined by the same things: "multiple victims (very young at the time), multiple offenders (part of an organized group), fear as the primary controlling tactic, and bizarre or ritualistic activity."[10] The Edenton Seven were but a few of the two hundred victims charged and prosecuted.

Defense attorneys Miller and Spivey rightfully questioned the reliability of child witnesses. They expressed concern about the complexity of lawyers defending someone charged with child sexual abuse because "the child is the principal, if not the only witness from whom information about the suspected offense must be obtained."[11]

According to the defense attorneys, the danger of "assumptions courts make about [a child's] abilities and comprehension to testify truthfully" was illustrated through the testimony of one of the children in Bob Kelly's trial. The prosecutor "employed blatantly leading and suggestive questions, including [language intended to encourage or guide] the child to remember what he had told his mother." And this was explicitly done "to have the child acknowledge offenses the prosecutor actually 'testified' about."[12] In simpler terms, the prosecutors suggested to the child what happened, and the child then confirmed what the prosecutor told them had happened. (The following is quoted directly from the trial transcripts in *State of North Carolina v. Robert Kelly Jr.*)

The prosecution asked one child if he remembered "Miss Debbie that lived down the street from you?"

"Yes."

"Okay. Did she do bad things to you?"

"No."

"Do you remember telling your mom that Miss Debbie stuck her finger up your butt?"

"No."

"Was Miss Debbie always nice to you?"

"I don't remember."

"Do you remember talking to your mom about Miss Debbie?"

"No."

The child was questioned nine times over the following three pages of testimony, asking if he "remembered."[13]

Loftus shares Spivey and Miller's concern about the reliability of the child's memory, and the "competency test" the court used showed little more than the child's ability to repeat what adults in positions of authority had told him or her. The state paid for the children to travel with their families to Farmville, North Carolina, to attend a "Court School" that would teach them how to answer questions "truthfully." If the Court School teacher held up a red object and said it was yellow, could the child correct the instructor? It truly was that simple to determine that a child was competent to testify. However, were their answers a test of the reliability of their testimony and memory, or were their answers influenced by what they had learned in Court School?

According to the North Carolina Rules of Evidence at the time, in "the past, if children below a certain age were deemed to be incompetent as witnesses," they were not allowed to testify. The courts eventually moved to determine "a child's competency as a witness . . . not by their age, but rather by the ability to understand the obligation to tell the truth." If they passed the test, they were then allowed to testify.[14]

Extensive research into these concerns was conducted in the decade leading up to the Little Rascals case in an "effort to determine the ability of children to remember and report accurately events they have experienced." Further, the research into child sexual abuse trials showed that the child witnesses were "generally involved in extensive and multiple pretrial interviews conducted by social workers, medical doctors, psychologists, parents, police officers, and prosecutors," which was undoubtedly true in the Edenton Seven case. Moreover, the studies showed that the children's memories were "influenced and distorted" by the "leading and suggestive questioning," and that there were "no neutral parties in child abuse trials."[15]

In addition to the constant, coercive questioning, psychologists Ceci and Bruck believe the social pressure on parents was profound. They had to believe their "children had been abused," and to deny it or refuse to go along meant "they became socially isolated." In fact, "It almost seemed that having a child suspected of being abused made one part of the 'in-group.'"[16] Naturally, people in Edenton were talking a lot about what they believed had happened, and likely spoke frequently in front of children.

It is not difficult to understand the impact of parents talking on the children, and more, the impact of the constant questioning and discussion that was obviously occurring in Edenton. In 2022, Peter Ornstein, professor emeritus of the Department of Psychology at the University of North Carolina at Chapel Hill, and his colleague Taylor E. Thomas wrote "A Constructivist Perspective on Mother-Child Conversations and Children's Eyewitness Memory." "It is well known that children's testimony can be influenced by suggestion" and that "adult-child conversations . . . can be critical in shaping a child's understanding—for better or for worse—of an experience," Ornstein and Thomas wrote. Through research, it was learned "how mothers navigate . . . challenging conversations" and the significant "influence mothers have on their children's views of [a] past experience," with "serious implications" for children's "testimony." And the more "highly elaborative" [animated in detail] the mother is, the "more likely [the child is] to make false reports."[17]

With that in mind, it seemed logical for me to consider a conversation with an Edenton native (he wished to remain anonymous) who lived in

Edenton at the time the case unfolded. He said the atmosphere in Edenton at the time was "highly charged, and people were utterly hateful toward anyone who questioned the accusations or supported the Kellys."[18] He also recalled that people openly ostracized and shunned many who had been their friends, from schools to churches, from grocery stores to the country club. They simply stopped talking to each other—parents *and* children—a pattern that has continued for thirty-five years. Children rejected other children whose parents refused to accept allegations of abuse, shouting things as cruel as "my mommy hates your mommy."[19] As a result, those children were excluded from birthday parties, dances, celebrations, and more. After more than three decades, many people continue to believe the abuse happened. They see those people who refused to side against Kelly and the others as pariahs and still avert their eyes or cross the street to avoid any contact with them.

For many residents, the pressure to acquiesce was powerful. Go along or else. Enough of the parents were wealthy, educated, and entitled. In fact, in their own words, they were "very well-connected," a detail that became paramount in Bob Kelly's trial. One father was quoted as saying, "They messed with the wrong people. We called the state representative, the mayor—we got straight to the governor, straight to [Attorney General] Lacy Thornburg."[20]

The prosecution asked one mother if she "wanted to believe [her] son had been abused." The mother responded that the pressure to believe was intense. She said to the prosecutor, "No, you are wording it wrong. It was once you got on this wagon that was going through town, sir, there was no way off. And if you jumped off of it like I did, then believe me, after people saw the way I was treated, then they didn't want to get off of it, and they weren't going to get off of it."[21]

One by one, parents and townspeople succumbed and joined the hysteria.

Chapter 13

The State v. Byrum

We didn't get these day-care panics until the so-called
therapists, so-called social workers, and so-called investigators began using questionable techniques.
—Richard Ofshe, PhD

Robin's lawyer, Jeff Miller, wasted no time. Within days, he made a general appearance in court and filed the following motions: a "Bill of Particulars" that requested information regarding the specific charges and offenses alleged to have occurred and of which Robin was accused, a "Motion for Bond Reduction," and a "Motion for Discovery" that requested disclosure of any statements or evidence that the state intended to use in her trial.

On January 24, Miller consulted with Dr. Hal Daniels from East Carolina University, an expert in speech pathology, regarding the statements from the children and the way they talked or spoke about things. In the letter, Miller wrote they believed "the psychologists, [social workers], and others had been 'co-opted' by the prosecution," raising an early red flag for the defense.[1] The theory about suggestibility was that children did not talk this way, and the statements were actually planted in the children. Daniels believed it was a "modern-day Crucible," which would prove to be prophetic.[2]

By February, it appeared to the defense teams that the state planned to try Robin, Shelley Stone, and Dawn Wilson together. Stone was already out on a $375,000 bond, but Robin and Dawn Wilson had been unable to make bond. Later, they decided they might be tried first, perhaps because theirs was the weakest case, so the attorneys for all three filed the first of many "Motions for Joinder" to try the cases together. This meant they could combine their efforts and resources to present a stronger defense. Miller wrote to Robin and her mother on February 7, reassuring them that he "shared [their] thoughts and feelings" about Robin's innocence. In that letter, Miller said he had "contacted several psychologists in an effort to get some idea as to the methodology used in interviewing the children." This would later prove to be invaluable when it came to light that the therapists and investigators may have used questionable and coercive tactics that Miller said "created a reality that [was] reinforced . . . repeated . . . retold . . . [and became] firm memories," and collaborated with the prosecution.[3]

As Robin faced "life imprisonment" for the charges against her, it became clear very quickly that her defense would need to employ all possible measures to prove her innocence. In a motion to the court, Miller stated that "THE DEFENDANT STEADFASTLY AND TRUTHFULLY ASSERTS THAT SHE IS INNOCENT OF EACH OF THE CHARGES AGAINST HER," and he requested funds to "employ experts," because without them she would be "deprived of a fair trial." He was justifiably concerned because he knew the state hired its own experts. And in fact, it was later disclosed to him and the other defense teams that all the children interviewed by the four state-paid therapists admitted to the abuse, yet all the children interviewed by outside, privately employed therapists denied any such abuse occurred. Miller asserted that there can be "no equal justice where the kind of trial a [person] gets depends on the amount of money [she] has."[4]

In a letter to District Attorney H. P. Williams, dated February 19, 1990, Miller reminded him of the fact that Robin continued to "stridently assert her innocence" and was "willing to undergo any type of examination to establish her truthfulness and lack of culpability." Furthermore, he reminded Williams that he was "supposed to be an advocate of fairness and justice for all the citizens of the state and Chowan County . . . and not for any particular interest group . . . or for advancing [his] political considerations." He went on to say that the indictment of Robin caused him to "question the validity of all the other indictments."[5]

By now, all the defendants, now widely known as the Edenton Seven, had been arrested and indicted. All remained in jail under significant bonds, except Shelley Stone and Darlene Harris, who posted bail earlier in the fall. Getting a fair trial was a pressing issue considering the nature of the cases and the publicity surrounding them. Hence, the attorneys of the seven defendants agreed their best chance was to join the cases together into one trial. The state had previously objected to Miller's request for joinder; however, it made sense because all were charged as "co-conspirators, and the state had failed to provide any specific dates or times" for the alleged offenses.[6]

The accusations and alleged offenses were a direct result of the defendants' employment or relationship with Little Rascals Day Care between August 1988 and December 1988. According to the attorneys' motion to the Superior Court, filed on February 19, 1990, trying the defendants collectively would prevent undue burden to provide "separate proofs, duplication of efforts, waste of assets, inefficient use of resources, and burdensome expense of time and money." The lawyers also had legitimate concerns about fair trials because of "pretrial prejudice arising from publicity" and "unfair saturation and [imitating] of evidence and testimony" from the children.[7]

In a motion submitted to the court, Miller argued that the defendants be tried together, writing he strongly believed that "the various conspiracy and substantive indictments [were] an attempt to create an interlocking matrix of alleged criminal responsibility which [necessitated] a joint trial."[8] He had learned that the district attorney intended to try Bob Kelly first, followed by a joint trial of Betsy Kelly and Scott Privott.

Miller was convinced that this was done intentionally for "the purpose of prejudicing each defendant." Miller wanted Robin to testify in her own defense. However, should she be required to testify in the trials before her own trial, her testimony might be used against her. And each defense attorney had indicated that they planned to subpoena her to testify. Likewise, Miller planned to subpoena the other six defendants to testify at Robin's trial. All of this would be unnecessary were they all tried together. Miller also expressed concern about preventing the stress on the "child witnesses who will be called . . . [and] . . . examined or cross-examined" multiple times.[9]

Miller cited the time needed for preparation for each attorney and case and the immense expenses and resources required for a trial of this nature as big concerns. He also noted the probability of polluted jury pools and the necessity for expert witnesses and investigators. These were legitimate issues, as Miller's Motion to the Court declared. On February 21, Judge Tillery ruled that the cases could be tried together, but that order was later vacated by an appellate court in September of 1990, and subsequently, Tillery resigned in October. In a defense brief from the 1992 Court of Appeals, Tillery complained, "I had served as a judge in the Superior Court for over 20 years and I never found it necessary to take such a step—neither have I ever been made to feel before that one side or the other considered me to be not only an adversary but also fair game . . . for reckless assertion" about the state's right to withhold evidence.[10] After Tillery resigned, Marsh McLelland was appointed as the new trial judge. This was a blow to the defense.

Chapter 14

Robin's Story—"The Thin, Gray Dress"

Bridget Bishop stands . . . Arms folded before her, she
stares down the gawkers . . . who gaze directly and smirk
to see her there . . . those who whisper to each other and
glance away as if fearful of her glance.
—Marilynne K. Roach, *Six Women of Salem*

The gloom of waiting in that jail cell was like stagnant air heavy on my heart. The sudden development of a medical issue meant that I had to be transported to the emergency room. I will never forget the horror of being in shackles, handcuffs, and that shameful orange jumpsuit as if I were some dangerous criminal. I was forced to walk through the emergency room, surrounded by people and their stares and gawking. I felt tainted. Never in my life did I feel like such a disgrace, like a complete failure. I was in terrible physical pain, but that didn't matter because the mental torment was far worse. The doctor examined me, and all I wanted to do was shout at him, "I'm innocent!" I wanted to plead my case, to tell him, "I don't belong in jail!" However, I just kept my silence and cried and cried.

I was diagnosed with an acute urinary tract infection and kidney infection, which I'm sure was from dehydration and stress. Regardless, I was not well. I was already slight, but my weight dropped drastically. Because I needed medical treatment the county jail couldn't tend to, they transferred me to Raleigh Central Prison for Women where there was an infirmary on site. This was three hours from my mother, my husband,

and, worst of all, my son. Three hours! I was even more devastated now because I knew I would see even less of them. As if I was riding in my own funeral procession, the long drive that afternoon from Washington to Raleigh Central Prison was beyond depressing. *Does Momma even know where I am? I wondered. How will anyone get in touch with me?*

Raleigh Central Prison was a massive compound compared to the jails in Chowan and Washington. There were lots of buildings, lots of fences, lots of inmates, and lots of guards. My first stop was at a small building used for admissions. It was nighttime when we arrived, and the first thing I had to do was get out of my orange jumpsuit and into an RCP uniform, which was a drab, thin, gray dress that buttoned down the front. That was it. But before I was allowed to transition into that dress, I suffered the unimaginable. Though I was sort of searched in the Beaufort County Jail, mostly it was just a pat down, but this search was different. They put me in a small room with one officer. I was ordered to take off all my clothes. Paralyzed with fear, there I was, standing completely naked when the officer ordered me to bend over so she could check my orifices for contraband. I was barely nineteen and had no idea what they were talking about. Was this really happening to me? Tears streaming down my face, I knew I must be in hell and somehow deserved this humiliation.

Once the officer finished searching me, I put on the gray prison dress they had handed me before. From there, I was thrown into a large, cold room with no TV, no noise, and only a few other inmates sleeping with their heads on the tables, all of us awaiting the admissions process. God only knows how long they had been there before I got there, or how long I would have to wait. I didn't utter a single word to any of them.

Honestly, I was scared to death and only imagined from reading and television what they do to people in prison who were charged with what I had been charged with. It was cold and drizzling outside, which compounded my feelings of despair and helplessness. After I got my papers, I was sent to the "safe-keeping" section of the prison. The only lights were on the walkways, but I could see the general population side of the prison as we slowly made our way down the dark hall. I later learned "safe-keeping" was where women were housed while awaiting trial. It was not meant for people to stay for lengthy periods of time. There was no heat, no air, and barely any running water. The toilets were just cement basins with a round base placed directly in the middle of the cells. Regardless of what this area was meant for, it would end up being my home for the rest of the year.

It was February 1990. There were about twenty cells, each housing four women, and we were all on a schedule based on even-numbered and odd-numbered cells. On my cell's day to be "out," we were sent to the lounge. We exited our cell at a specified time and remained out of our cell until lockdown that night. The good thing about being out was that it meant I could shower, eat at a table, and watch television. However, once we were locked down at night and after our day "out," we were then locked in for two days straight until it was our scheduled day to be out again. During my admissions process, I had to fill out a visitor's list and set up an account for the canteen, where I was only allowed to withdraw thirty dollars a week, regardless of how much I needed. It is no surprise that I spent most of my money on paper, envelopes, and stamps. Of course, I had to buy shampoo and deodorant, but mostly I just bought stamps, paper, and envelopes and then wrote . . . and wrote . . . and wrote a lot!

Most of the time, I kept to myself, and I was pretty certain Betsy and Dawn were both there too, perhaps housed somewhere in "safe-keeping" as well. I just had to find them. I found Dawn first, and from her, I learned Betsy was in some program that allowed her to leave "safe-keeping" for a little while each day. I couldn't imagine what that was, but a big part of me wished I could be out of that dark, cold place. My time there was as good as it could be under the circumstances. I made a few "friends" who believed me when I told them I was innocent. Some of them were there for murder, for trafficking drugs, or for driving drunk—and all of them admitted they were guilty and talked about changing if they ever got out. But me? I talked about my baby. I learned from these women that they may be guilty, but they were human. Even though I was innocent, there I was, just like them, sitting in Central Prison alongside the guilty. I didn't judge them. I just listened to their stories, and I certainly had plenty of time for that. Besides, listening to them helped keep my mind off my own problems.

Sometime near the end of February, they moved Betsy, Dawn, and me into the same cell. Why did they put us in the same cell? I thought it was odd, especially so soon after I arrived. I heard that once an inmate had a cell assignment, that's usually where she stayed until a court hearing. And we were to have many. On the days we had those hearings, we had to take everything that belonged to us to head out to court. Unfortunately, my court sessions were three hours away, and while there, I was usually housed in the Elizabeth City jail.

On return, we had to suffer the inevitable re-admissions process each time: surrender our belongings, get a new uniform, and submit to yet another body search. Every time. Nevertheless, I was thankful that at Central Prison I was finally in the cell with Betsy and Dawn, and we had one very important thing in common. WE WERE ALL INNOCENT! But still, it nagged at us. What was the reason for putting us together?

During the day, Betsy was out for the mental health program at the prison, but at night, when she returned, we talked. Mostly, we spent our precious time together comforting each other and catching up. The building where we were housed had been condemned a long time ago, so the walls were nothing more than cinder blocks with peeling paint. There was little to no light or heat, and huge cockroaches crawled and flew about us at all hours of the day and night. It was disgusting and terrifying. But to keep my baby and my family close, I stuck their photos on those nasty walls, silently forbidding those cockroaches to crawl on them. The three of us would read our Bibles and talk about the scriptures and our cases to comfort ourselves. Because we knew we were there for the long haul, it was important to us that we spent our time together supporting each other. We used ink and highlighters we bought through the prison store to mark the Bible passages that comforted us.

One day it was our turn for lockdown, and Betsy was gone again. They asked Dawn and me to step out of our cell, and suddenly the guards went in and ransacked our cell, going through all our things. What were they looking for? For some reason, they took our only possessions—our Bibles. We later learned the state wanted to see what satanic rituals we were involved in and thought perhaps they might find evidence in our Bibles. Seriously? Well, of course, they thought that. Didn't they think we were all child molesters? Monsters? Obviously, the state found nothing in our Bibles or in our cell, and they got nowhere with this intrusion. They were willing to go to any length to find something, anything against us. They ripped our lives apart, and now they had taken what little privacy we had, hoping to find some kind of evidence to use against us. They still had no case!

Overall, the day-to-day monotony in the prison was soul-crushing. The worst part was thinking about my baby. I could hardly bear to think about him and how he was growing. When I was arrested, he was only six months old, and now I was missing everything. My mother-in-law, Gloria, often wrote to fill me in, but it wasn't the same. It became important to figure out how to keep my sanity, so I was determined to try to accept I was there and not think about him. But I did anyway, and I cried every day. When I say that I cried every day . . . I mean I CRIED, often for hours at a time. Momma was always on my mind too. She never showed emotion because she didn't want people to see her break down, but both our worlds were collapsing. I knew how much she regretted moving me to Edenton.

In time, I discovered I could have my personal clothes from home brought to me, as well as some personal things, so I asked Momma for long johns to keep warm, tops and bottoms for under my prison dress, some daily devotionals, and my personal Bible. Just as important, I learned the routines of day-to-day life in safe-keeping. Food was a big problem. It was awful, and I wasn't eating well, mostly because of stress. However, I also watched how some of the "girls" operated when serving food. While we were in lockdown, other inmates were the ones serving our trays through small slots in the middle of the doors. I knew not everyone was a friend. Too many times I saw one of those inmates spit into another inmate's tray. I wasn't going to let that happen to me, so I wasn't eating. Even though most of the girls seemed to like me, I was worried there might be a new girl circulating the building who might assume I was guilty of child abuse before she knew me. She might spit in my tray as well, and that was just not going to happen.

One girl, Maggie, was very different from the others and from me in many ways. Most obviously, she was very tall. She must have been over six feet, and she was a prostitute with HIV and no education. But more importantly, she became my friend. She had no one on the outside to care about her or to give her anything, and it bothered me that I had what seemed to be so much while she had so little. I decided to help as much as I could by giving her a little money, shampoo, and deodorant. She also knew why I was there. However, she believed me when I said that I was innocent, and if another inmate caused me trouble, Maggie stood up for me. At one point, she almost fought with another girl who was running her mouth at me, which could have caused Maggie big trouble.

The months dragged on, and eventually, I was allowed to go into the same mental health program that Betsy was in, but I didn't know if I really wanted that. I hated change, and I certainly didn't want to put myself in a situation that would be worse than what I was already in. Reluctantly, I joined the program, and as it turned out, it was a bit of a blessing, if there was such a thing in prison. Finally, I was no longer locked down in a cell for thirty or more hours at a time, and I could walk . . . and walk . . . and walk. No one would understand that walking was such a big deal, but where we were held before, there was only a very small yard area. We were only allowed to sit outside or move around for about fifteen minutes a day. And if there weren't enough guards on duty, which there often weren't, we just weren't allowed to go out. Yet, in the mental health program, I was allowed to be free in a different way. It was a large building with a few instructors who gave us the chance to talk. We even had art and movie time. I'll never forget this was the first time I ever watched the movie *Pretty Woman*. All I could think was how amazing it was that the main character's life was so drastically changed—from a prostitute to a life of privilege—and she was with a man who loved her. It made me wish even harder for my life to change.

Being involved in the mental health program also helped me with something I was scared to death of—the general prison population. The mental health program was organizing an inmate fashion show, and I thought, *Boy, this is right up my alley*. We had to make our own outfits from whatever we could scratch together. So, I made a dress—I don't remember from what—and strutted myself right up there on stage in front of the entire prison community. Yes, it truly was funny; as shy as I was, I ended up doing well in the show. I knew I did a good job, and for the first time since I got to prison, something was fun, made me smile, and helped me forget about my troubles . . . at least for a little while.

During those long months in prison, people on the outside sustained me. Some of the most important ones were my attorney, Jeff Miller; his wife, Rachel; and Rachel's cousin, Sandra. Sandra worked in Jeff's law office. They were all an invaluable source of information and support for Momma and me. From the very first moment my mother hired him, Jeff believed in me, and he fought so hard for me. He and Rachel carefully kept us informed about everything that was happening. They provided my mother with copies of every document, every motion, every hearing, every meeting, every letter, and every single event that took place surrounding my case. My mom kept all those documents, though I wondered at the time if she read them. One risk was that she would not understand the legal jargon, and Rachel wanted to make sure my situation was clear to her. To help Momma, she wrote in the margins and put little Post-it notes on anything that might have needed expla-nation. These small gestures gave Momma comfort and helped her to know what to pay attention to in the documents and even if the motions were from the "good guys" or "bad guys." Rachel explained how to understand rulings, and at the same time, she encouraged Momma to be strong and keep her faith. To lighten Momma's pain, she occasionally sent funny cartoons hoping to make her laugh. As it turned out, all of it was important, and maybe, just maybe, she really did read all of it.

Like so many others, my Edenton and Kentucky church families also sustained me. They wrote to me often, and from those letters, we formed deep friendships. In particular, there was a dear sweet lady named Sheila who attended Aunt Penny and Aunt Sue's church and lived next door to Aunt Penny. I grew up around her, and I knew she loved me like another mother. After my arrest, she wrote weekly to remind me that God wouldn't forsake me. I read her letters over and over.

But honestly, I felt pretty forgotten in that awful place. I was innocent. Why did this happen? Why was it taking so long for anyone to believe me and set me free? Sheila's letters, words of encouragement, and the Bible she sent me all kept me breathing. But in the end, the only way I survived was to believe somehow that things were going to work out.

CHAPTER 15

ROBIN'S STORY—MY BOND

Excessive bail shall not be required, nor excessive fines
imposed, nor cruel or unusual punishment inflicted.
—Fourteenth Amendment, the
United States Constitution

I truly don't know what I would have done without Jeff Miller. As the weeks drifted slowly by, I sat in jail, unable to make a bond, awaiting a trial on something I didn't do, and facing the knowledge that if I was convicted, I might spend the rest of my life in prison. He never stopped fighting for me.

In February, Jeff finally succeeded in getting my bond reduced to $350,000, but we couldn't begin to meet our portion of the cash required for the secured bond. Every time he addressed the court and DA, he insisted I was not a flight risk, that I had a young baby and husband at home, and that I had no prior record that would indicate I might try to flee. Nothing. In March, Jeff even wrote a letter to the editor of the Raleigh *News & Observer*, hoping to elicit some sympathy from the public and addressing overcrowding in the "prison and county jail." In his letter, he shamed "politicians [who] overlooked the number of people who [were] incarcerated awaiting trial, many of these were 'innocent' [yet] incarcerated under huge bonds beyond their means" to pay. His letter closed by challenging that a "constitutional society which cherishes liberty and freedom, the fact that even one such innocent person suffers this 'punishment' ought not to be tolerated." The letter didn't help. I lingered in jail under a huge bond that was keeping me in prison and away from my baby.

After I was arrested, my Aunt Penny started a letter-writing campaign. She wrote and wrote. She wrote several letters trying to get someone to help with my bond. In particular, she wrote to North Carolina Governor Jim Martin, who thanked her and expressed his "[understanding] for her feelings regarding this matter" but added that he had "no authority to intervene." Sadly, I doubt he "understood" at all. She also wrote Pete Thompson, their representative from the North Carolina House of Representatives, whose reply was dated the same day as the governor's. He assured her that "H. P. Williams [was] acting properly in all his actions [as was] that of his staff, and that justice [would] prevail." Ironically, whether Williams acted properly would eventually be questioned by more than just me.

In the spring of 1990, Ofra Bikel and her team with PBS *Frontline* came to the prison to interview Betsy, Dawn, and me for the first airing of "Innocence Lost" in May of that year. We appeared on national television wearing our drab gray uniforms. It drew worldwide attention, and the reaction was unbelievable. I had some hope that with the documentary airing on TV and so many people knowing about the case, we would all be freed. I didn't know how long my stay in prison would be, but I tried not to give up hope. I was desperate for the nightmare to end so I could reunite with my son.

One woman from Cambridge, Massachusetts, wrote to me in June after watching the *Frontline* program, stating that she thought all of us were "victims of a classic 'witch hunt.'" That wasn't the first or the last time we heard that. She went on to say she was so troubled by what she saw that she "sent for the transcript . . . to make sure [she] hadn't missed something . . . recognizing that we were victims of one woman's psychotic reaction amplified by mass hysteria." Unfortunately, it would take more than one woman's moral outrage or a documentary to end this for me. I just wanted to get out on bail, and we couldn't understand the state's resistance to reducing my bond. Was it meant to pressure me to accept a plea bargain and testify against the others? I was not going to testify to a lie.

Jeff Miller entered a "Second Motion and Request for Bond Reduction" based on the same facts he argued in the first Motion: I was nineteen years old, unemployed, unable to afford the bond, had a ten-month-old child, and was declared indigent by the court. I steadfastly and truthfully [asserted] that I was innocent of each of the charges against me; I agreed to a polygraph; I freely and voluntarily spoke with investigators prior to arrest; I made no attempt to flee prior to being charged, even though I knew it was coming, and because I was innocent of the allegations made against me; I had no prior criminal record; the weight of the state's evidence against me was weak and insubstantial, at best; all my family and financial ties were to Edenton; and the district attorney and special prosecutor were clearly seeking high and unobtainable bonds for the improper purpose of punishing me prior to trial and inhibiting my ability to prepare a defense. A total of twelve pages were in that motion with eighteen substantial, significant, and carefully elaborated facts presented for the court to consider to "modify" my bond and the conditions of pretrial release.

It was denied.

In December 1990, the three of us got another court date for bond reduction, and we were transported from the Raleigh prison back to the Pasquotank County Jail in Elizabeth City to prepare for it. Betsy, Dawn, and I were inseparable by now, and we had been dragged in and out of courtrooms, county jails, and back to Central Prison so many times that we lost count. Was this going to be the last time for me?

Our appearance mattered when we went before the judge, so for the first time, we were able to browse a clothing catalog to select something other than those awful gray uniforms for our court appearance. It was up to our families to have the new outfits ready for us when we arrived at the courthouse. After all, every court session was televised live—which meant more publicity.

The courtroom was bursting with bright light, a very different atmosphere from our oppressive prison cell, but that wasn't what grabbed me. As the officers paraded us into the courtroom and past the audience of day care parents, I felt the heaviness of their hate. Their stares were agonizing, judging. I refused to be defeated by them. I was exhausted, but I was determined to hold my head high and be strong for the two people in that courtroom who were there for me, Jeff Miller and my momma. Our eyes met, and Momma's beautiful smile reassured me that "everything would be okay." The judge did reduce my bond, but it was still so high, and I felt even more defeated. I knew my family didn't have that kind of money, and Momma was already crumbling under the weight of legal fees. All I could think was, *How will we ever make that kind of bond?*

After the judge handed down the new bonds, the officers took us to the back of the courtroom to see our families. I wasn't handcuffed at this point, and I was crying. Momma grabbed me, hugged me tight, and whispered, "You will get out soon, very soon, I promise. Pap-pa and I will wire the money to Edenton tonight." Was this really over? Was I going to be holding my baby tomorrow? I held on to Momma's words as the three of us were escorted out of the courtroom.

The next two days were the longest of my life. I heard nothing. We were transported back to the jail in Elizabeth City, the closest female jail around. It was incredibly small and housed about ten female prisoners total. There we were again, with no shampoo and no change of clothes— every time we entered a different facility, we were stripped of everything we came with and had to start over again. I was determined not to buy one more shampoo or deodorant. I don't even recall if there was a shower.

Every few hours, a jailer would walk by the cells, and we would hear someone's name, the keys clanking, and a cell door opening, but our names were never called.

Until, finally, there it was: "Robin Gail Byrum." Like a puppy at the shelter, I ran to the cell door.

"You're bonded out," the guard said. "Get your things."

It was finally happening. But I suddenly felt torn. There was a real sadness knowing I had to leave Dawn and Betsy behind. I was the first to get my family back, but I knew Dawn's family was working hard to get her out. I also knew Betsy was likely going back to Central Prison and safe-keeping. I hugged them both, turned, and left with the guard, not having a clue what was ahead of me.

They took me back to the Chowan County Sheriff's office, where officers and bondsmen were everywhere. Reporters and television crews were swarming the sheriff's office, and I was told to move quickly into the building. Several officers then escorted me into an office filled with even more officers, and I wondered, *What in the world is going on?* I had no idea that bonding me out was so involved, or if there was a threat. Was my life in danger? Did Momma know what was going on? I tried to call her from the sheriff's office, but the bondsman grabbed my hand and aggressively shoved the phone down. I was in tears. I wondered if I was going somewhere that I didn't understand. Then one of the officers said quietly, "We'll fill you in soon."

There I sat in another jail cell. Waiting. Wondering if I really was going to be bonded out. Finally, on December 20, 1990, four long days after my bond reduction hearing, 345 days after my arrest, 345 days without my precious baby, and 345 days without my freedom, my grandparents and my mother were somehow able to come up with the money to get a secured bond for my release. I learned later Momma borrowed $10,000 from Aunt Penny, $5,000 from Aunt Sue, and $25,000 from my Pap-pa. The bond also required quite a few bondsmen. But I believed Momma was going to keep her promise. Maybe I really was going to be home by Christmas. I could only hope.

When I walked out of that jail, I was met by Herb Gardner, the bondsman, who escorted me into a huge, black Lincoln Continental. I was terrified. What was this unmarked car? We were in that car for over an hour. It was dark. It was late. I was disoriented. Where were we?

Suddenly, we pulled up to Jeff Miller's office. I was utterly bewildered. What were we doing there? But the moment he opened the door to the car, I was met by my mother, Kevin, Rachel, Jeff, and a few others, all there to welcome me with balloons and gifts and tears. I was overcome with emotion that this was all for me. But wait. Where was my baby? I was completely crushed that he wasn't there.

As it turns out, Kevin wanted time alone with me that night, so Rachel and Mom arranged for us to stay at a local hotel that first night. I was devastated. I thanked them, but I was sure they all saw the disappointment on my face. Mom was just happy that I was out of jail, as was I, but I just wanted to hold my child. To really hold him, and not like in prison. Kevin and I went to the hotel, where I'm sure he wanted his night with me, but quite frankly, intimacy was not on the table. If I couldn't have my baby, I just wanted a long, hot bath where I could finally, after nearly a year, shave my freaking legs! Kevin knocked . . . many times . . . but when I finally came out, he was fast asleep.

The next morning, Kevin and I were supposed to go to his Aunt Tricia's house, where we would set up camp until we knew our next steps financially and mentally, and where we could work. Tricia lived in Tarboro, located about thirty miles from Greenville. In the meantime, Rachel, friends, and family all donated items to get us started, and for that, I couldn't have been more grateful. But my mind was still focused on my child. I only wanted to get to Tarboro to get my hands on him. It was nearly Christmas, and I knew Tricia's house would be packed with family, something I was not looking forward to. In the end, I was thankful for all the welcoming family members, some of whom I had never met before. There was goodness in that house surrounded by trees wrapped in yellow ribbons in support of me. In fact, yellow ribbons were all over her neighborhood and a real home-cooked dinner was on the table.

Finally, Kevin's mother and sister arrived from Edenton, and there in Gloria's arms was my little baby. This was the moment I had waited for an entire year, but instead of pure bliss, it was painful and awkward. My baby had been six months old when I was arrested. He was now eighteen months old. He didn't know me, so at first, he rejected me. I was afraid our bond had been irrevocably broken, and it was hard for Gloria too. I was grateful she stepped in when my world fell apart, but now she had to let go.

Afterward, I think Gloria resented me for their separation, but I also think she resented that my mom had to work instead of helping with the baby. Kevin had moved in with his parents in Edenton so Gloria could take care of the baby, but he didn't step up to do his part. Momma had to sell our trailer and furniture to pay the attorney's fees. She quit the hospital to freelance because it paid better, and she couldn't stay in Edenton and do that. Besides, as part of my release, I couldn't return to Edenton, where Momma and I had a home. She owed a lot of money to her family in Kentucky, and she was now supporting all three of us. Kevin and I moved in with his aunt for a few weeks until Momma could rent us something in Tarboro. We had nothing.

While I was trying to get my life together, I never stopped thinking about Dawn and Betsy, who were both still at Central Prison. Two months after my release, Dawn finally made bond, more than two years after her arrest. She was scheduled to be tried next. Betsy remained in prison for eight more months, and on October 4, 1991, her family was able to secure her bond. On October 9, she was released from jail to return to her ten-year-old daughter. Betsy Kelly spent more than two years in prison awaiting her trial.

CHAPTER 16

ROBIN'S STORY—TRIALS AND PLEAS

*A lie can travel halfway around the world while the truth
is still putting on its shoes.*
—Mark Twain

Bob Kelly's trial was moved to Farmville, North Carolina, based on a petition by the defense team that he would be unable to receive a fair trial in Edenton due to pretrial publicity and prejudice. That courthouse was much larger, which meant more people, but it also meant room for more Little Rascals parents and even grandparents. I was scheduled to testify, but it took a while for that to happen. I wanted to be in the courtroom every day. I wanted to hear what the prosecutors said. I wanted to hear what the parents and children were saying we all did. I was on trial there as much as Bob was. On July 22, 1991, the state began its efforts to prove that Bob Kelly was guilty of the one hundred counts as set out in his indictments. It started with jury selection, which took until August 12. Then, on August 19, the state began putting on the evidence against Bob, which did not conclude until December.

Next, Mike Spivey and Jeff Miller (he was the co-defense counsel in Bob's trial) began to put on their defense. By the time I testified, my anxiety was through the roof. I wanted to shout everything I knew—I wanted to shout the truth. But instead, I answered question after question. I believed right up to the very end that Bob would be found not guilty.

In March 1992, the defense rested their case, but the prosecution team took more time to rebut the defense before Judge McLelland charged the jury and sent them out for deliberations on March 30. Twenty-two days later, the jury came back: "GUILTY" . . . "GUILTY" . . . "GUILTY." They found him guilty of ninety-nine of the one hundred charges. His defense team appealed that same day.

For eight months, while I awaited my own trial, I sat in that courtroom every single day. For eight months I listened to the lies against Bob, against Betsy, against all of us . . . against me. Jeff and Mike worked so hard to prove Bob's innocence, but the state won. Regardless of their efforts or the lack of physical evidence or eyewitness testimony, it ultimately resulted in a guilty verdict and twelve consecutive life sentences for Bob.

Afterward, I felt like I was trapped in a tidal wave, and wherever it landed was how my life would be. I was depressed, confused, and cried for days. I couldn't eat or sleep, and I couldn't imagine what I had done to deserve this. Most of all, I couldn't understand how God would let this happen to me.

My marriage was just awful. We were not even friends anymore. It was just a relationship of convenience. He didn't stay around much and didn't even try to get a job that paid better. He was only making about $100 a week, and I was getting health care at the local health department, receiving Medicaid, and getting food stamps. He was happy spending what little bit of money we had on frivolous things and doing what he wanted. In turn, that pushed me even further from him. Momma was our provider. She was working in Greenville during the week, living in a hotel room. Then on the weekends, she stayed with us, financially supporting the three of us, and Kevin took advantage of that.

People saw Kevin's outbursts and behavior, but I felt sorry for him. Our marriage never really had a fair chance. I never thought about straying from my marriage. I just wanted to know how to get out of it. But I was out on bond, had twenty-three felonies hanging over my head, and didn't have anywhere else to turn. The waves just continued to crash in on me.

After Bob's trial, the lawyers speculated that I would be next because I was the state's weakest link. At the time, Jeff believed the state thought if they could get the biggest and the weakest convicted, the rest would crumble in between. Although I didn't understand why that wouldn't be Darlene, Jeff kept telling me, "Be prepared to be called next."

The state again offered me another plea bargain: "Confess and save yourself a trial. You will get a small number of years." Jeff had to relay every one of those pleas to me, and he knew my answer every time. No matter how tempting it was to not have to go to trial, to put this behind me, there was no way I was going to make the previous two years of my life a lie. I did nothing wrong, and if I was meant to go to trial, then so be it. So we waited to see if I was next.

We were wrong; it wasn't me who was tried next—it was Dawn Wilson. Initially, she considered accepting a last-minute plea deal the state offered her. Plead guilty, testify against Betsy Kelly, reduce the sentence to time served, and go home. It was agony for her. She was only twenty-two when this all began and the single mother of a toddler. Unfortunately, she also became pregnant while she was out on bond. She talked to me about whether to accept the plea deal so she could have this "all behind" her. She asked me what I would do. That was an easy decision for me. I simply and honestly told her that it was her decision, but I could never do that "because it was a lie. I couldn't live with myself." In the end, she decided to plead not guilty and went to trial. We were all convinced she would be found not guilty. Like Bob Kelly, her trial was moved, this time to Hertford, North Carolina. And as in Kelly's case, no one believed she could get a fair jury in Edenton because of all the publicity.

Dawn's trial began on November 2, 1992. The state produced the same evidence from the same children and parents, and the same interrogators testified. It was all the same lies. The same hysteria. Unlike Bob's trial, hers lasted only a few months. I couldn't sit in the courtroom every day for her trial because I was in school by then, so I went on the days I testified. On January 26, 1993, Dawn was found guilty and convicted on all but one count. After just over two months, she was sentenced to life in prison. My hope and belief in justice were fading rapidly. Her attorney,

Bo Simmons, appealed, and she was eventually released on bond pending her appeal. The state also offered her many opportunities to bargain, to testify against the Kellys, but like me, Dawn was not going to lie to save herself, even though she had a toddler and a brand-new baby waiting for her outside. She refused to sign her name to the lie.

Later in 1993, *Frontline* aired the second of four episodes in the documentary series. In this one, the crew covered the verdicts from both Bob and Dawn's trials. In those interviews, Ofra Bikel exposed several troubling facts about the jurors. Judge McLelland expressly instructed the jury not to read or watch anything that could prejudice them, not to talk to anyone about the trial, and not to go to the day care. Imagine the shock for all of us when we learned that three jurors admitted in the interview to behavior that would be considered "misconduct." One juror admitted in the documentary that he had been sexually molested as a child. Another admitted to bringing a *Redbook* magazine that contained an article about pedophiles into the jury room while they were deliberating. And a third juror admitted to getting into his car and driving to Edenton to see the boarded-up day care for himself. So much for a fair trial.

Betsy's trial was next. She had suffered beyond imagination. While awaiting trial in Central Prison, the state had her moved from "safe-keeping" to some worse place in prison. Then, at the last minute, on January 21, 1994, she surprised almost everyone except her attorney, Joe Cheshire, and the defense team, when she entered a plea of no contest to the charges against her. In her address to the court, she insisted she was "not guilty of any of the charges" . . . but she was "tired" and couldn't fight anymore. Had she been tried and convicted, she would likely spend the rest of her life in prison. She just wanted to go home to her young daughter, who had been living with her sister, Nancy. Betsy wanted it over. In the months that followed, Betsy Kelly served a shortened sentence of eleven months as part of her plea deal and was released in July.

Scott Privott, the son of a judge, wanted it over too. He took the same option and pleaded no contest on June 6. He had already served more than three years in jail awaiting trial because he couldn't make bond—that is, until a Raleigh businessman read about his difficulty making bond and posted the money. Privott was out on bond when he appeared before the court to enter his plea of no contest, and he was released on time served. Like Betsy Kelly, he was weary and just wanted his life back.

All of this was so surreal. Now what? Bob and Dawn's cases were under appeal, and there I sat, with more waiting, more wondering. All I could think was, *What is going to happen to me?* It was two more years before I got an answer to my question

CHAPTER 17

THE BOX OF EVIDENCE

Perhaps only one simple and straightforward claim can
be made about the accuracy of children's testimony: not
all statements made by children are true.
—Gabrielle F. Principe and Erica Schindewolf

As the attorneys for Bob Kelly and Dawn Wilson were preparing for
the appeals, they knew they had to consider which facts to argue to the
court, and they had to assess the role of the prosecutors and judge in the
original Kelly case. This in turn influenced the remaining defendants of
the Edenton Seven. It has been argued that there were concerns about
prosecutorial misconduct in the original trials that should have been
considered at the time. Those concerns eventually were addressed by the
appellate court.

Legal and ethics experts Paul Roberts, a professor and associate editor
of the *Wall Street Journal*, and Lawrence Stratton, a professor of ethics at
Villanova University, viewed the Little Rascals Day Care Case as one of
the most abusive and unjust prosecutions in the country. In their book,
*The Tyranny of Good Intentions: How Prosecutors and Law Enforcement
Are Trampling the Constitution in the Name of Justice*, they specifically
addressed the Little Rascals cases, saying they believed the prosecutors
were "responsible for . . . the latter-day Salem witch trials . . . and for
ruining the lives of so many people." In general, their position about
prosecutorial overreach is that "government prosecutors, manifesting
a win-at-all-costs mentality, sacrifice the quest for truth in order to

advance their careers." They concluded, "Prosecutors get away with their violations of justice, law, and ethical behavior because no one is prepared to hold them accountable" and wondered why these same prosecutors "did not go to jail for withholding exculpatory evidence, for suborning perjury, or for prosecuting a case they knew to be false."[1]

Certainly, in the case of the Edenton Seven, the prosecutors and law enforcement ignored conflicting evidence that did not support the allegations, dismissed a complete lack of physical evidence or eyewitness accounts, and misused interviews-as-interrogation that traumatized the young children to create the reality they sought. Roberts and Stratton observed that even in the "total absence of any physical evidence . . . [the prosecutors] presented preposterous charges, extracted from the children by 'child advocates' and 'child specialists.'" It would appear that in the prosecutors' minds, Kelly and the others were guilty, and they only had to frame the case to sound like they were guilty to convince the parents and public that all the accusations and, therefore, the charges were true.[2]

All along, the defense knew that other records existed. Where were the interviews with the other kids, all those not named in the indictments?

After Kelly's original trial, Jeff Miller was in the Pitt County Clerk of Court's office when the clerk asked him about "all those boxes" stored in their office. Some were closed and sealed, clearly intended for the appeal. But there were several unsealed boxes, so Miller opened one and took out a file. He realized what he was looking at—exculpatory evidence that was never turned over to the defense. He returned the file immediately and called the appellate attorneys, Malcolm Hunter and Mark Montgomery.

Judge Tillery's final order before resigning from the case required the state to turn over all exculpatory evidence for "in camera review," a process during which the records are viewed privately in the judge's chambers or in a courtroom void of all spectators. The purpose of this was for the judge to determine the admissibility or use of the records in the proceeding. Was there anything in there the defense team had a right to access? Tillery's order was that the state had to present any and all "identifying information, medical and psycho-therapeutic files, DSS files . . . notes, reports, or recordings . . . for children named in the indictment . . . as well as all materials in their possession" for children not named in the indictment.[3] Tillery would have been the judge to view that evidence, but when he resigned, Judge Marsh McLelland was required to abide by that order.

After Miller's tip, Montgomery went to Pitt County to review the boxes of evidence stored in that clerk's office. He opened several boxes containing trial exhibits, none of which were sealed, and one of the boxes contained twenty-nine files labeled with the names of Little Rascals children. As he reviewed some of the documents, he realized he had never seen these files and immediately requested the box be sealed and transmitted to the North Carolina Court of Appeals for review. Montgomery and Hunter subsequently argued on appeal that the files contained "undisclosed information that would have been material to the defense."[4] It turned out that the boxes contained testimonies of children who, when interviewed, insisted nothing had happened. The discovery of the failure to disclose that evidence, never reviewed by Judge McLelland per Tillery's pretrial order, may have been essential to the defense teams in preparation for representing all seven defendants. McLelland "refused to review the contents of the box either before trial or during trial except for one file on a single non-testifying indictment child, which [McLelland] claimed he reviewed *in camera* . . . and determined that no material evidence existed to warrant giving the file to the defense."[5]

While attorneys were preparing for an appeal, an article in the *Virginian Pilot* revealed that barely more than a month after Kelly's probable cause hearing, parents of ten of the children began pursuing monetary damages in June 1989 from the insurance company that covered Betsy Kelly and the day care. Most of the children had yet to suggest anything had happened. Only a few had begun therapy with Abbott, Robertson, and the others. But by the end of the trial, twenty-eight parents of forty-two children seen at UNC Children's Medical Evaluation Program had joined the class-action lawsuit. The insurance claim in the suit was that Betsy Kelly "was negligent in allowing her husband to be at the day care center, failed to tell the parents about the molestation and failed to control her husband."[6] In 1994, five years later, a three-person panel consisting of a former judge, a child psychologist, and a retired insurance adjuster authorized an insurance settlement of $1 million to be distributed to the forty-two children in an undisclosed amount in damages. When questioned about the lawsuit, one parent asking not to be identified said, "We just don't want to say anything. This is something we wanted to be private."[7] That seemed an odd statement considering the most private parts of their children were displayed in the courtroom in order to get that conviction.

Meanwhile, Robin awaited her trial, and the North Carolina Court of Appeals was hearing the cases against Bob Kelly and Dawn Wilson. On May 2, 1995, six years after Bob Kelly's arrest, Chief Judge Charles Arnold, speaking for the North Carolina Court of Appeals, overturned Kelly's conviction for the following reasons:

Judge McLelland was bound by Judge Tillery's order to review "certain privileged information" *in camera* and McLelland refused to look at the materials in the box. Tillery's order was affirmed by the North Carolina Supreme Court, and "Judge McLelland was bound by the order." Tillery had directed the state to turn over material on non-indictment children it had in its possession, including medical and psycho-therapeutic files and Department of Social Services files for *in camera* review, and the judge was required to review those files in chambers.

The Court of Appeals found that Judge McLelland allowed into evidence "improper lay opinion" from the parents. For example, one parent testified that his child was examined by a physician who claimed to find evidence of abuse, and the parent stated to the court, he knew "beyond a shadow of doubt Bob Kelly raped my daughter." That testimony could only be admitted through an expert.

Judge McLelland erred by permitting certain testimony from Chris Bean, former defense attorney for Bob Kelly and parent of a child identified in the indictment. The North Carolina Court of Appeals ruled that "the prejudice inherent in having [his] former attorney, once [his] champion and defender, announce his knowledge of [his] guilt to the jury, is blatantly obvious."[8]

In addition, the Court of Appeals overturned Dawn Wilson's conviction for the following reasons, according to Chief Judge Arnold:

As in Bob Kelly's case, Judge McLelland was bound by Judge Tillery's order to review "certain privileged information" *in camera*, and he refused to look at the materials in the box.

The cross-examination of Dawn Wilson about prior drug use was irrelevant and inadmissible. The testimony was prejudicial, particularly when there were no witnesses other than the children, and "scant physical evidence" supported the charges against this defendant who vehemently and consistently denied all charges.

The Court found "prosecutorial misconduct with . . . gross improprieties in the state's closing argument," ruling it was "a grossly improper argument" by acting like they were explaining the law but, in fact, were actually introducing new and improper evidence to the jury during their closing argument.[9]

The Court of Appeals decided that McLelland should never have allowed Bean to testify against his former client. Apparently, Bean was subpoenaed by the state. Over the defense team's objections, Judge McLelland permitted him to testify. Clearly, Bean should have asserted attorney-client privilege to anything involving confidential communication or his work for Kelly. He could have petitioned the appellate court for a review if McLelland tried to force him to testify about those matters. The problem with his testimony was not that he disclosed privileged information, but rather that in effect he believed Bob Kelly was guilty.

In the Court of Appeal's decision, Judge Arnold said, "We take this occasion expressly to disapprove of the foregoing arguments by the prosecutor in that they mislead, misstated the law, and are calculated to demean defense counsel."[10] Later, Mark Montgomery said, "Those files were bulging with exculpation, conflicting claims, evidence of hysteria, and eyewitness testimony that nothing happened."[11] Three decades later, Montgomery continued to criticize the state for not turning over the exculpatory evidence.

Shockingly, those documents withheld from the defense team showed that the children likely were coerced into admitting something happened to them. The box under appeal contained, among other things, therapy notes and medical notes on the twenty-nine indictment children, twelve of whom testified at both Kelly and Wilson's trials. Extensive research into the tactics therapists and investigators used during their interviews supports this assumption. And sadly, in many cases, the children were verbally or physically rewarded for saying what the interrogators wanted to hear. In her own notes, Betty Robertson documented that she told one child in a therapy session, "You're doing a good job, young lady. You're telling me lots of important things today, aren't you." In another session, she noted that the child received a "glow in the dark" item that he took home and shared with a family friend. Notes from another session revealed that the child received "treats of the town—Burger King, Tons-o-Toys, etc."[12]

Even more shocking was that the therapists were reporting information from the sessions directly to Brenda Toppin and the prosecution team. Robertson noted sending Toppin a memo of what a child said from "sessions 5/8, 5/18, 5/24, and 5/31." On July 10, 1989, Robertson wrote that one particular child "would not be an adequate witness in court because of his anxiety level and fantasy and if he was able to progress beyond 'I don't know' or 'Nothing happened' responses, his accounts might be difficult to follow." In that same notation to Toppin, Robertson recommended "that he be interviewed [again] by Brenda Toppin in six to eight weeks." That child ultimately did go on to testify for the prosecution.[13]

On September 15, 1989, Robertson made a note regarding that same child that said the "mother signs release for info to go to D.A."[14] Was all this to ensure that the child had been sufficiently programmed so that he could give the prosecution the responses they wanted? That same child was named in the indictments and testified against both Bob Kelly and Dawn Wilson. Bob Kelly's trial began in July 1991, and these materials were not handed over to the defense until the night before testimonies in October 1991 and December 1991.

How could the defendants' attorneys mount an adequate defense when information trickled down to them, or worse, was withheld from them? Did the prosecution team deliberately withhold the evidence that may have led to "not guilty" verdicts in the original trials? Experts know that young children often have difficulty distinguishing between an actual event and what they have been told happened. The indictment children ranged in age from three to five, which is the range that researchers have expressed concern about children's susceptibility to being misled. But older children were interviewed, yet they were not named in the indictment. Why? What were their statements? Were the younger children simply less able to withstand the assault of suggestions, prompting, and repeated questioning so that they told the best version of the stories the prosecution wanted to hear? Was the urge to use interviews from the youngest subjects part of an agenda? Why wasn't each and every child interview recorded and transcribed so they could be analyzed by outside experts? What the defense team received in October, November, and December of 1991 were pages of typed notes transcribed into Toppin's words and the therapists' versions of what was said. How did anyone know what the children really said in their own words in those interviews? Why did the therapists never testify?

In *Tyranny of Good Intentions*, Roberts and Stratton said that among the plethora of child sex abuse cases across the country during the 1980s, prosecutors did not go to jail for "withholding exculpatory evidence, for suborning perjury, for prosecuting cases [they] knew to be false, or for any other crime [they committed] in [a] drive to ruin as many people, guilty or innocent, as [they could]."[15] In the Little Rascals case, they exploited children and convinced the families, the public, and the media that something must have happened. That abusive and unjust prosecution was done at no cost to themselves, except a verbal admonishment by the Court of Appeals.

CHAPTER 18

THE COURT OF PUBLIC OPINION

The fear of abuse translates into a belief in abuse.
—Mark Montgomery, Appellant Brief,
State of North Carolina v. Robert F. Kelly Jr.

Leading up to and during the time of the trials, news coverage was omnipresent and public opinion was tainted and potentially damning. Overall, there is little doubt that the media played a significant role in the events from beginning to end. In the words of Mark Montgomery, these cases "came along at a time when no one was really paying attention to the law regarding child sexual abuse. What they were paying attention to was the publicity around the country, and child sexual abuse hysteria was running rampant."[1] Authors Roberts and Stratton were especially critical of the media and believed that the jurors in the Little Rascals case and other "fabricated sex abuse cases" were absolutely "swayed by irresponsible media."[2]

The most compelling media program to cover the case was the previously mentioned eight-hour long documentary, which aired on PBS's *Frontline* and began with "Innocence Lost." The second in the series was "Innocence Lost: The Verdict, Part 1" and "Innocence Lost: The Verdict, Part 2." The finale of the series was "Innocence Lost: The Plea." Bikel, documentary journalist and producer of the series, hired Rachel Dretzin, an associate producer with extensive experience filming cases about child sexual abuse. The two set off to Edenton "blind . . . not knowing anything about the case," as they reported in the TV series. Their team was looking for a small town about which to film a documentary on the "anatomy, workings, and values" of a small town—one Bikel could examine "like a foreign country."[3] What she found was something else. They intended to stay for about three weeks without preconceived notions about guilt or innocence. They never expected to still be there six years later.

When they arrived in Edenton, Bikel and her team found a town consumed by the child abuse scandal. On July 20, 1993, Charlie Rose interviewed her on his weekly signature television show just as Part 2 of "The Verdict" was airing. She told Rose what she found were "lots of questions [but] not many answers." When Rose asked Bikel if she believed the charges were true, she paused, then said, "It could have happened . . . but Bob Kelly did not get a fair trial . . . there was no way of knowing because there was no physical evidence. No adult saw anything." When Rose pressed her further on that point, she said, "No, I do not believe anything happened."[4]

Bikel's concerns were many. She thought the parents "believed in their hearts that a great evil had been done to their children. They were good, loving parents." But she condemned the therapists, seeing them as the "villains" in this case who never had to testify to any of the information that came from their interviews with the children. Yet those interviews were the only damning evidence against the defendants. She was also concerned by the ferocity with which the prosecutors were determined to "win at all costs," and that the jurors admitted in the series to voting "against their beliefs" because they felt ill or wanted out. Even more, she was troubled by a fact raised repeatedly: not one parent immediately went to their private doctors or pediatricians to have their child examined, even in light of the very serious allegations they were raising against the defendants.[5]

The documentary drew both criticism and praise, but without question, it created quite a battleground as people took sides following the airing. The prosecution was unhappy with Bikel's documentary, and in the opinion of the prosecutor, Nancy Lamb, *Frontline*'s coverage had "'tainted' the Little Rascals case by portraying the prosecutions as analogous to the 'Salem witch hunts of the 1600s.'"[6] According to the interviews with the people of Edenton, they were bitter and highly resented the film because they felt it portrayed their small town as not a very nice place. The families of the alleged victims were the most aggrieved by Bikel's documentary, calling it "a hatchet job." One parent, Gary Smith, who was also interviewed on the *Charlie Rose Show*, said he believed "it was apparent that there was context maneuvering," suggesting that there was "cut-and-pasting made to support whatever it was Ms. Bikel wanted to portray." He asserted that there was "a lot of evidence and proof that was not portrayed in that documentary."[7]

Smith did not make it clear in the interview what specific evidence he was talking about. He said he resented the implication made in the documentary about the therapists leading the kids; he believed they were there "to help my young daughter work through [the abuse], not to come up with stories" to plant in the children's heads. His child was four at the time of the alleged abuse, but she did not testify until nearly three years later in Kelly's trial. Smith questioned, "Why would anybody put themselves through this?" if they did not believe their children.[8] The parents complained on Rose's show that the documentary failed to present the parents' points of view. Instead, they believed it made them appear hateful and vindictive.

But it was not just the producers of *Frontline* who were enthralled by the story. Media outlets far and wide were engaged in a feeding frenzy with the charges and trials. The daily coverage in the local Edenton and Farmville papers alone kept the community and the Associated Press (AP) saturated with coverage and opinion.

A significant amount of coverage came from the newspaper in Greensboro, North Carolina. In fact, the Greensboro *News & Record* seemed preoccupied with the case, and in 1991, ran the first of many articles about it. An AP piece the paper published featured an interview with Debbie and Jay Swicegood, whose child was named in the indictment. They were more than willing to offer remnants from their testimony. The all-caps headline read, "FATHER: TODDLER SCREAMS WHEN HIS CLOTHES WERE REMOVED," drawing the reader into the horror of the alleged abuse. In the lead sentence, Swicegood was quoted saying that his child, "allegedly abused at the daycare, screamed when clothes were pulled off his body so a doctor could examine him." Later in the article, he suggested that his child had been taken to a local hotel where "the abuse happened." He didn't know when the incident at the hotel happened, and the only evidence of that allegation was the child's interview with the therapist—even though no one had noticed his child being whisked away from the day care to a "local hotel."[9]

In February 1992, Betty Ann Phillips testified on behalf of the defense, and parts of her testimony were published by the *News & Record*, which just happened to be the hometown newspaper of Judge McLelland. The compelling article described Betty Ann as a worker at the day care and the mother of a child in Robin's classroom who was implicated by other children in the abuse accusations. In the article, Phillips said that she told District Attorney Williams all along that she was "concerned the charges were false." But then Williams instructed her "not to go out on the street and say that. You know, all the children are saying you were the lookout."[10]

The coverage of her testimony continued, and in the article, Phillips said neither she nor her husband had "consented" to their child being included in the indictments. Later those charges were "dropped." She said Williams told her, "The charges would help you out when people started talking about you." What exactly did Williams mean by that? Phillips agreed to leave her child in therapy with the state-hired therapist Judy Abbott but also said, "I was scared they would come and arrest me too." After four hours of cross-examination by Bill Hart, the special deputy attorney general who was assigned as a special prosecutor in the case, Phillips asserted that she "never saw Kelly hit a child" or anything else. Phillips later reflected on an ominous threat from another mother,

Patricia Kephart, who quietly warned her, "I will make sure they come for you."[11]

The newspapers were not focused solely on the children. Sean Bailey, a staff writer for the *News & Observer*, wrote an article criticizing Hart for his admitted "relationship with that same Patricia Kephart, mother of a six-year-old girl allegedly sexually assaulted by Kelly." In the interview, Hart assured the reporter that "the relationship with her did not pose a conflict of interest in the case." Plenty of people in the legal community thought otherwise and saw this as a significant ethical problem. Nevertheless, Hart's old boss, Attorney General Thornburg, saw "no conflict in the relationship at all;" after all, they "were both consenting adults." Moreover, H. P. Williams said it "had no influence on the trial." But many disagreed with Williams and Thornburg, saying Hart had a "duty to avoid the appearance of impropriety . . . because [these] parents [were] a special type of victim because of the mental anguish they endure[d]."[12]

Months after the interview with the Swicegoods, the *News & Record* ran yet another article on March 31, 1992. Loraine Ahearn, a staff writer, interviewed Judge McLelland while the jury was out deliberating the fate of Robert Kelly. In the interview, the reporter noted the "amused McLelland" said he believed "the state's longest and most expensive trial would have ended" months earlier were it not for the "extraneous detail" and children's testimony about things like "whether the center served cheese puffs." Seemingly joking about the case, he went on to say, "I realized I was a little flip when I said 80 percent of the evidence is trash, but it is. I thought sooner or later, some editorialist was going to write, 'That sorry judge should have done something.' And yet if I stopped it, it would have been a problem in an appeal."[13]

McLelland also went on to openly criticize the Bikel documentary, recalling "the cross-examination of a Salt Lake City psychologist hired by the defense [who said] the documentary convinced him that Kelly was the innocent victim of a witch hunt." McLelland said the documentary was "a right good TV show, but hardly one that was balanced in any sense." And he indicated to the reporter that he would "likely be the trial judge for the others" when they came to trial, which of course included Robin's case. His expressed concerns at the end of the interview were for the jurors, stating, "Look how difficult it's been for them."[14]

McLelland's lack of judicial restraint seemed to many an ethical problem as he was making jokes, talking to the press about a case that had yet to be decided by the jury, and expressing his personal opinions about whether the documentary was fair. Sadly, he did not express concern for the children at any point in the interview, which seems troubling even three decades later.

National news publications like the *Washington Post* covered the case broadly. On May 10, 1991, Megan Rosenfeld wrote an article implying there were two Betsy Kellys . . . one who was a "degenerate" and the other "your best friend." Of course, the "degenerate" accusation dominated the article by referring to Betsy Kelly as "drab and pale . . . expressionless . . . and guilty." Rosenfeld claimed there "was no real vehicle for sorting out the truth . . . and it was more about 'winning or losing' than determining what really happened." Of course, the Court of Appeals would later make a similar charge against the prosecution. In the article, Rosenfeld concluded that it was about "knowing and being known" in this small town, implying that some of the parents may have been influenced by "belonging" to a clique. To Rosenfeld, one mother claimed that she too could "quiver [her] bottom lip," implying that Nancy Smith, Betsy Kelly's sister, was faking it in her interview on *Frontline*. Rosenfeld explored the back-and-forth of the evidence, but ended with one final condemning statement related to the night terrors the children allegedly experienced: "How does one explain the scream in the night?"[15]

The *Chicago Tribune* and the *New York Times* printed articles and editorials that deliberated "facts" and "accusations" in an effort to determine if any of the charges could possibly be true. The story resonated with the public and the media alike, but it was impossible not to taint the public with insinuations of guilt. In one *New York Times* article by Ronald Smothers on March 23, 1992, Smothers quoted William Hart of the prosecution team in saying that "the state had presented enough 'consistent themes' through the children's testimonies to show them credible," dismissing any possibility raised by any "expert witness" who testified that the children had been coached or led into repeating the accusations. He wrote earlier in the article that "the little children 'with gentle coaxing' gave prosecutors one version of events two years earlier and another version to defense attorneys who [sought] to highlight the suggestibility of the children."[16]

Prosecutor Nancy Lamb was all too willing to diagnose the abuse when interviewed, saying, "Experts for the prosecution have testified that behaviors don't prove abuse but are red flags. Their reactions fit the pattern of a traumatized child. They are a consistent picture that paints abuse."[17] The case was everywhere on the national news by the close of the trial. Prosecutors planned to use the same evidence and testimonies against Robin and the other remaining defendants when they went to trial. Could they possibly receive a fair trial, with an unbiased, unblemished jury pool?

The media coverage of the Little Rascals case was so intense that many sensed it contributed to a monumental miscarriage of justice. Christina Gutierrez, a defense attorney also interviewed on the *Charlie Rose Show* with Bikel, expressed deep concerns about the defendants' ability to get a fair trial while facing the "most dangerous accusations" one can face, accusations that carry a life sentence as punishment. How and where the information is shared matters. Parents talk in the day care, in the church, in the grocery store, and around the county. Gutierrez told Rose, "Parents carpool their children to therapists. Therapists talk to each other," and then, as in this case, they talked to law enforcement.[18] And the media covered it relentlessly. All of this made it difficult or even impossible to discern truth from rumor.

As he watched the documentaries and read newspaper articles, journalist Lew Powell began amassing thousands of documents about the case, dating from 1989 to 2012. Powell said his desire was "to bring attention . . . to the irregularities in its investigation and prosecution," which he believed "to be a gross miscarriage of justice." Like so many, Powell believed the most telling fact was that all of those "charged maintained their innocence from the beginning and never brokered plea deals to testify against the others in exchange for lighter sentences" or freedom.[19] In Betsy Kelly's case, she chose to plead no contest to the charges because she had a ten-year-old child at home, and rather than risk multiple life sentences, she wanted the case over. With the no contest plea, she served an additional year and went home to her child. Scott Privott also entered a no contest plea and was given credit for time served. Both have always maintained their innocence. Bob Kelly also continued to maintain his innocence, refusing offers for a plea bargain. When asked how he felt about the verdicts, Kelly later said, "I would rather spend the rest of my life in jail for something I did not do than admit guilt to a lie and have to live with that the rest of my life."[20]

The public reaction kept the media well supplied with subjects for commentary. The phenomenon known to sociologists as "moral panic" was just as much driven by religious zealotry, lies, paranoia, and coercion in 1988 as it had been in Salem in 1692. Rumors and stories of satanic cults were raging all over the country, newly ignited and fueled by the McMartin Preschool case and covered relentlessly by the media. According to Lew Powell, a "confluence of unlikely events—religious involvement, talk shows in their heyday, a fascination with Satanism," and the media's willingness to cover it without concern for the truth—all contributed to the widespread hysteria.[21] Unfortunately for Robin and the others, these things created a perfect storm in Edenton. The media openly sold this frenzy to an insatiable public.

David Loomis was a graduate student at the University of North Carolina at Chapel Hill in 1997. His dissertation, "Modern Witch Hunts: How Media Have Mishandled Ritual Child-Sex-Abuse Cases," examined the role of "news media coverage . . . of Witch Hunts—also called 'delusions,' 'moral panics,' and 'political hysterias' . . . that exhibited repeated shortcomings . . . evident in [recent] cases brought to courts nationwide involving sexual abuse of preschool-age children in day-care settings." His case study of local newspaper coverage of the Little Rascals Day Care Case showed the media "may have contributed to avoidable injustices that exercise of the press' watchdog responsibility could have prevented." According to Loomis, the very first reports of the alleged sexual assault at Little Rascals were in a local paper based in Elizabeth City, a nearby community. He found that "media attention peaked in 1992 when [Kelly] was tried, convicted, and sentenced to twelve consecutive life sentences."[22] He also found that news coverage continued until the next trial but dwindled significantly after the conviction of Dawn Wilson. It decreased even more after Betsy Kelly and Scott Privott pleaded no contest. By the time Robin's case was considered years later, the news focus had shifted and, in some cases, disappeared. When questions finally began to arise about the investigation and the prosecution, much of the news media, especially the local news, still failed to examine the questions and bring them to the front of the press coverage.

Loomis's inquiry compared the striking similarities between the Little Rascals Day Care case, the witch hunts of colonial America, the 1950s House Un-American Activities Committee hearings (led by Senator Joseph McCarthy), and the McMartin Preschool sexual abuse trial of the 1980s. In each case, the media was biased against the defendants from the beginning; however, Loomis's examination also showed that, ultimately, reporting in these cases shifted in the other direction and turned against the prosecution after a period of time. Still, overall, the media utterly "failed to provide basic fairness and balance."[23]

Ultimately, Loomis found that the local paper in Edenton "exhibited no skepticism about [the] alleged conspiracy involving seven adults serially raping, torturing and photographing scores of three- to-five-year-old children during broad daylight at a centrally located day care in a small town . . . without a single witness or a shred of physical evidence. That lack of skepticism also was evident in the Edenton paper's failure to detect and report broader societal currents" that fed and fostered the witch hunt. Ultimately, he hypothesized that the "news media favored the views of authorities over the individual," a view that would eventually be held by many. Loomis concluded, "The Edenton day care story was one in which press coverage [reflected] a failure to apply the McCarthy period's lessons and to avoid the errors of the past."[24]

In September 1996, the *Virginian-Pilot* ran an AP article on Shelley Stone, "one of the three forgotten defendants," along with Robin Byrum and Darlene Harris. In the article, Stone said she spent seven years waiting for a trial that she believed would absolve her of child sex charges, and she feared that she "was going to die with this still going on." So did Robin. Still out on bond, Stone and her husband could not find work because of the stigma of the case, and they were "forced to go on public assistance."[25]

Like Stone, Robin also could not move on. Though the article did not express an opinion about blame in the case, it did shed light on the continued tragedy and legacy of the case. In the article, Nancy Lamb, the lead prosecutor for the case, said she still hadn't figured out "what to do with the three forgotten defendants." Seven years and she still had not figured that out? Three months after the charges against Robin, Stone, and Harris were dismissed, Lamb told the Associated Press, "We didn't bring charges in 1989 and 1990 thinking these people weren't guilty. Why would we do such a thing? We had enough evidence all along to convict all three, or we would not have brought the charges." [26] But did they really have the evidence they needed?

Contrary to the overtly biased media coverage of the Little Rascals Day Care case, almost without exception, everyone seemed to consistently praise the quality, fairness, and ethical reporting of Ofra Bikel and the *Frontline* crew. Though one retired journalist from Edenton said he believed Bikel went into her project with "a jaundiced eye," Bikel disagrees.[27] She believed it was her moral obligation to present the facts as objectively as possible, and most agree that she accomplished that.

CHAPTER 19

TRIAL BY AMBUSH

If it is not right, do not do it. If it is not true, do not say it.
—Marcus Aurelius, *The Meditations*

For the Edenton Seven, because there was no verifiable physical evidence of abuse or eyewitnesses, the state pressured the defendants to "confess," which none of them did. The state needed the parents to believe what the children told their therapists, and the testimonies from the children were critical in trying to prove to a jury that abuse occurred. That said, the defense attorneys believed the state "began reconstructing the events at the day care . . . [to encourage the children] to remember things that seemed innocent at the time, but appeared sinister in retrospect."[1]

The parents accepted suggestions from "the experts" that violent, heinous, evil abuses occurred against their three-, four-, and five-year-old children, under the watchful eye of a small, closely knit community, in the middle of downtown with windows open and parents coming in and out, without any verifiable physical evidence, traces of blood, unusual bruising, tears to the vaginal or anal area, missing babies, or anything else that indicated a traumatic, violent act had occurred. Imagine the damage to a three-year-old that would come from anal or vaginal penetration with scissors, not to mention any of the other horrific charges leveled against the Edenton Seven.

It cannot be overstressed: these were very young children, and the parents had the right and obligation to investigate the accusations. However, nothing about this case fits what experts believe to be confirmed patterns of behaviors attributed to adults who sexually victimize young children. Even Roland C. Summit, the controversial psychiatrist and leading expert witness for the prosecution in the McMartin Preschool case, which took place five years before Little Rascals, wrote that the "perpetrator is most often in a trusted, loving position" (for example, a father, stepfather, sibling, or grandfather), and that the abuse usually occurs as "an intruder in the night," rather than in broad daylight at an open day care.[2]

What techniques did the interviewers and therapists use in the Little Rascals case to elicit the eventual accusations, and were those questions legal, moral, and ethical? What were the accepted standards at the time by which they should have conducted those sessions? If the information was obtained through repeated, delayed, leading, biased, or even coercive methods, as suggested by experts such as Maggie Bruck, Elizabeth Loftus, and Kenneth Lanning, one could assume there was a strong probability that the accusations were false. According to Judith Adams, forensic and clinical psychologist, the "number of interviews to which the children [were] subjected, the repetition of questioning across and within interviews, the delay of . . . interviewing, and the types of questions"[3] mattered greatly. In some cases, those interviews lasted hours, and the children continued to be questioned for many months, beginning in January 1989. The repeated interrogations went on for five years beginning with the first allegation and lasting until Kelly and Wilson were eventually convicted. By then, the children believed what likely had been suggested to them by Officer Toppin; the selected therapists Abbott, Robertson, Childers, and Zimmerman; and prosecutors like Nancy Lamb.

Richard Gardner, a child psychiatrist who appeared on the *Charlie Rose Show* with Ofra Bikel during Kelly's trial, took it further. He questioned "people's judgment," suggesting that the "hysteria impaired the parents' judgment." He believed "emotions were so high that they [could not] think logically." They thought someone could actually "feed children feces and have them drink urine." Someone could put "all kinds of objects in their vaginas with no medical findings" . . . and all while so many "people were coming and going with endless opportunities to see something." Yet no adult ever saw anything. All they had, Gardner said, were the "validators, the therapists . . . the ones who 'found the sex abuse.'"[4]

As early as July 1990, the defense attorneys appeared before the court to present a motion to compel the state to provide them with all materials, documents, transcripts, and medical records, especially materials from the social services and therapists, so they could subpoena relevant material witnesses. The indictments were so vague that defense attorneys could not tell exactly which of the indictments pertained to which defendant or specifically when the alleged offenses were said to have occurred. The state withheld from the defense access to critical information needed to defend their clients. The defense knew prosecutors had all the details and reports, yet the state asserted it was privileged information. The defense knew at least two doctors had seen the children and had reached different opinions. They knew social services had done an investigation into at least one child. They knew there was information about the interrogations and the questions and asked the court to grant them access. Did they get what they requested? Clearly not.

So what chance did Robin have to defend herself against these allegations? In September 1990, Jeff Miller wrote a letter to Dr. Moisy Shopper of the St. Louis School of Medicine and Psychoanalytic Institute regarding the accusations against Robin. Based upon his review of the facts, medical reports, and various "expert opinions," Miller told Shopper he was absolutely convinced that his client was innocent and "a victim of hysterical contagion," contaminated and suggestive investigative techniques, and unprofessional "expert" therapies "co-opted by the investigatory process." He was troubled by the "trial by ambush" used by the prosecution, and literally "begged" for Dr. Shopper's assistance.[5]

Shopper agreed to help. He examined and studied hundreds of documents, testimony, and therapists' reports as part of his tasks as an "expert" for the defense in all the Edenton Seven defendants' cases. He primarily focused on what he called a "created reality" where children are coached into becoming "honest liars." He believed the efforts of the professionals and authorities to create the reality they sought in this case was in an effort to get a guilty verdict at all costs and with "gross miscarriage of justice" based on two criteria—an error of massive proportion that impacted both the individual and society and egregious procedural errors in the judicial process.[6]

In Shopper's opinion, they all suffered from "mono ideational thinking," where they got an "idea in [their] minds and excluded everything else." If it didn't fit, they didn't "want to hear about it." It was striking to him "how long the children maintained . . . that no sexual abuse had taken place . . . in spite of the prolonged insistence by parents and therapists to tell the 'secrets,' in other words that the sexual abuse actually had taken place."[7]

As Shopper reviewed the testimony of Audrey Stever, he focused on her admission that she questioned her child night after night and then reported her findings to Officer Toppin. Shopper was concerned that after only "six days, Officer Toppin determined that sexual abuse had [in fact] occurred." However, at this point, neither she nor anyone from the Department of Social Services had "interviewed a single child or employee" of the day care. Toppin also admitted that her official interviews with Stever's son lasted "more than two hours," yet the tapes and notes from those interviews mysteriously disappeared.[8] Also troubling: the more she questioned the child, the more he named other children. Toppin quickly advised those parents to interrogate their children, even coaching them on how to approach the questioning.

Eventually, all the children identified as victims of the abuse were sent to be interviewed by one of the four therapists hired by and paid for by the State of North Carolina. According to Shopper, these four therapists were "overzealous and inadequately trained" and "proceeded in an unethical fashion" of reporting their findings to the prosecutor's office.

Shopper found of the children who testified, "The therapists were not treating the children psycho-therapeutically . . . but rather, were agents of the prosecution in preparing children to testify falsely."[9]

As a result of this trauma, the children's symptoms and behavior changed dramatically. One of the many things that bothered Dr. Shopper was the misuse of the therapy sessions. In his testimony, Shopper expressed concern that "the harmful part of the so-called treatment is that there was no attempt to help the [children] with their reality testing so that manifestly implausible things like 'My head was cut off, My arms were cut off, We were drowned, or Mr. Bob killed babies in outer space' . . . were simply accepted at face value." In his opinion, the professionals were "not doing [their] job as a therapist . . . and they actually did [harm] to the children . . . and [their symptoms actually] got worse . . . and in many ways, *they* did the children harm." The therapists had an ethical responsibility to "do the patient no harm." However, in this case, did they, as Shopper questioned, become forensic examiners and work for the court acting as inquisitors and part of the prosecution team?[10]

Shopper would go on to say that the "confessions" by the children were a result of "the repeated, forceful, and coercive interrogation techniques used with these preschool children," and the "Little Rascals children who testified were severely traumatized, that is, overstimulated children who had lost parental protection from adult sexuality, and whose omnipotent, grandiose, and hostile fantasies were excited and accepted as fact."[11]

The children's created reality would then be replaced by what Shopper called the "community's collective created reality." In the case of the Edenton Seven, this created reality was sexual abuse. Period. Shopper hoped the parents would come to their senses and seek help for their children for the "horrendous trauma perpetrated on them . . . by law enforcement, prosecutors, therapists, and parents."[12] In the words of Robin Byrum, "The parents did this to them."

Later, Shopper reflected on his testimony, stating he "felt like a feeble voice against the roar of an airplane . . . because the judge and the jury had already arrived at their verdict—guilty." He felt neither "roughed up by the prosecution . . . nor depressed" after the verdict, but rather "enraged . . . that the perjured testimony of a police officer, the unprofessional conduct of the therapists, and the questionable legal tactics of the prosecution" led to the wrongful conviction of Kelly and the condemnation of Robin Byrum and the others by a community made sick from a created reality and hysteria.[13]

On the same day that Miller wrote Shopper for help, he also wrote to Dr. William Kenner at the Vanderbilt University Department of Psychiatry, asking the same of him. He advised both doctors that there was no money to pay them, but he hoped they would find it a "worthy and valuable cause." Kenner also agreed to help and poured through mountains of evidence, including seven videotaped DSS interviews of children from another sexual abuse case that were "made at the beginning of [that] outbreak before the children and their parents' memories were distorted . . . by the interviews and the trials three to four years later."[14] But he went further. He also examined medical records and court documents for all the children named in the indictments.

Kenner focused on the "hysterical contagion" that Miller cited in his letter. He noted that "one sees this in one case . . . followed by sympathetic attention and widespread publicity." He explained that when a new case arises, an investigator can trace the spread of fear and anxiety within the group. "Short-circuiting" then occurs as the group fails to seek an explanation through logic. In response, the victims jump to "generalities and misconceptions." This is when the rapid build-up of cases occurs. Authorities then do one of two things. Hopefully, they take a "thoughtful and reasoned approach," gather facts, and the outbreak ends. However, Kenner said, when the more sober and rational approach does not occur, the result is a "breakdown" that explodes into a massive outbreak, as in the Salem witch trials.[15]

In an effort to understand the techniques used to interview the children, Kenner and Shopper studied and then testified regarding what they observed in videotapes of interviews with children in a child abuse study at the University of Tennessee. All the interviewers were given instructions on how to interview the children without using leading questions. Yet consistently, those interviewers showed a "pattern of leading, cross-germination, and suggestion," in which the children "showed clear evidence of stress and anger at the process itself." One child, in particular, reacted to the interview technique by "screeching in a falsetto voice and hiding in the corner." Kenner and his team agreed that the child was reacting to the "aggressive, non-empathic treatment by the DHS interviewer and colluded in by the parents."[16]

Ultimately, Kenner and Shopper agreed that the "perpetrators of abuse in this case were, in fact, the overly zealous, academic and criminal investigators, and the therapists who were swept along in the outbreak of hysterical contagion. The children in the taped interviews "showed evidence of PTSD . . . brought on by the interviews themselves . . . and guilt-laden, angry parents . . . who in turn caused 'complex changes' that damaged the children's lives."[17] Furthermore, after viewing the tapes, Kenner wrote that they were both more convinced of the "inquisitorial method of investigation" that was likely used by parents, police officers, and the four therapists in the Little Rascals case.[18]

This method was not new. It was a technique dating back to before the seventeenth century, used against medieval heretics accused by the church of practicing witchcraft and Satan worshiping. The inquisitors used interrogations and even torture to "elicit confessions," thereby "confirming their assumptions" about both the crimes and the guilt of the accused.[19] According to the Innocence Project at Duke University, the doctors believed the Little Rascals children were victims of a witch hunt, and when the kids "weren't coming forward, they were drawn in after months and months of interrogations."[20]

According to Anna Twiddy in the University of North Carolina's *People, Ideas, and Things Journal* in 2016, from the start, this case was "influenced by mass moral panic, poor instructions to the parents by the therapists, invasive and suggestive questioning, harmful pressure on the children, and conditioning to offer up evidence against the defendants." And the "various actions taken by law enforcement, prosecution, and parents were highly inappropriate," and the "highly coercive techniques" used by the therapists conditioned the children to believe something had happened that had not happened. Twiddy wrote further, "The Little Rascals case serves as clear proof that the use of children's testimony in criminal cases must be heavily monitored and regulated, ideally through legislation, which would provide a uniform framework for handling such controversial cases. In the Little Rascals case, not only did the four therapists evaluating the children use inappropriate methods to advance the prosecution's case, but it appears they manipulated the children into giving them the desired responses, and their involvement went virtually unregulated due to other mishandlings of the case by police, prosecution, and parents."[21]

According to Shopper, "The children's therapists failed to follow safeguards" against using suggestive techniques.[22] He went on to suggest that "there was no attempt to help the child with their reality . . . so a lot of these children got worse in the course of treatment . . . and in many ways did the children harm."[23]

Unfortunately, operating out of their fears that their children may have been abused and in their search for answers, the parents ended up opening their children to trauma when there had previously been none.

CHAPTER 20

ROBIN'S STORY—DISMISSED!

I will say it, if it was my last time, I am clear of this sin.
—Mary Towne Easty, April 1692

December 1990 to December 1996 stretched over my life with a thick blanket of lies and accusations. The monstrous charges lurking in the shadows of my own life were a ball and chain, trapping me to my past, a past I did not choose or cause. It kept me locked in a limbo that I wasn't sure I would ever be able to escape. I knew I needed to move forward. My marriage was crumbling, and I had to be able to take care of myself if that happened. But how?

I spent the first eighteen months after I was released from prison just bonding with my baby and sitting in Bob Kelly's trial every day it was in session. I had to do that. It was *my* future too. I needed to know what they were saying about me. But once Bob's trial was over, I knew I needed to better myself. I wanted to go into nursing, but being out on bond was going to make school extra difficult, so I went into health information management instead. In 1992, I enrolled at Edgecombe Community College and got a Pell Grant to pay for it.

This all created another dilemma for me. It meant I had to put my baby in day care. "Day care." That word alone meant facing the monster called fear. I worried daily that someone would recognize me or call me out. What if they rejected my baby because of me? My image and charges had been plastered all over the media, and I believed everyone knew me, knew about me. Insecurity was my middle name. And what about making friends? Had they watched the news? Did they know about me? How was I supposed to move on?

I was right when I thought it was going to be hard. Dealing with a baby, an uncooperative husband, and school was almost impossible. I studied while the baby slept, and Kevin watched TV, pacing by me and "chuckling," or turning the volume all the way up, all done to make it more difficult for me. He told me I would fail. He told me going to school was "useless" because I would "be next to be tried." But I was determined to prove him wrong.

I had an amazing instructor, Dottie Tolson, who encouraged and pushed me. She knew learning was my escape, and she was a godsend to me. While I was pushing myself as hard as I could, Kevin was taking the only money we had and spending it on stereos and boats. How could he do that? I told myself he loved me, and he loved our baby, but did he? Life was impossible.

I finally graduated in September 1995 with a 3.89 GPA, and with Dottie Tolson's help, I already had a job. Kevin, the baby, and I moved to a new town and got a little house. My mother had moved back to Kentucky, thinking it would help our marriage if she wasn't around. But then in late summer, I found myself pregnant again. I was happy because I didn't want my baby to be an only child like I was, but Momma was devastated, and Kevin could not have cared less. Our marriage got worse, the physical abuse started, and I was still waiting to be tried for something I did not do.

Of course, also during that time, the state sent more offers through Jeff Miller to push me to accept plea deals. Freedom for confession. Freedom for admission. Freedom. No! I would not. I could not. I was not guilty. None of us were.

On December 13, 1996, seven years after the Little Rascals nightmare began, Bikel and her *Frontline* crew were at my house to film the final segment of "Innocence Lost." This day was a testimony to Bikel's commitment to not only document the entire ordeal of the Little Rascals

Day Care case, but also to show the truth to the world about the impact on all our lives—the Edenton Seven, the children, our families, all of us.

Bikel had remained steadfastly in our corner from the night the documentary first aired in May 1991 to the final segment, scheduled to be released that spring, seven long years later. The crew was set up and ready to begin filming me with my boys. Kevin and I were still together, but only barely, and he wasn't at home at the time. The crew was trying to document where my life was after years in limbo awaiting trial. It had been six months since the cases against Bob and Dawn were overturned by the Court of Appeals, but mine still lingered in what seemed to be an endless wait. For months, I had heard nothing from the state regarding my charges. The last plea offer was months earlier when they asked me to plead no contest, and in exchange, I would receive no time. This meant no trial! Was it tempting? Perhaps momentarily. But of course, I refused. I didn't go through all those years of hell to have a no contest plea next to my name.

In the middle of filming, the phone rang, and I was thinking it was probably Kevin. He had gone to a job interview, and I thought perhaps it was him calling with news of how it went. I stopped the interview so I could answer the phone. I'm happy I did. It was my attorney, Jeff. The first thing I heard was, "Hi, Robin. This is Jeff. Are you sitting down?"

"No," I replied. Suddenly, I felt a wave of something coming, so I leaned against the kitchen counter.

Jeff continued, "All the charges against you were dismissed . . . today. All twenty-three charges are over."

IT WAS OVER!

Frontline filmed the entire conversation as I burst into tears, real tears. Tears that hadn't fallen in such a long time. Nothing was staged. It really was over. And Bikel got it on tape, our evidence that it was over. Our proof.

Over? What did that even mean? It only meant that the court battle was over. But I thought, *I will likely have to deal with this for the rest of my life.*

PART II
THE TRUTH

Chapter 21

Twenty-One Boxes

Judges should not hesitate to require the disclosure
where it appears to them to be necessary in order that
the truth be known and justice be done.
—Justice Clifton L. Moore,
Sims v. Charlotte Insurance Co., 1962

After that chance meeting with Robin in April 2022, I became obsessed. Each time I thought I was close to completing the writing of this book, another detail would emerge, and my understanding of Robin's old, unhealed wounds would burst open again, raw and raging. The push to answer the questions—*how* and *why* this had happened to her—lingered mercilessly. I could no longer delay a trip to Duke Law Library, where I hoped to discover what those long-ago preserved documents could reveal. The library staff constructed an inventory list and gave me access to the artifacts. They had never had the extra staff necessary to digitize the collection of 24,000 pages of transcripts, which meant poring over the documents one page at a time.

There it was—Robin's history. The twenty-one boxes waited silently on a rolling cart—a dinosaur holding the truth hidden away for more than three decades.

"No one has ever asked to see those documents," a librarian told me.

Shocked to hear that, I hoped to find answers somewhere in those boxes. Perhaps some were the files Jeff Miller and Mark Montgomery discovered in the Pitt County Courthouse in 1992 that had been withheld from the defense.

Each prison-gray box was carefully identified with a label: "J. MICHAEL GOODSON LAW LIBRARY, DUKE UNIVERSITY SCHOOL OF LAW, Little Rascals Day Care Case Papers *State v. R. Kelly.*" They were numbered 1 to 21. Each was a sort of sarcophagus waiting for the contents to be revealed. Inside were aging legal folders carefully organized, each hand-labeled in #2 pencil. And inside each was a piece of the Little Rascals story: handwritten notes, letters, typewritten documents, and old faxes, all relics of a story gone silent.

Though this collection of files was mainly from Bob Kelly's trial, it all pertained to Robin and the other defendants. The first document I pulled out was the motion from Jeff Miller about their struggle to get information from the state. In it, he was "seeking . . . [all] material relevant" to Robin's defense. He and the other lawyers knew the accusers had "been interviewed by DSS, SBI, law enforcement, psychologists, social workers, and medical doctors" about the "allegations of child sexual abuse."[1] Robin said at our first meeting, and repeats even now, that she still wants to confront the people who said she did those horrible things. Now I knew who they were.

In 1990, Miller told the court they needed those documents to mount Robin's defense and to ensure that justice would occur. The Constitution and due process guaranteed that she and her co-defendants had the fundamental right to face their accusers, but the prosecution prevented that from happening. Miller, Spivey, and the other defense attorneys were justifiably concerned that a "substantial body of information and records . . . had been withheld" from the defense. It was imperative that "the evidence used to prove the state's case must be disclosed to the individual."[2] This was the only way they could construct a defense against the accusations.

The truth was waiting there about what really happened to those children. Inside Box 14 were the "Children's Statements," and inside the folders were pages and pages of transcribed parents' journals, notes from the children's interviews with law enforcement, notes from therapy sessions, and more. Screaming at me in black-and-white all-caps was a document ominously labeled, "ABUSERS FROM ABBOTT, CHILDERS, ROBERTSON, ZIMMERMAN REPORTS." The name of each defendant the children christened as an abuser was there, and under that were the names of the children who named them. A second list, labeled "Honorable Mention," held each indictment child's name and the other children they named as co-conspirators. A third list contained more than a dozen names of other adults accused during the therapy sessions, yet only seven were indicted. And finally, there were the names of sixteen children who mentioned Robin.[3]

In her indictments, nine little children, some not even in her classroom, accused Robin Boles Byrum of unthinkable crimes of conspiracy to commit indecent liberties with a child; indecent liberties by touching; indecent liberties by sexual offense; indecent liberties by urination and defecation on a child; indecent liberties by crimes against nature; and indecent liberties by being nude in front of children, all with no specific date, no specific place, no specific time, no physical evidence, and no eyewitness.

CHAPTER 22

"I Don't Remember"

It is well known that children's testimony can be influenced by suggestive interviewing, but now we know . . . conversations with mothers have the potential to distort children's accounts of their experiences.
—Peter A. Ornstein and Taylor E. Thomas

Childhood should be about chasing butterflies, playing tag, making up magical stories, and giggling until your tummy aches. It is about getting potty-trained and then slipping backward and wetting your pants or throwing temper tantrums for no apparent reason. It is about saying mean things that hurt people's feelings, but not understanding why it hurts. Most importantly, childhood is about trusting the adults around you to protect you. It should never be about facing a predator or fearing violation in unimaginable ways.

Sadly, children sometimes are abused. But what about the ninety-two children in Edenton, North Carolina, between September 1988 and December 1988? In truth, were those three months filled with molestation, perversion, terror, rape, and unthinkable crimes against their tiny bodies?

On any given day before, during, or after those three months, did any parent see physical evidence of horrifying trauma even once, let alone four hundred times? Was bedwetting, wetting pants, or constipation proof that a toddler had been sodomized? Were nighttime "bad dreams" evidence of rape, or just part of a typical childhood experience? Was a toddler's fear of being left at day care evidence of an evil plot, or a symptom of separation anxiety that all children experience? Was a four-year-old stating she did not like a particular adult a sign of something sinister? Or could it be that little children sometimes suddenly do not like even their mommies and daddies? Do children that age intentionally lie, or do they simply lack the brain development to distinguish between truth and fiction? Can they easily be convinced something happened when it did not?

The pursuit for answers to these questions led me to the now-grown Little Rascals children, hoping to learn the long-term impact this had on them—my own sort of "longitudinal study." And like others who tried before me, I thought their voices could help in ongoing efforts to get exoneration for the Edenton Seven. In 2019, Lew Powell wrote letters to each of the now-adult children who were cited in the indictment, but his efforts failed. Lee Coleman, the author of *Has a Child Been Molested?*, wrote an open letter asking them "to seriously consider if justice could be served" by them "coming forth." In the letter, he assured them they had "done nothing wrong," but they had only listened to the adults around them. He did not seek their "memories of what did or didn't happen" at Little Rascals. Instead, what mattered most was "how they were interviewed" and by whom and how often.[1] Powell, Coleman, and I all understood we were unlikely to get responses. In the words of the uncle of a child named in the indictment, they had "put this behind themselves long ago." He, too, would not speak with me.

But the luxury of burying the past was impossible for the Edenton Seven.

As it turned out, three of the Little Rascals "kids" were finally willing to revisit the memories when I reached out to them. One now-adult child (name withheld to protect identity) named in the indictments responded within days of my request only to say, "I would not be a good resource. I don't remember anything from that time. Nothing."[2] This person had not one shred of a memory. True, it had been over three decades, but not one memory of the alleged trauma lingered? Not even the grueling interviews? Lucky him.

A second now-adult child (name withheld to protect identity), one who was interviewed by Toppin and Abbott but never named in the indictments, was more willing to talk. We had a lengthy, lighthearted chat about their life, family, and parents. For more than an hour, we spoke with no leading questions necessary. Instead, we simply let the conversation evolve slowly to the day care. What did that person remember? They laughed and said their recall was little more than a "clip of a memory . . . something about a boat . . . nothing more."[3]

This person had been a child in Robin's three-year-old class when the charges were made. It was about two months into the allegations before their name was mentioned. Looking back, they doubted anything had ever happened. And in fact, they had "absolutely no memory of any kind of abuse" at Little Rascals. Instead, they vividly remember the "blonde lady questioning them repeatedly over many weeks," and her demanding again and again that the child "answer the questions," which they consistently refused to do.[4] The child's parents were always outside the door, listening and questioning. Why was that child never named in the indictment? Probably because that child never gave "the blonde lady" the answers she sought. Even now, the child doubts the memory of the boat was real. Was that just an idea planted in their mind through hours of interrogation?

The parents of a third child, not named in the indictment, say they feel fortunate they never got "pulled into the delusion. It just didn't make sense." They sat through the dozens of the parent meetings, the state-hosted meetings, and the pressure sessions. In fact, the father still questions "where in the world it came from," blaming Mabry for the hysteria and feeling certain that her agenda "was something other than a slap." He continued, "It was just a feeling, something I couldn't confirm, but she just seemed motivated by something else . . . jilted, perhaps?" Regardless, the now adult-child and her parents painfully recalled the spitefulness waged against anyone who didn't go along with the hysteria. And they remembered Lamb "as particularly vicious and cruel to them."[5]

The mother of this third adult-child said her family lived only a short walk from the day care, and she was "in and out of that building at all times." Though Edenton, located directly on the Albemarle Sound, had easy access to the water, this mother said there was "little possibility [abuse] could have happened without someone seeing something. Absolutely no way." Incredulously, these parents asked, "Did folks really believe Kelly took little children out and threw them off the side of boats? Absurd!"[6] But folks did believe it.

The topic of boats came up time and again. The archived documents showed a consistent list of themes that ran throughout all the children's interviews: secrets, fire, scissors, hot-air balloons, shark-filled water, trained sharks, a man named black Abe, a man named white Abe, the fat man, the mean man, pills, poison, pirates, alligators, snakes, ropes, rabbits, licking, and BOATS! It became clear why some children were named, while others were not. Did the therapists plant those themes as the experts suggested? Did they create memories for the children, leading those who accepted the suggestions to contribute to the story-truth? Did the children and parents who cooperated become pawns? Even more, what role did the mothers play in suggesting something happened that perhaps did not?

Significant studies have been conducted on how accurate or true children's testimonies are. According to researchers Gabrielle Principe and Erica Schindewolf, each of the previously mentioned sources of suggestions can significantly impact children's memories and their "abilities to provide accurate accounts of the past."[7]

Principe and Schindewolf's research shows that the "suggestive features of interviews" can "lead to entirely false accounts." They wrote that "memory is constructive," and misinformation can be introduced to children either "deliberately" or "unknowingly" through something they called "conversational contamination." It seems that young children are "especially vulnerable to the contribution of others" in constructing their memories. The studies showed that memories can come from the way the investigators constructed those memories and by suggesting to the children that something happened. The memories can also come from interaction with peers through play as children share "collaborative stories." Suggestions can come from rumors, or "reports of an event" that the child did not actually participate in, but rather the memory is planted suggesting that they observed something they did not. This is especially true when overhearing a detail from adult conversations. Perhaps the most interesting possibility from the Principe and Schindewolf studies was that of "maternal suggestibility." When parents have "preexisting beliefs about what has happened to their children, they are prone to shape their interviews with their children to elicit untrue statements consistent with their beliefs." The studies also suggested that "maternal style influences how children remember," and those Principe and Schindewolf called "high-elaborative mothers . . . those who hold false beliefs . . . may be more likely to weave their own beliefs" into the construction their children's accounts of events.[8]

The hours and days I spent in a small study room at the Duke Law Library left me exhausted yet driven even harder to continue my search through the journals and testimonies, hoping for some understanding of what role the therapists and parents played in the children's stories from this case. In one mother's entries, she wrote that in mid-May 1989, her child mentioned boats to her. She wrote that she immediately went to another mother to ask if her child "had said anything about boats." Then the second mother began asking her child about boats. At first, there was nothing, but eventually, boats appeared in interview after interview. Many weeks later, one of the children's stories took an ominous turn about Mr. Bob taking the two children out on a boat, where Kelly "threw the little girl into the water." That three-year-old boy remembered on the witness stand, "I jumped in and saved her." His story had slowly morphed into a bizarre tale of "sharks, and white Andre," and more. How much of that child's memory about the boats came from his mother's account of what happened?[9]

A suggestion from one mother to a second mother, and a frantic suggestion by the second mother to Toppin, and suddenly boats became a reinforced idea in all the subsequent interviews. This was the "mono-ideational thinking" Shopper talked about, where the interrogators fixated on one thing only and disregarded anything that refuted it. But the parents believed their children, and as late as June 1990, that first mother was still searching all around Edenton and Chowan County for the boat and the place where the abuse could have occurred.

The first child who mentioned the boats would later testify in Kelly's trial. (The following quotations come directly from the transcribed testimony in *State of North Carolina v. Robert F. Kelly, Jr.*)

In response to Spivey's questioning if he "remembered" telling Mr. Hart about "going on a boat with Mr. Bob," the child said, "Yes, he pushed me in the water, and he said, um, there's a shark, and he really did that at night time, he . . . he tricked us . . . and it was fake."

"'Who was there?'"

"The other kids, Ms. Betsy, Ms. Dawn, the big fat man, and all the other people who worked there."

"What did Mr. Bob do after he pushed you in the water?"

"They laughed at me."

"What did you do after he pushed you in the water?"

"I climbed back up."

The child went on to tell the court he swam back to the boat, "pushed" himself up, helped Bob load the boat on the trailer, and went back to the day care until his "mommy and daddy picked me up." This same child is the one who accused Kelly of sticking "a play knife up my butt."[10]

Time matters. What really happened in all those months before the trials two years later? By 1991, all twelve children who testified to reclaimed memories with the help of the therapists that they were on "boats"—speed boats, tugboats, houseboats, marinas—yet every child told a different version, and all were bizarre at best. Could those memories have been planted? One mother's transcribed journal indicated her son was not interviewed until well into the investigation when another child named him. That mother's notes revealed that they then met with Toppin and the therapists. Like the others, it was many weeks before that child made the first accusation.

According to research by Judith Adams, if a child spontaneously reports being abused, "especially [if] the child provided consistent, credible details of the incident in age-appropriate language . . . it is very likely credible." Further, her studies suggest that "interviews within a week after an event can be reasonably accurate."[11] But that did not happen in the Little Rascals case. Weeks and months lingered before any of the children told tales of boat rides, touching, sodomy, and rape, which allowed plenty of time for ideas to be planted into their memories.

Don't forget. These children were required to attend "Court School," where they were not only interrogated but coached on how to respond in the courtroom. In a *Virginian-Pilot* interview in January 1995, Lamb admitted that the use of those "court schools for young witnesses"[12] was first tested in the Little Rascals case, and the effects of those coaching sessions had never been challenged. What effect did all that have on how the children framed their stories? Before they ever entered the court system, they had already experienced months of repeated coaching by therapists and parents. Confirmed in the artifacts at Duke, in each instance, the children refused repeated bribing, pleading, coaxing, and threatening until well into the therapy.

Toppin and the therapists encouraged the parents to keep journals, which they did, and those transcribed journals, filled with details the jury should have heard, were withheld from the defense team. The parents' journal entries made clear how the convictions were accomplished and who the key players were. Mabry never testified, yet she was mentioned by parents throughout the journals as an instigator of the claims of abuse. The journals also suggested some parents believed Audrey Stever was at the center. Stever began journaling at the suggestion of her friend Brenda Toppin, with her first entry dated November 7, 1988, long before the first formal accusations and before any other parent began journaling. She continued journaling until March 14, 1990. Parent journal entries, brief notes from Toppin's interviews, and notes from therapists' sessions all implied "conversational contamination."[13]

The boxes at Duke produced more troubling details. Shortly after Stever made the first allegation against Bob Kelly, the Department of Social Services issued a statement that they had "contacted all the kids about the alleged abuse and there were no further additional reports about neglect or abuse."[14] Yet, only three days later, the DSS mailed a letter to all the Little Rascals families inquiring about "alleged abuse." Why? What changed in three days? The rumor mill had started, and intense pressure was building. Suddenly, parents were networking, making frantic phone calls, having meetings, and comparing "symptoms." Stever wrote that she called multiple mothers, who then called other mothers. Within days of the DSS letter, dozens of panicked parents reached out to other panicked and suspicious parents, and the firestorm could no longer be contained.

And there was more. When Chris Bean was hired to defend Bob Kelly, his wife, Grace Bean, wrote in her journal and later testified that there was intense pressure from the community for Bean not to defend Kelly. People stopped talking to her. She felt she was "ostracized"[15] by her friends and community, which must have been a harsh blow to a woman with her social standing. Soon after Chris Bean withdrew as defense counsel, Grace Bean wrote her first entry—May 2, 1989—in a near-daily journal, which she continued until February 1991.

Grace Bean also journaled details of learning about the abuse. It was clear that H. P. Williams and Brenda Toppin had warned Chris Bean, but who else suggested to the Beans their little boy had been molested? On the witness stand, Grace Bean recounted a visit from Lynne Layton, who went to the Beans' home, but Grace was not there. Layton stayed, chatting with Chris while she waited for Grace to arrive home. According to Grace, it was that day that Layton told them in detail about gruesome allegations involving their young son. How did Layton know about those lurid details? How did she benefit from that moment? Did it connect her socially? Did it give her a sense of power? It was shortly after that visit that the Beans put their son in therapy.

Grace Bean documented events, meetings, discussions, and frequent family sessions with their young son. In her first entries, she wrote that their son repeatedly denied anything happened at Little Rascals. But there was more revealing information in those journals. She wrote extensively about Betty Robertson's evaluation sessions—what Robertson said in them, what she discovered, and what she shared with the state. The evaluation for the Bean child's therapy began on May 8 and continued for four weeks. Robertson used a stuffed rabbit, drawings, and homework assignments to elicit information from the young child. By June, Robertson told the Beans she was confident their son had been a "victim of touching" and would need three to six months of therapy. As the months of therapy rolled on, the entries revealed his allegations grew more sexual, sinister, bizarre, and more similar to the other children's.

Near the end of June, Grace Bean writes about them questioning their son at the dinner table about "secrets" and his "private parts." He refused to answer. Robertson's therapy notes from July 20, 1989, indicated that she believed he had "repressed the scariest parts" of the abuse.[16] Then the notes revealed more. In court, Grace Bean stated under oath that her child "had been abused in ways he [did] not even remember; that he had 'repressed' some of what happened to him." Did this theory come from Robertson? The defense repeatedly objected to her offering expert testimony. She was a mother, not a psychologist. However, Judge McLelland overruled their objection and denied the motion to strike it from her testimony. When the prosecution asked Grace about her son's memory regarding the day care, she speculated that her child "has repressed . . . a lot of what must have happened . . . that he has disclosed as much as, I think, he's capable of doing in handling it. He has pushed it away and has actually forgotten things because it was so traumatic. And those have been his coping skills."[17] The North Carolina Court of Appeals later ruled this was "illustrative of a non-expert [or lay person] testifying to matters reserved for expert testimony," and her testimony was "nothing more than speculation."[18]

In another crucial entry, Grace Bean wrote the following about an exchange between Chris and his son. On November 14, 1989, five months into therapy, they were on a car trip with their son to attend another session with Robertson. Grace wrote in a long, loosely constructed journal entry that Chris told his son, "Mr. Bob is pleading not guilty and says he did not touch the children." The child responded, "He did . . . Mr. Bob has been lying to you." Yet Bean "points out" to his son that he said previously that "Mr. Bob wouldn't do anything like that." According to the journal entry, the Beans continued to question the child about why he said that. He eventually replied, "Because Mr. Bob told me if I told, you wouldn't love me anymore." Grace noted there was a long pause, and then their son responded to their silence with the words:

"Mr. Bob didn't do what you think he did."[19]

The entry goes on to describe that Chris Bean continued prodding and questioning about Mr. Bob "touching at naptime and in the bathroom." His son replied, "A little bit." Bean asked, "What about Shelly [sic]?" The boy responded, "She was nice," and said he "didn't remember her touching the children." Bean then asked him why he said earlier that she was "touching the children?" He replied that he "didn't remember saying that."[20] The entry ends shortly after that.

Grace Bean's final entry was three months later, on February 7, 1991, almost two years after her first entry and five months before the trials began. In her journals, she also confirmed that "Robertson reported"[21] information to the prosecution team. One must wonder, did the Beans know as early as November 14, 1989, that it was possibly all a lie?

Another mother began her journal about the same time in May 1989. Like the Bean child, her young daughter denied for weeks that anything happened at Little Rascals until Betty Robertson began drawing pictures of private parts and using "the dolls" to coerce the child into saying she had been "touched."[22] Still another mother kept a journal of her daily drilling sessions from January 26, 1989, to July 8, 1991. Michelle Zimmerman, the therapist, suggested it would help her child eventually "tell the truth about how some secrets are not helpful."[23] The mother of still another child, one who accused Robin of kicking her, kept a journal from January 25, 1989, to July 26, 1991. She journaled that Nancy Lamb actually came to her house to "take [her daughter and another girl] out to lunch."[24] Both girls were named in the indictments, and both had accused Robin. Were there witnesses to that lunch date? Recordings? Notes? What did Prosecutor Lamb say to those two little girls?

Then, two-and-a-half years after the abuses were alleged to have occurred, these children took the witness stand in the trials against Bob Kelly and Dawn Wilson. Their testimonies centered around both what their mothers wrote in their journals and testified to on the witness stand. (The following dialogue featuring the direct and cross-examination of the children is quoted from the trial transcript in *State of North Carolina v. Robert F. Kelly Jr.*, July 1991 to April 1992.)

On examination of one accusing child, the prosecutor asked: "Do you remember a lady named Ms. Robin?"

"Yes."

"Who was she?"

"I don't remember."

Yet only a few moments later, this same child testified to doing arts and crafts in Ms. Shelley's room, and when asked if Mr. Bob was there, the child replied, "Yes."

"Ms. Betsy?"

"Yes."

"Ms. Robin?"

"Yes."

Further into the examination, the child testified that Mr. Bob and Ms.

Betsy took the child upstairs at the day care and began inserting needles into him.

"Where did they get the needle?"

"I don't know."

"When they put the needle in you, what did the other children say?"

"They didn't say anything."

"What were they doing?"

"I don't know."

Another child was asked, "Do you remember telling Ms. Judy they killed babies at the day care?"

"Yes."

"Tell me about that."

"I don't remember."

Yet another accusing child was asked, "Did you like Ms. Robin?"

"No."

"Why didn't you like Ms. Robin?"

"Because she did bad things."

"What bad things?"

"She would kick the people that [were] in her classroom."

"Did you see who Ms. Robin kicked?"

"Some children."

"Did you know their names?"

"No."

"Did she say anything when she kicked them?"

"No."

"Did she do other bad things besides kick them in the stomach?"

"No."

"Did Ms. Robin kick a whole bunch of children or just one?"

"I think she kicked a whole bunch. . . They were in her room."

"Where were you?"

"I was walking in the hallway."

"What did the children do when she kicked them?"

"They were screaming."

That child went on to testify that she was walking down the hallway with her teacher and her entire class going outside to play.

"And why didn't the teacher see anything?" the prosecutor asked.

"Because she was looking forward."

Moments later, as she was questioned about whether she knew who Ms. Robin's husband was, the child testified she did. When asked if she liked him, she said, "No."

"Why?"

"Because he was on Ms. Robin's side . . . he liked Ms. Robin."

Yet another child was asked, "Did you like Ms. Robin?"

"No."

"Why didn't you like Ms. Robin?"

"I don't know."

"Did Ms. Robin ever do anything bad to you?"

"She touched me."

"Where were you when she touched you on the bottom?"

"In the bathroom."

"Whose room was the bathroom in?"

"Nobody's room."

When Spivey cross-examined one child about the burning flower stems that Mr. Bob was accused of inserting, he asked if they burned the child's bottom.

The child responded, "I don't remember."

"Did you ever see bad things happen to other children?"

"No."

"Did you ever see Mr. Bob hurt 'R?'"

"Yes."

"What did he do?"

"I don't remember."

"Did you ever see Mr. Bob hurt anyone else?"

"No."

Did you ever . . . did you ever . . . did you ever?

Another child was asked, "Did Ms. Robin ever hurt you?"

"I don't remember. I don't remember really."

The questioning continued later: "Did Ms. Robin ever stick you with anything? Do you remember telling Ms. Judy that she stuck some scissors in your privates?"

"No."

"Did Ms. Robin stick scissors in your privates?"

In a very child-like explanation, the tiny witness said, "She did really … like … stick them in there; she just … like … putting them up to it; like them on it."

And supposedly she did this sometimes upstairs and sometimes in Ms. Shelley's room.

"What did Ms. Shelley say?"

"Nothing."

"Did she see her when she did it?"

"Yes."

"What did the other children say when she did it?"

"Nothing."

"Did all the other children see her do that?"

"Not all of them, a couple."

"What did Ms. Robin say when she did that?"

"Nothing."

On examination of even another child, the prosecutor said, "Sometimes when you were at Little Rascals . . . you said . . . Mr. Bob put things in your bottom . . . could you tell me where you were when this happened?"

"I don't remember."

"Were you in Ms. Shelly's room or some other room?"

"I don't remember."

"Was [Child X] there?"

"No."

"Was [Child Y] there? Were any of the other children there?"

"No."

"Was anybody there when this happened?"

"No."

Later: "Did you ever go away from Little Rascals with somebody besides your mom or dad?"

"I don't remember."

Later: "You told Ms. Betty you went out on a boat with Mr. Bob one time . . . What kind of boat was it? Just tell me what it looked like."

"It was a tugboat."

"And who went with you?"

"Nobody."

Later: "Did [Child X] go with you?"

"I don't remember."

"Did [Child Y] go with you?"

"I don't remember."

"Did any other children go with you . . . did any other grownup go?"

"No."[25]

The painful chant of "I don't remember . . . I don't remember . . . I don't remember" and "No . . . No . . . No" were reminiscent of the repeated denials from the children in the beginning of the investigation. Over and over, it appeared no one saw or heard anything other than the testifying child. No other teacher? No grownup? No other child that they could remember? When Robin and Shelley were supposedly dancing around naked in the check-in room, no one saw anything? When Bob and Betsy Kelly inserted needles into a toddler, no one screamed? No one heard anything? No child went home at night telling anyone terrifying details of abuse with needles, scissors, and burning flower stems? Things happened nowhere and everywhere, upstairs and downstairs, on boats, and in check-in rooms?

After the trial ended, two parents raised serious doubts about the abuse claims. The mother told Bikel of Frontline that she "had many doubts" . . . and their son was "a changed little boy" after "being investigated by Judy

Abbott." During the interview, the father uttered some prophetic words. He believed his son was "over-brainwashed" because everywhere they turned, they were being told, "Your child is sexually abused." He was certain that his son was "fine" until after Abbot "questioned and almost interrogated him." That was when the child "started acting [that] way." The father believed his child "understood enough to know what they were trying to get at. If he said 'no' enough, and they said, 'that's not the right answer,' you figure he'll try 'yes.'" He did not believe his child was abused, nor did his son. None of the stories they filled him with "would come back" . . . and he didn't "think they ever would."[26]

Of the now-adult Little Rascals children I spoke with, after all the accusations, their memories never returned. If they remembered anything, it was the memory of being repeatedly interrogated. One child ensnared in the delusion recounted that the most traumatic thing she recalled from the day care were "the pears they served with lunch."[27]

CHAPTER 23

CHRISTOPHER BEAN FOR THE PROSECUTION

A lawyer shall not reveal information acquired during a
professional relationship with a client unless the client
gives informed consent.
—North Carolina Rules of Professional Conduct 1.6

The fact that Chris Bean took the stand and testified for the State of North Carolina against his former friend and client continues to raise condemnation from his legal peers across the state. Over the objection of the defense counsel, Judge McLelland allowed Bean to testify. Though legal and ethics experts like Paul Roberts and Lawrence Stratton were more critical of the prosecutors, whom they said had a "win-at-all-cost" attitude and functioned in a "culture in which the pursuit of convictions has replaced the pursuit of justice,"[1] it was McLelland who allowed Bean to testify against his former client. Later, the North Carolina Court of Appeals ruled that McLelland was in error to allow certain testimony from Kelly's once "champion and defender."[2] (What follows in this chapter is directly quoted material from Christopher Bean's testimony in *State of North Carolina v. Robert F Kelly Jr.*, July 1991 to April 1992, Volume 43, pages 10,273–10,334.)[3]

As H. P. Williams questioned Bean about his background and history as a lawyer, Bean told the court that after leaving the district attorney's office in Elizabeth City, North Carolina, in 1977, he went to Raleigh to work for the North Carolina State Bar, which at the time "had created a new section for disciplinary actions for lawyers." He was one of two attorneys who prosecuted those lawyers charged with violating the Rules of Professional Responsibility. Two years later, he moved to Edenton to practice law and eventually testified against his former client. Bean could have appealed the subpoena. Questions remain as to whether or not he had to testify against his former client, but he chose not to protest it and instead willingly took the stand and gave what turned out to be shocking testimony.

Anyone who has raised children can attest to the fact that they sometimes behave in the most bizarre ways when under duress. When their lives are disrupted by confusion and change, toddlers often respond in ways we cannot rationalize as adults. As the mother of three and the grandmother of two little boys who are currently the same age as the Little Rascals children, I know personally how unpredictable young children can be, even when life is normal. They can fall apart over anything—or nothing. But when faced with changes in their lives, they often act out, regress, scream, rant, cry, and more. Ultimately, the Beans' opinions regarding their child's behavior were ruled as prejudicial and inadmissible as evidence.

Early in Chris Bean's testimony, he said his son began attending Little Rascals at the new building on a regular basis in the fall of 1988. He testified to family disruptions: they had a new baby, "they built a new house" that went "way over budget," and "Grace had to go back to work." All of these were huge changes in their lives. Added to that, the boy was now attending day care, and because the child "had been with his mother from the beginning of his life, he was very close to her," as Chris Bean said, so it would make sense that the child was confused and anxious.

The testimony reveals the stressful details of how this three-year-old child spent his day split between three different day cares. He started each day at Little Rascals around 7:00 a.m. or 7:30 a.m. On Mondays, Wednesdays, and Fridays, he left Little Rascals to attend a separate preschool program from 9:00 a.m. to 11:30 a.m., and on Tuesdays and Thursdays, he attended yet another preschool from 9:00 a.m. to 11:45

a.m. Sometimes he ate lunch with a friend, and Chris would pick him up to return him to Little Rascals for the remainder of the day. Bean said he usually walked the child in, as "it was a busy time at Little Rascals because it was lunch time." Bean recalled walking in and seeing his son's friends eating, and it was "real quiet . . . very orderly." He then entered an opinion to the court in hindsight that the "quiet" was a sign of something else. Bean added the child "never wanted to go to Little Rascals. Instead, he wanted to know why he couldn't go home. Some days he didn't put up much resistance . . . other days he did."

According to Bean, about the time his son began Little Rascals, he also started having issues with his bowels and developed temper tantrums, nightmares, and other behaviors. They believed it "was some phase he was going through," and they thought "he was having a hard time adjusting." Bean again added, "He had always been really close to his mother." Bean further added his opinion that the bowel issues and night-mares decreased by February 1989 and linked that changed behavior directly to when "Bob Kelly was no longer supposed to be at the day care."

In describing the child's behavior, Bean said they worried about their child just "[falling] apart" for things that were "relatively minor," and he constantly had to "reassure him" that they could fix it. At one point, he said the child "was constantly asking Grace 'do you love me?'—but he didn't ask me that." He even testified that at one point his child "stopped letting me touch him." He questioned his son, "Have I done something to make you mad?" The child said, "No." Bean then asked, "Why won't you give me a hug?" The child was silent. Bean told the court, "I didn't know what I had done. I wanted to make it right." Bean offered his lay opinion, but was he legally permitted to suggest that these were signs of abuse?

Bean offered more opinions to the court regarding the child's behaviors. Were the child's changes because Bob Kelly was no longer at the day care, or could it have been because of fewer disruptions? Was the child suddenly lapsing "into baby talk" because he had been sodomized, or because he had a new baby brother at home? Perhaps it was because he was being interrogated over and over? Were the behaviors indicative of a toddler being over-stressed by a mother who was suddenly absent and leaving him in the care of others, or because he was being abused? One incident Bean testified to as troubling was when his son wrapped his mother's ankles in rope. Could that have been because of his childish obsession "with bandannas" and playing "Davy Crockett," or because someone had tied him up to rape him?

Williams began to question Bean about when he first learned his child had been implicated. According to Bean, on Tuesday, April 25, 1989, Brenda Toppin told him his child "had been named and may have been abused." By that Friday, the day care was closed. Layton then came to their house to tell them in "very graphic detail" what her daughter said happened to his child. Bean declared, "There's no way in the world a child that age could have known that unless that child had actually experienced it or witnessed it."

But what was "that?" What was the "very graphic detail?" What did Layton tell him? His testimony never disclosed to the court what Layton said happened, only that her child was "three at the time." He claimed she did not tell him who named their child, but then testified, "The next day, Marjorie Hollowell told Grace that if there was any way in the world [Bean] could get out of being his attorney, he ought to."

The most prejudicial testimony was the moment Bean declared he had "never been so shattered." Bean said to the court, "I had believed adamantly and completely in Bob Kelly's innocence. And for all those months . . . from January through that day, I had believed in his total innocence. And for me, I've never been so shattered, I don't think, in my life as I was on that Saturday, that to face the possibility that the allegations—whatever they were because we still didn't know—could be true. It was the first time that I had admitted to myself that it might be true. And then to think that my own child had been abused. I didn't know whether he had been. I—I selfishly prayed that he hadn't been, but thought some of the others had been. But I thought maybe he had escaped it. And I know Grace and I stood in the kitchen—and we cried. And we held on to each other."

Christopher Bean, Bob Kelly's previous attorney, testified under oath that he believed the allegations "could be true" . . . and he "thought some of the others had been as well." I tried to imagine the reaction of the jury when those words were entered into testimony.

During direct examination, Williams asked Bean about what he'd told his son about him representing Kelly.

"Did you talk to [him] about the allegations?" Williams asked.

Bean said he did. He also asked his son, "Did Mr. Bob touch you anywhere he shouldn't have?" and "Have you seen Mr. Bob touch any other child anywhere that he shouldn't have?" His child responded, "No," and walked out of the room.

Williams then asked, "End of discussion?"

"End of discussion," Bean said. "That's the way [he] deals with things if he doesn't want to talk about it."

And what was the implication? Was he suggesting something happened that he did not want to discuss, or was he just being bluntly honest? This was one of many moments in Bean's testimony where he added his non-expert opinion about what he believed the child's behavior meant.

Furthermore, during direct examination, Bean testified that he and his wife reached out to a friend who recommended a psychiatrist, who in turn referred them to Betty Robertson. Bean "reached out to her on May 1," testifying that he "was concerned about children being led to say things by adults." He assured the court they had said nothing to their child at this point "other than that first question" asking if Mr. Bob had touched him, to which his son had answered, "No."

Bean testified that no one from the police or DSS had yet interviewed his son, telling the court he wanted his child's "mind clear of any suggestion of abuse." He further testified that he told Robertson he did not want her "putting any suggestion" in this child's mind, and that she "assured him that the evaluation process . . . was not to suggest to the children anything had happened." In his words, she needed four sessions to "test him . . . but not to suggest to him any specific acts."

Then Bean's testimony took a turn. He testified to another lengthy exchange between his wife and their child. "That night, as I was putting our younger child to bed, I overheard a conversation between Grace and [their child]—I heard her say something about Little Rascals—my ears perked up—I heard her ask if he had been upstairs at Little Rascals—what happened up there—and he described being tied up with bandannas— he wore a bandanna a lot—every day. I then heard her ask him if 'Mr. Bob is a nice man or bad man' and he said, 'Bad man.' She asked then, 'What had Mr. Bob done?'"

Bean continued that his son told his mother that Kelly "bopped me on the nose," and the mother then asked what *he* had done—a question that seemed to be seeking the child's reaction to the "bop." Bean added his child told Grace that he had "thrown Mr. Bob out of the window, tied him up and thrown him out the window."

Bean's testimony continued. He testified that a few days later, he and his son were returning from a trip to Rocky Mount when he began to question his son about the day care's "upstairs." He told the court he suggested to his son that another child, a close friend of his, said they "had been tied up by Mr. Bob—and upstairs, at the daycare." When Bean asked his son if that was true, he said the child turned to him and said, "'Mr. Bob's a nice man—he wouldn't do anything like that,' and turned his back away . . . end of conversation."

We know Chris Bean told Betty Robertson he did not want her "putting ideas in his head." We know she assured him that the evaluation was only to test him, but not "to suggest" any "specific acts." Yet from Chris Bean's testimony, we also know the Beans asked the child "if Mr. Bob had touched you," before he ever met with Robertson. We know that Grace Bean asked the child if Mr. Bob is a "good man, or a bad man." We know Chris Bean asked the child if Mr. Bob tied him up in the upstairs at the day care. All these ideas had already been planted in the child's mind before Robertson even began evaluating him.

Williams examined Bean about the evaluation sessions with Robertson that began on May 8. Bean explained to the court how Robertson told him the evaluation sessions would be different from therapy if she determined he needed that, which, of course, she did recommend.

Williams asked, "Did she indicate—how [they] would be different?"

Bean responded, "She did—the therapy session was to bring out of the child what was inside the child's mind to deal with the problem the child was having because of what had occurred. Ah, so the procedure would obviously be different in the therapy than it would be in the evaluation because you have to, uh, reach into the child's mind, you have to ask them, uh, more leading type questions in therapy in order to be able to find out what's causing the problems and to be able to deal with the problem."

Bean admitted under oath that Robertson used leading questions to probe the child's mind and "find out what's causing the problems." It proved that the therapists did coerce the children and plant ideas in their minds.

Further, Williams asked Bean, "In other words, you would have to give them the ideas to think about?"

Bean responded: "I would think so."

Added to this, Bean testified that during the evaluation period, the family frequently talked about Mr. Bob and Little Rascals at home. Further, he said, Robertson "as a rule [talked freely in front of the child] because he was her patient." In addition, Robertson gave them homework assignments to "talk about things" that had been discussed in the child's sessions with her. This all provides more evidence that ideas of abuse came from the adults and not the child.

The Bean child started therapy with Robertson at the beginning of June, four weeks after his evaluation period, and the following conversation occurred eight weeks into his visits with Robertson. That was after eight weeks of leading questions to "give them ideas to think about." For eight weeks, Robertson used "leading type questions" to suggest to the child that more happened than he was admitting.

On July 27, Bean said his child made accusations that "Mr. Bob touched his privates" in the bathroom in Miss Shelley's room.

Williams asked, "At this point, did you begin to understand why [the child] had had the bathroom problems?"

Bean's response was, "We discussed his fear of the bathroom . . . I think I realized that that's why he was afraid of the bathroom because of what happened to him at Little Rascals."

Bean later testified about his son being "preoccupied with jail," and that he was worried if "he was going to jail" too. Bean said he "assured him children don't go to jail in North Carolina." The child "was just obsessed with the jail." But why? Was jail something he learned about at Little Rascals? Or did he hear about it because the adults around him were talking about it constantly? Bean said he took his son and four other indictment children to visit the jail in hopes that it would satisfy the child. That is when the children met Sheriff Spruill. Bean said the sheriff let these four little children go inside a cell and closed the door behind them, and he said his child "never asked about children going to jail again." Strangely, after that visit, the sheriff was named as an abuser. Like many others whom the children named, Sheriff Spruill was never charged.

Bean testified that finally, in late September, he told his child that Betsy had been arrested. The child asked, "Why? She hasn't done anything?"

Bean said he assured him, "Shelley and Dawn have also been arrested."

His son told him, "Daddy you have to go tell the judge to let them out. They haven't done anything."

Bean asked him, "Well, didn't you have to lick Miss Dawn's vagina?" *Leading question?* He then testified the child said, "Miss Shelley tried to stop Mr. Bob from doing bad things" and "that's why you have to tell the judge to let them out."

H. P. Williams asked Bean, "Was it your impression he saw Shelley and Dawn as victims as well?"

Bean responded, "That's exactly what my impression is because when I asked him about Dawn, which is obviously a terrible thing—he didn't see that as wrong because she hadn't wanted to do it."

Perhaps Betty Robertson did not want the Beans planting ideas in their son's head, but did they? Did both the parents and therapist suggest something happened? The children went from evaluations into therapy, and Bean's testimony confirmed all the suspicions by experts like Lanning, Loftus, Shopper, Kenner, Coleman, and others. The therapists' testimonies were not available, nor were their verbatim transcribed notes from the therapy sessions. There were no videotapes of their therapy sessions. What was available was Christopher Bean's testimony, under oath. From that, we know they did guide the children into providing the information they were seeking. Christopher Bean admitted under oath that the therapists "had to use leading type questions in the therapy to be able to find out what happened." He testified that he believed his child and others had been abused. He testified that he knew best what his child really meant when he said something—or said nothing. And last, Christopher Bean violated the most sacred trust between a lawyer and his client.

In the words of Judge Arnold as he entered the Court of Appeals ruling, "The prejudice inherent in having his former attorney, once his champion and defender, announce his knowledge of his guilt to the jury, is blatantly obvious."[4]

CHAPTER 24

THE MEDICAL EXPERTS

This court has permitted an expert to testify to a
diagnosis of sexual abuse ONLY where there has been
some physical evidence on which to base this opinion.
—*State of North Carolina v. James Clayton Clark Jr.* (2022)

The twelve compelling testimonies by the children of Little Rascals Day Care had been bound together and stored away, silenced by time. As I read them, I understood how difficult it must have been for the parents to hear their children's stories, regardless of the absurd and irrational nature of the accusations. But in order for the prosecution to prove what the children were saying was true and to convince a jury "beyond a reasonable doubt," they needed expert testimonies. They found four: Desmond Runyan, Jean Smith, Doren Fredrickson, and Janet Hadler. (Testimony in this chapter is directly quoted material from Drs. Runyan, Smith, and Fredrickson's testimony in *State of North Carolina v. Robert F Kelly Jr.*, July 1991 to April 1992, Volumes 57–59, pages 13,088–13,663.)

In the 1970s, child welfare agencies for the State of North Carolina were concerned that potentially abused children might not be seen by properly trained physicians, so they created an extensive roster from across the state of what they deemed qualified, experienced physicians. Places like Elizabeth City Medical Center, East Carolina University's medical school, and the University of North Carolina's medical school had verified physicians who agreed to participate in the program.

In 1987, Dr. Desmond Runyan, who was a UNC School of Medicine faculty member, wrote a grant to open a "referral clinic" at UNC Hospital that specialized in "extensive evaluations" of children referred to them as potential victims of sexual abuse. The clinic was open for four hours on Friday mornings, and the doctors saw a few hundred children in the first two years it was open. Regardless of who or what agency made the referral, all children who came to the Child Medical Evaluation Program (CMEP) were already suspected to be victims of mistreatment and/or sexual abuse. The grant included an application for funding for a "colposcope—for looking at skin in more detail" and for "videotape equipment with a microphone to tape interviews" so they could teach learners how to conduct the interviews.[1]

Runyan, who became the CMEP director, explained recently in an interview that on Friday mornings the clinic usually saw about "six or seven children scheduled for an exam." They were assigned to a staff of two physicians, a psychologist, a social worker, a rape crisis volunteer, and sometimes a medical student or resident to help with the exams. According to Runyan, the goal of the program was to provide medical intervention that was "sensitive, picking up any possibility of the problem, rather than . . . specifically determining if the child with a normal exam *does not* have the problem."[2] A normal examination absent physical evidence did not mean that no abuse had occurred.

But was it also possible that it meant abuse *had not* occurred?

Was the program's actual purpose to *find* abuse, rather than evaluate? Runyan said there were earlier forms used to determine the presence of physical signs of abuse, but they needed something better. So they developed their own form over time using protocols collected from programs across the country, and in 1988, he and his team ultimately designed a form that aligned with "what CMEP wanted to look for"— physical signs of abuse. This intake form created a "protocol" that "shortened the process of collecting" histories from the patients. He said they set up a "sort of production line" so that while one child was being interviewed, the doctor could see another.[3]

Months after Little Rascals closed, the head of Chowan County DSS, the Edenton Police Department, and the DA's office referred forty-two children from Little Rascals to CMEP. The program was overwhelmed by the large number of children involved in the referral. Runyan said, "It took a long time to get through that many examinations."[4] None of those CMEP physical examinations were performed until six or more months after the day care closed, and nearly a year after the alleged abuse supposedly occurred. Only the three physicians—Runyan, Smith, and Fredrickson—performed all the examinations.

In our interview in February 2023, I asked Runyan whether all the Little Rascals children went through the same process, and he responded that "a considerable period of time had passed" for these children and when seen at CMEP, they had already been interviewed by several people. He said he and his staff decided in those cases "not to make the kids go over the history again."[5]

However, the CMEP doctors' testimonies indicate that they did interview a significant number of those children. Runyan said in our interview that they also chose not to gather histories from some of the parents but instead just talk to the parents about "behaviors they observed."[6] Yet again, the testimonies revealed something quite different. Runyan testified that "talking to the parents was one of the more important aspects to find out how the child was doing" and confirmed that "the children had been through a lot."[7] And some of the diagnoses of abuse were made based on parent histories alone.

What behaviors did Runyan testify were consistent with abuse? According to court documents, he cited "poor appetite, temper tantrums, not trusting the parent, blame, anger, lack of control, dogmatic about how their room is arranged, regression, sucking a thumb, losing control over bowels and bladder, yelling, being inconsolable, and screaming."[8] I couldn't help but wonder, *Could any or all these behaviors also be consistent with typical, non-abused three- and four-year-old children?*

According to Runyan, David McCall, the head of Chowan County

DSS, told him that "the kids hadn't had any physical exams."[9] Granted, when Runyan told me this in 2023, it had been more than three decades since the trials, and memories fail. However, in the trial Runyan's colleague, Dr. Jean Smith, testified to something different. Once the court accepted her as a qualified expert, the state questioned her about whether the children had been seen by other doctors before the visits to CMEP that began in the fall of 1989. She said that their program did not require medical records if the children had been examined by their primary care physician. When asked why, she said it was because "this is a referral itself for . . . a medical evaluation of possible maltreatment."[10]

According to summaries of parents' journals archived at Duke, at some point after the accusations began, a few parents did take their children to primary care doctors or pediatricians, only to be told there was "no evidence of abuse."[11] Therefore, those parents then made calls to CMEP and took their children to Chapel Hill, where CMEP staff set up the examination schedules, assigning different pediatricians to different children. In our February 2023 interview, Runyan said that "the CMEP doctors were careful not to confer with each other about the individual cases so [they] would not have any conflict."[12]

When we talked, Runyan said the CMEP doctors were "provided short paragraph summaries of the history of abuse"[13] for each child. But what or who was the source of those histories? Runyan thought he remembered that it was DSS, but Smith testified at Kelly's trial that the CMEP staff did conduct many interviews. They had an in-house staff member, Janet Hadler, who had a master's in social work and whose "duty as part of the CMEP protocol . . . was to conduct in-depth interviews." Further, according to Smith, Hadler "was the only one that did" such interviews except for being assisted by Nancy Berson, "who was associated with the Department of Psychiatry" at UNC. Smith further stated that Hadler's role "at the time was to gain information from the child in an open-ended fashion to let the child say in their own words what may or may not have occurred."[14] But was that later contradicted in testimony?

Runyan later testified at the trial that another associate, Shelly Johnson, a psychologist, also assisted Hadler and Berson in conducting the intake "medical history interviews," but that they were not "a mental health interview."[15] Hadler and Berson used CMEP's checklist of physical findings to evaluate the children. One of the things the evaluation was supposed to ask was how many times the children had already been interviewed. Smith testified she did not have any prior knowledge about how long or "how many times a specific child had been seen by Judy Abbott" or the other therapists.[16] But later, she testified she did have conversations with Hadler in advance of the physical examinations of the children about things such as the "prior interviews with Abbott and the other therapists." During cross-examination, the defense attorney asked Smith, "Who was present in those interviews? What questions did you ask the children? What did the parents say? What did Ms. Hadler say to you?"[17]

Smith consistently answered she did "not recall" because she "did not write it down."[18]

When Prosecutor Nancy Lamb questioned Smith about whether Hadler had "exchanged the information [from the interviews] with the attending physician," Smith responded that Hadler "would often talk to me before she saw the child." As it turned out, some of the children refused to be interviewed because, she said, "They didn't want to talk about it anymore." In those cases, the physicians "were assured the children had already been interviewed prior to the CMEP interview."[19] What happened to the records of those interviews? When were they conducted and by whom?

On direct examination, Smith testified that the information from the CMEP interviews was "very helpful" in deciding if the "medical exam alone [would] confirm the presence or absence of abuse." She then expanded on that, saying, "The history was very critical" in determining if there had been abuse and that "important information gathered from the history—may be very helpful in making an assessment of probable sexual abuse even if" they found "nothing during the physical exams" of the children. Smith further testified that the history could weigh as much as "100 percent in the absence of physical findings" in an examination. Smith explained that the program had developed a "set form, a set number of items [they] would ask on past medical history evaluation—a checklist of yes-no questions about hospitalizations—developmental behavior—and changes [parents had] witnessed."[20] This information, combined with the information gathered in the examination, was how the doctors ultimately made a diagnosis.

Along with the physical exam of the genital area, CMEP doctors used another checklist to document physical signs of abuse and to make a diagnosis from "possible, to probable, to definite." After examining one of the girls, Smith checked "NO" to every question about visible physical signs for that child. However, on the signed and affirmed checklist document, she wrote that she "could not rule out penetration, but the findings are *consistent with* penetration. But it was not a *diagnosis* of penetration."[21]

Was that even scientifically possible? And what does *consistent with abuse* mean? It could be anything from fondling, which could leave no physical evidence, all the way to penetration, which could leave tears and scars before healing. How did the protocol Smith testified to allow her to conclude that it was "*consistent with* penetration"? And what protocol did the CMEP doctors utilize in their analysis? Smith testified there was no specific formula to apply from child to child, nor was there any "uniform system for every doctor [or for] every hospital."[22] They did not use the same positions, the same techniques, or even the same tools for measurement. If there was no specific or consistent formula, how could they concur on their findings, which they did?

Of the forty-two children referred to CMEP for evaluation, only a handful of those examined were diagnosed as "*consistent with abuse.*" Their diagnoses were based on physical examinations of vaginal and anal openings using evidence that is no longer accepted by medical science.

The tools the doctors used to make measurements were a measuring tape, Q-tips, and Polaroid pictures taken from the colposcope. They admitted that the information obtained from parents weighed as much as 100 percent in determining abuse.

How could that be admitted as evidence into a court of law? In the words of Lee Coleman, "Medical examiners often label normal examinations as consistent with abuse, but that is not evidence of abuse." He continued, the term "*consistent with*" had become a "linguistic *tour de force*," and "law enforcement and prosecutors took them at their word."[23]

How could the CMEP doctors' willingness to make diagnoses be done with such confidence? They asked both the children *and* their parents specific questions outlined in the form they had created, and because the children came to UNC because they were referred as victims of sexual abuse, was it possible that the questions might bias the examination?

When the prosecution asked how long an examination took, Fredrickson testified that the full exam didn't take long—"maybe fifteen minutes," he said. Conducting the actual physical exams took "maybe nine or ten minutes."[24] This was a detail Smith had concurred with in her earlier testimony. Without question, the doctors knew beforehand what to ask. Then they consulted with one another about their findings after the exams. In her testimony, Smith admitted she "consulted with other people in [their] field to discuss their findings" in each case.[25] Fredrickson testified he was "able to conclude . . . from published reports coming from other centers that it is so common not to have physical findings" that it made him "more confident about saying there had been abuse" even in the absence of "any findings of physical abuse." In the case of two children examined by Fredrickson, he testified, "There was no sign . . . the [physical] findings were normal, but with the histories and behavior issues, I concluded there was sexual abuse."[26]

From the results of his examinations, Fredrickson attempted to assure the court about the quality of the pictures from the colposcope, which even Runyan testified were difficult to see because of "reflections that can cause glare."[27] Still, Fredrickson's explanations raised more questions. The pediatric sexual abuse experts from which they drew their knowledge were Astrid Heger and Bruce Woodling of the McMartin Preschool case—the doctors who dominated the diagnostic arena in the child sexual assault hysteria. After the McMartin case, Heger and Woodling had been highly criticized by their peers for their practices with the colposcope and their recommendation that it was *the* way to find evidence of abuse. Given the outcome of the McMartin case, should this have raised questions about the reliability of the research techniques on which Fredrickson relied?

In testifying about the use of that procedure, Fredrickson testified sarcastically that it "takes a darn good photograph and they're magnified . . . but you can look and see exactly the same thing with the naked eye that you can see with a colposcopy." He further quipped, "Nobody likes to get that close to anybody's bottom to take pictures with a camera you have to hold on to."[28]

The doctors testified they did not perform colposcopes on the children if they determined they did not need them. Of those who were examined, the doctors presented slides made from photographs of four little girls' hymens. From those slides, they determined that the shape, thickness, and notches of the hymens were sufficient to conclude that the examination results were consistent with abuse.

The physicians certainly had a duty to try to find physical evidence to make a diagnosis in cases of suspected child sexual abuse. In examining at least one male child named in the indictments, Fredrickson testified that he "reviewed" the family physician's medical records prior to the exam. Those records showed the child as a "normal little boy" with a history of only minor ear infections. Fredrickson then fully examined him and found "nothing unusual." The genital and rectal exams were "all normal." Yet in court he offered a diagnosis of "consistent with abuse" that was based solely on his discussion with the parents, who expressed concern that constipation, painful bowel movements, tantrums, and bad dreams were signs of abuse. Combined with "what the [child] told his parents and the psychologist who interviewed him," Fredrickson believed he was "able to conclude penetration was possible even if all you have is the history." More than seven months after the alleged abuse was said to have occurred, and in the absence of verifiable physical evidence of trauma, Fredrickson testified he "decided there had been sexual abuse," and his diagnosis was based on interviews *alone*.[29]

In the CMEP examinations of the girls, Dr. Jean Smith entered her medical opinion that the "thinning in the hymenal area" was, in her judgment, "consistent . . . with penetration by a penis . . . and a finger."[30] She and the other doctors regularly referred to and relied upon questionable research studies by Heger about the use of colposcopy for identifying subtle abnormalities of the prepubescent hymen as evidence of penetration.

In order to determine the evidence of abuse, Smith examined two of the girls, using the "frog-legged position" for one and both the "frog-legged and knee-chest position for another" as well as "the knee-chest" for one boy.[31] Through that, she concluded abuse had likely occurred in all of them.

Both Smith and Fredrickson agreed that their physical findings were consistent with what the patient reported as sexual abuse. Fredrickson further concluded that "the [lab] cultures were pending and even if negative, they [did] not negate the patient's verbal and behavioral evidence of sexual abuse."[32] Once again, the diagnosis was based entirely on the words of little children who had been in therapy for more than two years and the parents' assessment of what they believed happened.

Fredrickson testified further: "Sexual abuse is such a broad term— but—it's consistent with small objects being put in his rectum; they're consistent with fondling; they're consistent with oral sex; they're consistent with a whole bunch of things that don't leave long-lasting damage."[33] Perhaps. But what about burning flower stems? Or scissors? Or six-inch plastic knives?

Desmond Runyan was the last of the three doctors to testify for the state. He confirmed previous testimony that all the children they saw were "referred by other physicians or social services or police . . . occasionally families who refer themselves . . . as well as prosecuting attorneys." His early testimony focused on statistics and studies about how often sexual abuse occurs, the long-term effects on adult survivors, and the difficulty of collecting data and information because of the stigma of sexual abuse. He told the court he believed the numbers were "absolutely staggering . . . and as much as 27 percent of adult American women . . . and 15 percent of adult American men" had been sexually abused. He also admitted that "how [victims] are questioned is clearly important."[34] *What effect would this have had, if any, on the juror who later admitted in the* Frontline *interview that he had been abused?*

According to Runyan, his opinion was the same as Fredrickson's: the colposcope was unnecessary because "if you can't see it with the naked eye, it probably isn't there with the colposcope either." He used it in some but not all cases, and because he believed "the knee-chest position makes many children feel vulnerable," he preferred the "separation technique because that's the one in which the standards for measurement are described . . . and the majority of information can be collected." He testified, "Everyone has been doing it for so long . . . and they know what the structures look like" and how it should be measured.[35] His testimony indicated that the colposcope was unnecessary to see the injury. Then why was it relied on so heavily by the prosecution? *Did the doctors use consistent techniques to assure the accuracy of their results and diagnoses?*

How did Runyan measure a child's hymen, which is the opening to the vagina? He testified that he used the separation technique to spread the children's legs, and then used a "tape measurer marked off in milli-meters and [held] up in front of the opening, and eyeballed . . . from side to side." The little girls were flat on their backs. He examined them from the perspective of a clock and testified that if a penis or object penetrated that area, it usually "causes damage at what is called the 6:00 area on the hymen . . . where they then look for tears" that he then said would only be visible if the exam were conducted within hours after penetration. He went on to say that "penetration from a legal standpoint can happen without ever entering into the vagina," which is technically correct because in North Carolina, penetration can occur "however slight."[36] But like a Q-tip or Polaroid photo, does a measuring tape meet what would be considered a high standard of precision? *Why didn't the three doctors use all the same protocols and techniques to conduct the examinations to ensure consistency in the program and their diagnoses?*

Nancy Lamb questioned Runyan on how to determine if there had been penetration, to which he said that the examination seeks to determine if the hymen is attenuated or ripped, if it healed against the vaginal wall, or if the hymen has been interrupted in some other way. In his opinion, "Only 50 percent of abused children have evidence of penetration," and the "hymen can heal without any physical evidence." During his testimony, he told Lamb, "You never really want to rely only on physical findings with nothing else to support it." When required to make a diagnosis, he said, "I put my best assessment on the basis of what I know and I express that either it is quite clear from the history, it's quite clear the physical exam supports that, or it's very strong, then I'll state it with definite certainty" that abuse has occurred. He also expressed frustration at doctors who "hide their conclusions in medical jargon" and said he "jokes with my staff that some doctors need to have a spinal transplant to make a decision." Because of *that*, CMEP doctors had "redesigned the form to make it easier . . . for physicians to draw some sort of conclusion to help social services."[37] *Was that conclusion and form directed toward a positive diagnosis that abuse had occurred?*

At this point, it seemed apparent that the form and process at CMEP were indeed predetermined to find abuse. On August 21, 1989, Runyan was assigned to see one of the indictment girls in the Little Rascals case, and he was assisted by Dr. Elizabeth Blair, a young female resident at the UNC medical school. Because the little girl was nervous, Runyan asked the resident to conduct the examination and said he only came in for the colposcopy. In this case, the child was interviewed first by Berson, who then shared the information from her interview with Runyan in advance of the examination. He also testified that he met with the parents and questioned them about their own history and found "nothing worrisome at all"[38] in their family history.

Runyan and Blair went on to conduct the colposcopy on the little girl. They put her in the "dorsal lithotomy position" on her back. He separated her vaginal area, placed the colposcope in position, and took pictures. He submitted the photographs from that examination as testimony. In his testimony, Runyan said that parts of her anatomy were unclear and "a little hard to see," so he directed the jury to the magnified view of her hymenal area in which he saw "several things: a crescent-shaped hymen that measured five millimeters, a notch, neither of which were clearly diagnostic," but he said it fell under the category of "suspicious." Though medical experts for the defense asserted that notch also appeared in children with no history of abuse, Runyan testified to the court that in his experience, they see it "more often than not in children who have a history of penetration."[39]

Because that particular slide was not clear, with Runyan saying there was a "glare" that obstructed the view, he explained, or rather described to the court, what they were looking at, saying "that the . . . edges were smooth and round . . . not knife-like . . . and it isn't quite as thin as one we see on a normal hymen."[40]

Lamb then asked Runyan, "In your opinion, would that be consistent with a history of penetration by either a finger or a penis?" Runyan stated under oath that he thought "the combination together made it seem likely there had been penetration, not absolutely clear, but quite likely." On a second child, he testified that "the hymenal ring is developed into five centimeters," suggestive of vaginal penetration. It must be noted that the current medical conclusion is that crescent-shaped is the most common hymen shape and five centimeters is normal. But Runyan claimed that there were "subtle" changes in the genitalia of four of the little girls that "could indicate or be consistent with" some type of penetration. Therefore, he "determined the children had been abused" and testified to that "fact,"[41] one that Smith had testified to earlier.

Lamb asked Runyan one very revealing question about the slides from the colposcopy: "Does it make something look like it was there that wasn't there?"

Runyan replied, "Yes, there can be reflections that can cause a glare."[42]

Did Nancy Lamb ask the prosecution's witness if "it looked like something was there that wasn't there?" Yes, she did.

In reviewing all these documents, the questions kept mounting. *How did the interviewers conduct the sessions with the children? How often were the children questioned? How did the interviewers ask the questions? What was their body language? What techniques did the interviewers use to elicit responses from the children? How did they use techniques such as anatomically correct dolls? Clearly, Hadler and Berson did interview the children prior to the examinations by the doctors. What impact did their reports have on the doctors as they examined the children? Did Hadler and Berson use leading questions to obtain histories that could have contributed to Smith, Fredrickson, and Runyan determining penetration had likely occurred? Did the doctors ever consider the possibility that perhaps there were no physical signs because there had been no abuse?*

THE DOLLS!

Preschools in this country . . . have become a ruse for
larger unthinkable networks of crimes against children.
—Kee MacFarlane, creator of the
anatomically correct doll

As it turns out, the interviews were a very important part of the examination process at UNC CMEP. Janet Hadler was the medical health consultant for the team and was the first person to have contact with the children and their parents. She was called to testify on behalf of the state in Robert Kelly's trial, and the first six pages of her testimony under direct examination by H. P. Williams were for the sole purpose of establishing her credentials as an expert witness. Hadler stated to the court that it was her role to "provide consultation" and to determine whether a referred child was "going to need treatment."[1] In regard to her role, Runyan had testified that these interviews were for "medical evaluation," not "mental health evaluation." (What follows in this chapter is directly quoted material from Janet Hadler's testimony in *State of North Carolina v. Robert F Kelly Jr.*, July 1991 to April 1992, Volume 40, pages 9,534–9,737.)

While on the witness stand, Hadler was asked to testify about a specific Little Rascals child she saw on July 21, 1989, which would have been more than seven months after the alleged abuse. When Williams asked her if she usually videotaped the interviews, she admitted she did not videotape many of the interviews with the children because the equipment was often not available. It may have been already locked up for the day or was being used by someone else. But in this case, she did videotape the interview. Williams asked about protocol she used for the interview, and she explained what she did in general with the children when she saw them. As she described the videotaped interview with this specific child, her descriptions fell back into vague generalities, telling the state that "sometimes I will," and "I try to" and "most of the time," but never what she specifically did with that one child.[2]

During his direct examination, Williams asked her about how she used the dolls. Hadler testified, "I use the dolls as—to give the child an opportunity to demonstrate or show us something that they are describing verbally." This was likely not the first time the children had seen them. In fact, Toppin testified to using them. The therapists also confirmed they used them. But Williams asked, "Based on your training and experience—the studies that you've done—or have you examined studies on whether or not they're improperly suggestive?"[3] Hadler said she believed the dolls were appropriate in these cases. Williams did not ask her if the child had previously been exposed to those dolls, by whom, how often, or in what way. *Is it possible the state already knew the answer to these questions?*

Hadler referred to "a study done by Dr. M. D. Everson and B. W. Boat, with the UNC program," on the uses of anatomically correct dolls and "seven other [unnamed] studies" of a total of 322 children, abused and non-abused. She testified that five children in the Everson/Boat study, who were "thought to be non-abused . . . demonstrated sexual intercourse with the dolls," but she then went on to add her opinion that "children who demonstrate explicit sexual contact are doing that demonstration because they have some actual knowledge of adult sexual behavior."[4]

In cross-examination, Mike Spivey challenged her on the studies she referenced regarding "children's knowledge about sex." Hadler told the court that her "interpretation of the studies" was different from what Spivey's question suggested. Spivey suggested that the study found that children "had so much greater sexual knowledge at that age than they had previously thought."[5] But what other experts had Hadler relied upon for her opinion? She referenced Kee MacFarlane from the McMartin Preschool case—the creator of the anatomically correct dolls.

Later, as Spivey questioned her further about the use of the dolls, Hadler admitted that "it is not uncommon for children to place the dolls in the missionary position," which she called the "suggestive intercourse position." Challenging her in cross-examination, Spivey went on to ask if she recalled that "37 percent of the children, ages three to five years old," from the Everson and Boat study, placed the dolls in "that position?" Did she recall that "they were thought to be normal . . . non-abused children?" Spivey asked if "one of the more common behaviors they found was that 50 percent of the children were interested in examining the genitalia . . . and about 50 percent put the penis in the mouth" of the other doll? Did she recall that they also "frequently inserted their fingers in the vaginal and anal openings? All this behavior was witnessed during a play period prior to any interview between an examiner and the children."[6]

Spivey cited statistics from a number of studies, including one that determined 40 percent of three-year-olds had more sexually focused behavior after exposure to the dolls than they'd had before.

Hadler responded, "That may be true. I don't recall that."

Spivey asked if the study showed "70 percent of four-year-olds had more sexually focused behavior after exposure to the dolls?"

"I have read that study . . . I don't remember the details."

"You used the dolls [with the child] in the interview—on the videotape. Were these introduced to her for the first time in the room—in the videotape we saw?"

Hadler replied, "I don't recall."

"You said you asked her in the interview if she had been exposed to the dolls before and she told you no."

"I may have asked her—I don't recall."

Spivey then handed her the transcript. She responded, "No." She had not asked the child if she had been exposed to the dolls previously. "It's often a question I ask, but I don't always ask." More statements of "I don't recall" and "I don't remember" followed.

Spivey then asked, "Now, you do recognize that these dolls cannot be used as a diagnostic test for sexual abuse, don't you?"

She said, "I use the dolls, as—to give the child an opportunity to demonstrate or show me something that they are describing verbally."

"Well, my question was do you recognize that these dolls cannot be used as a diagnostic tool for sexual abuse?"

"Yes, I would agree with that."

"And would you agree that one has to be very cautious in using the dolls with preschool children?"

"Ah—cautious as regards to, to what specifically?"

"Cautious with regards to the manner in which they are used?"

After a several-minute exchange about the studies, Spivey asked Hadler again if she was familiar with a "follow-up study" that the children's "sexually focused behaviors increased after exposure to the dolls." She said she was aware but "didn't recall the details."

He then asked her if she knew how many times the child being discussed had been interviewed by Judith Abbott.

"I don't know," Hadler said.

"By her parents?"

"I don't know."

"By Ms. Toppin?"

"I don't know."

"By the SBI?"

"I don't know."

Did she know how many times "the sexually explicit dolls had been used?"

"I don't know."

Like the others, Hadler had no handwritten notes and could not remember.

Though Hadler had testified initially on direct examination by Williams that the CMEP "have a general protocol" they follow when a child comes to them, during Spivey's cross-examination, he asked her specifically if she followed any published protocol or guidelines for the use of the dolls.

She replied, "Well, there are published guidelines."

Spivey pressed, "Do you use them?"

"I think my interview style is, ah—is very consistent with some of the interview guidelines."

Spivey then asked, "Which ones do you think your style is consistent with?"

She responded, "Boat and Everson have written guidelines about interviewing using anatomical dolls. Um, I think there probably are some things they have written in their guidelines—uh, which I—I do. There are probably some differences—some variations."

Spivey then asked her about the importance of following guidelines in the first interview, about taking care not to suggest or lead a child.

She responded, "It can be an issue."

"What about—after the tenth, fifteenth, or twentieth?"

She testified that it depended on how close the child was to revealing the abuse in the fifteenth instance.

"In the case of [this child] do you know how many interviews were done?"

"At this point I don't remember that information."[7]

Hadler had seen this particular child one time, and according to her testimony, she said the interview was specifically to "assist the pediatrician in making a diagnosis of whether or not sexual abuse had occurred." She went on to offer more opinion about how children reveal abuse, about "possible behaviors" in abused children, about "indicators" in young children, about possible "imagining and fantasizing," which meant, therefore, they are "not going to be talking about explicit adult sex unless they have gained some knowledge about that."[8]

But clearly, they do. And were the interviews truly for "medical evaluation," and not "mental health evaluation?" Was "imagining and fantasizing" about "adult sex acts" appropriate for a "medical evaluation?"

Williams, in his re-direct examination of Hadler, asked, "Did you observe any of those behaviors, or were you told of any of those behaviors?" She did not hesitate. She said the parents told her about stories of "pictures being taken, adults dressing in costume, being taken out on a boat, Mr. Bob peeing in her mouth, digital and penile penetration, knives, ropes, and threats . . . and the house catching on fire."[9] Yet, as in all the cases, there was no physical evidence of any of the accusations the parents made and no eyewitnesses to any of the charges. But those recurring themes and those recurring questions remained. *Did Hadler, Berson, Abbott, Robertson, Childers, Zimmerman, or Toppin present questions in any way that led to allegations of abuse in any or all of these cases?*

During another re-cross examination, Spivey returned to the specific interview with that particular child in the videotape. Did Hadler take any notes during the interview except for the chart that she completed weeks after the interview?

"No, I did not."

"So there were no handwritten notes ever taken; the sole record of her interview with you would be the videotape and the chart notes prepared from that."

"That's correct . . . the only existing record is the medical chart."

"No other records were created"—that is, until the week before the trial when Hadler went back, at the request of the state, *to create* a "transcript of the videotape." Spivey asked if Hadler had any "occasion to obtain information from any other source in connection with her evaluation . . . social services or law enforcement?"

Hadler said, "I may have had a conversation some months later with Brenda Toppins [sic]." The fact is that she mailed her chart notes to the district attorney in October and previously admitted to having a conversation with the doctor before the physical examination.

Spivey questioned if stress can be imposed on the children by their parents or interviewers.

Hadler testified, "That certainly could contribute to—that child's stress."

Spivey asked if it could lead to a child being "fearful or frightened."

"It could certainly add to a child's feeling of anxiety," Hadler answered.

Spivey asked if this meant anxious parents, or pressure by parents?

Hadler said, "Yes."

Then Spivey asked her if children are "susceptible to suggestions through the interview process?"

Hadler replied, "To—to some extent."

He then asked if it was possible a child "will want to please or accommodate the person conducting the interview in terms of the responses they give?"

Hadler said, "It's certainly possible."[10]

It turns out Nancy Berson, Hadler's colleague, also interviewed this child, but she did not testify. Instead, Runyan testified on her behalf, stating that Berson told him the child showed what he called "alarming behavior . . . with the dolls." According to Runyan's testimony, Berson handed a male doll to the child and "identified it to her as Mr. Bob. That child then began to jab Mr. Bob in the eyes, hit him in the head, throw him down, and said, 'You're going to the police station. You're dead.'" Runyan then explained that using the doll, Berson asked the child to show her "what Mr. Bob had done to her." She had the "female doll put her mouth on the male doll's penis."[11]

Was it possible this child was parroting the behavior she had seen her mother exhibit? Evidence from the therapists' notes raised significant questions about why this child may have behaved as she did. Judy Abbott made a note on June 14, 1990, that the mother showed that child a picture of "the Kellys on TV, in handcuffs, and the mother punched the TV." Abbott noted that the child then also "punched the TV."[12] *Were these ideas planted in the child's head?*

Runyan further testified that the little girl told Berson that someone applied "lotion to her buttock." He told the court that Berson said she pushed the child to "clarify what happened and whether that was actually before" someone inserted something into her bottom. He then testified that Berson said "[the child] indicated it was before something was inserted in her hiney."

Williams asked, "Who inserted something in [her] hiney?"

"OBJECTION," the defense said.

Judge McLelland replied, "OVERRULED."[13]

Runyan then testified that Berson told him the child "identified Mr. Bob as having done that."[14] We do not know what the grounds were for McLelland to allow Runyan to testify on Berson's behalf; however, it raises questions about hearsay testimony. Where was Berson? Why didn't she appear in court to be cross-examined?

I found troubling evidence in that child's records stored in the Duke archives. Dozens of entries from May 1989 through January 1990 implied that Abbott and the child's mother may have guided her into making admissions about the Edenton Seven. The journal notes showed that just after the therapy sessions had begun, Abbott suddenly inserted suggestions to the child about Robin's husband, who had never been mentioned. She asked the child what she thought "about Kevin? [Robin's husband]." Abbott also quizzed her if she'd seen Robin and Kevin doing "things together that aren't nice." The child's response was a simple, "No." Abbott even asked if she went out on a boat with someone named "Mr. John," likely one of the many Edenton people named but never charged.[15]

It suddenly seemed more than obvious where the suggestions began that the child had been sexually abused by Kelly and eventually by Robin. By September, months later, the child asked Abbott in a therapy session when "Miss Robin and the others would be arrested." By October, she had accused Robin of "putting scissors in my privates."[16] By January, the following exchange occurred in a therapy session, according to Abbot's notes:

"Guess what, my mama said Miss Robin is in jail."

"She's in jail. Should Miss Robin be in jail? Why should she be in jail?"

"Because she be bad to everybody . . . she pinched, pulled hair, put everybody on the ground and made them bleed."

"How did she make them bleed? Did she make you bleed?"

"Yeah. She put me down on the ground and shot a gun on me."[17]

Did any of this happen, or did Abbott suggest to the child that this happened?

The exchanges between Abbott and the child continued over many months. The sessions were not videotaped or recorded. Instead, Abbott's interview notes were summarized in Abbott's own words, and neither she nor any of the therapists ever testified. Without exception, similar accusations like those about Kevin appeared in other children's interviews. Susan Childers, one of the four therapists, wrote of one child that "she said Robin and Kevin abused the children . . . by penetrating their 'hiney' with a stick."[18] At this point, Kevin was named by several children, but he was never indicted. Childers also never testified.

"The State has no more questions."

Chapter 26

The State Rests

The way to combat falsehoods, is with the truth.
—William O. Douglas

It was time for the defense to put on their case. (What follows in this chapter is directly quoted material from expert witness testimonies for the defense in *State of North Carolina v. Robert F Kelly Jr.*, July 1991 to April 1992, Volume 40, pages 9,534–9,737).

Defense Attorney Jeff Miller and Mike Spivey, his co-counsel, called Dr. Thomas Grant Irons, a professor of pediatrics at East Carolina University's medical school. He was an expert for the child abuse program, a leading expert in child abuse prevention, and creator of the Child Abuse Program for the United States Army. The defense asked Irons to review all the photographs and evaluations submitted by the CMEP doctors, and he agreed to do that. After reviewing it, Irons challenged all their conclusions about evidence using the colposcopy photograph and the shape or thinning of the hymen. He also challenged Fredrickson's testimony and testified in direct contrast to the CMEP doctors, stating that the examinations he performed on children suspected of abuse "are exhausting and sometimes take hours to complete,"[1] rather than the minutes Fredrickson and Smith testified to.

Irons testified that, in his expert opinion and based on widely accepted studies and protocols, he concurred that the "colposcope and its magnification is not significant in finding abnormalities" any better than the naked eye, but his agreement with the CMEP doctors ended there. In doing these forensic exams, Irons testified that the "guidelines recommended by the Academy of Pediatrics Committee on Child Abuse and Neglect"[2] do not even recommend the colposcope in the examination to determine if there was an injury to the hymen. He reviewed reports by Dr. Lane from the Elizabeth City Children's Clinic and agreed that Lane's examinations "indicated the children had normal exams with no sign of abuse." Beyond the use of the colposcope, Irons disagreed with every finding by the CMEP physicians who each testified to the presence of scars, adhesions, or synechiae as being *consistent with abuse*. Irons said, "They simply were not present."[3]

Dr. Robert Brayden testified after Irons. He was on the faculty at Vanderbilt University, board certified in both pediatrics and behavioral psychology, and had extensive training in "clinical matters concerning children who were presented with suspicions of sexual abuse." He trained under researchers who were international leaders in child abuse and neglect and had achieved that level of recognition on his own. Notably, he had extensive experience and published research into the use of colposcopy in child sexual assault cases. He testified, "In my opinion, there is no significant difference in finding evidence of injury in children when using the colposcope or when using the naked eye."[4]

Brayden was also asked to review the evaluations from Runyan, Smith, Fredrickson, the local doctors, the parents' journals, medical records, and the videotaped testimony from Smith. He also reviewed the photographs of the "hymenal anatomy of the children involved,"[5] and the testimonies of Runyan, Smith, and Fredrickson based on their examinations and medical reports.

Brayden gave his opinion to the court that all three exam positions were necessary and in fact recommended by research experts to observe the anatomy and to determine if there has been penetration. The hymen changes shape and appearance based on the child's position during the examination. The knee-chest position is essential when there is suspicion of sexual abuse. In the other supine and frog-leg methods, it is common to see "concerning conditions in normal, non-abused children."[6] Therefore, completing the exam with the third position, the knee-chest, is necessary for a full picture of the vaginal or anal tissues.

The measurement of the hymenal opening must be done with precision and accuracy, he said. When asked about using the Q-tip to measure the hymenal opening, Brayden was "very concerned" about that technique, stating, in his opinion, that it was "neither precise nor accurate to the level necessary for an argumentative judgment."[7] He disagreed with Runyan and Smith's opinions on diagnosing injury based on that technique. In fact, he disagreed with every medical finding from Runyan, Smith, and Fredrickson—from measurements to labial adhesions, which he said are very common in young female children and can result from infection, scratching, or even minor trauma. The medical records of the child with adhesions showed a history of lesions from vaginal infections from infancy. Her mother used creams to treat that condition for at least three years prior to the allegations of abuse.

In another child, the synechia was likely misdiagnosed as a tear when it was a normal "intravaginal ridge" or structure and not synechia at all.[8] The enlarged blood vessels found in the one child? Normal in 30 percent or more of prepubescent children, Brayden said. Thinning and thickening of the hymen? The hymen changes with the presence or absence of estrogen, Brayden said. Anal dilation in knee-chest position? Normal, according to Brayden.

To illustrate his opinions, Brayden brought slides of normal, non-abused pre-pubescent girls from his research to compare with the slides from the CMEP examinations. His testimony was to measure the accuracy of the CMEP doctors' measurements in millimeters and compare the hymenal anatomy between the research slides and those from CMEP. He presented several slides, and the photographs were of the same child in the three different examination positions. In his opinion, they "accurately depicted the hymenal anatomy."[9] He also presented slides of a child the same age who had sustained a penetration injury by an adult male, and that showed clear tearing and clefting of the hymen. Further, he presented slides of a male child, non-abused and normal, and an abused child with signs of penetration, taking time to walk the jury carefully and thoroughly through a discussion on each of the slides.

Later in Brayden's testimony, he compared his findings with the slides of the four Little Rascals girls examined and photographed by CMEP doctors. Contrary to Smith's testimony, Brayden determined from the slides that all the girls were examined using only *one position*. He testified that "in my opinion [the slides] were not consistent with penetration by a penis [nor] did they suggest any abnormality, or indication of digital penetration." Referring to one child examined by Smith, Brayden didn't understand "how she came to the conclusion *or* statement" that she couldn't see the hymen because of scarring, which he noted did not exist the way she described it. He saw "no evidence of injury;" "no evidence of adhesions" consistent with penetration; "no evidence of asymmetry that caused concern;" no evidence of "abnormal measurements" or "abnormal vascularity;" "no synechia;" and "nothing that caused him to believe there had been hymenal trauma or injury."[10]

Brayden then placed the slide of one of the abused girls on top of the slide of a non-abused child from his research. They were nearly identical in appearance, ridges, asymmetry, and measurements. Next, the defense team put up another slide marked with the name of a child named in the indictment—a slide the state for some reason did not present as evidence. Using a different slide from that child's case, Smith had testified there were tears to the hymen consistent with penetration. As Brayden explained to the court, in his opinion, there was no presence of the tears or synechiae that Smith testified to. Furthermore, he also saw no evidence of the adhesion she testified to. As he compared the two slides, he testified that the only difference was the shape. He did testify, however, that there was a clear presence of a "finger" in the slide that was pulling or "putting tension on the area," causing the blood vessels to bulge from the pressure asserted by the finger.[11] According to Smith, her examination record stated the child had an 8 mm hymenal opening, yet no one was ever charged with penetration of this particular child.

In the fourth little girl, Smith testified she did the knee-chest examination, but Brayden said her photographs showed no evidence that Smith performed that type of examination. There was no evidence of synechiae, lacerations, turning inward of hymenal tissue, or any of the observations Smith testified to as present in the examination. "Nothing in those photographs clearly showed" abnormality or trauma by "penetration," but rather they were consistent with a normal, non-abused hymen, Brayden said.[12]

Jeff Miller asked Brayden about his review of the CMEP medical records. Was there any evidence the CMEP doctors used the knee-chest as recommended when there is suspicion of abuse? He testified, "No." In terms of the slides he looked at, he said, "All of the slides were in the supine position. There [were] no knee-chest slides presented,"[13] except for one boy who was examined *only* in the knee-chest position.

In explaining his concerns about how the CMEP doctors conducted examinations, Brayden used a videotape of an examination of a non-abused child the same age as those in the Little Rascals case. In the video, he used each of the three positions. As he walked the court through the examination, they could observe the changes in the angle and effect of gravity as the doctor moved the child from supine to frog-legged to knee-chest. Brayden described in detail what the hymen looked like in each position and how it changed depending on the child's position. There appeared to be a suspicious area on the hymen in the first supine position. By the next position, the frog-legged, it changed shape considerably, and by the third, the knee-chest position, the hymen changed dramatically. It was clear what they observed depended on the position they placed the child in, and that light and gravity impacted what they saw. Based on Brayden's testimony, there was no verifiable physical evidence of the alleged sexual abuse on any of the children from Little Rascals Day Care in 1988.

Miller began his questioning. "Now, Doctor, based on your review of the record in this case, including your review of the medical slides from Chapel Hill, do you have an opinion satisfactory to yourself and to a reasonable degree of medical certainty as to whether or not the hymens for [the four girls] show evidence or physical indications of having been penetrated?"[14]

"Yes, I've formed an opinion."

Miller asked, "What is that opinion?"

"That opinion is that I see no evidence on review of the colposcopic photographs, of the review of these testimonies and medical records presented, both from CMEP program and other medical doctors, I see no evidence that suggests to me that these children have sustained hymenal injuries."

"Doctor, in your opinion would the fact that these children have normal appearing hymens make it less likely that they sustained digital penetration of the hymen?"

Brayden responded, "I believe it does, yes."

"Doctor, in your opinion would the fact that these children have normal appearing hymens make it less likely that they have been penetrated by a finger repeatedly and by different people at different times on different occasions?"

"Yes, I believe it does."

"Doctor—are there any groups of behaviors or behavioral indicators that are of diagnostic significance in a medical examination for the purposes of assessing or determining child sexual abuse?"

"In my opinion there is no cluster of behaviors that are diagnostic for child sexual abuse."

"Doctor, in your opinion, is child sexual abuse a medical diagnosis?"

"In my opinion, child sexual abuse is not a medical diagnosis."

Brayden went on to say, "It should be considered a legal determination based on the evidence—collected by an examiner—carefully documented, if not by audiotape, by videotape—documenting evidence of injury."[15]

That never happened.

The defense called Dr. Leibert Devine of Edenton, a family practitioner and the medical examiner for Chowan County. He was the doctor for four of the "indictment children," and he had been treating each of them from their births (in approximately 1984) until May 1989. Other than treating the children for routine medical issues, such as coughs, fevers, ear infections, and the like, he testified he "never observed anything that indicated sexual abuse."[16] The children had "no complaints of any type" other than routine problems with bed-wetting, toothaches, fussiness, and bowel movements that one mother thought were "too large."[17] He had regular occasions to fully examine both the boys and girls during routine exams, including inspections of their genitalia. He knew those children very well and had examined them from head to toe.

Miller also called Dr. Robert E. Lane of Hertford, another family medical practitioner, who had treated one of the little girls named in the indictment. He treated her from 1985 to late 1988 for "continued vaginal adhesions" from a yeast infection that he treated with "Premarin estrogen cream," and for abdominal pain due to something unrelated. Because of the chronic labial adhesions, he had to regularly examine her vaginal area. His last examination of her was on April 27, 1989. On that date, he conducted a full vaginal examination. He testified that "had there been any evidence of penetration, the hymen would have been disrupted."[18] There was no sign of abuse.

In their testimonies, Smith and Fredrickson both made definitive diagnoses of abuse on two boys based on the history and story provided to them by the parents and child. In the case of another child, Fredrickson made a definitive diagnosis of abuse without any physical evidence or a statement by the child. His diagnosis for that child was based solely on the history the parents provided. In yet another child, Runyan made a definitive diagnosis that the physical evidence (a 5 mm hymenal opening, a notch that could not be seen because of glare, and a thinner than normal hymen) was consistent with digital and vaginal penetration.

The prosecution asked Runyan if he had seen Smith's reports on six of the children and if he agreed with her diagnoses. He testified that he did agree with all six of her examination results.

The CMEP doctors stated categorically that the word *"'undetermined'* [was] the medical standard for the country" in sexual abuse cases in 1989 and 1990. They testified that they did adhere to standards and protocols for the examinations according to national standards of the time for identifying child sexual abuse trauma. However, Brayden said he also absolutely adhered to nationally accepted protocol standards for examining prepubescent children suspected to have been sexually abused, and his medical opinions were diametrically opposed to those of the CMEP team.

The testimonies revealed that the role of the CMEP doctors and interviewers contributed significantly to the conviction of Robert Kelly. These doctors and professionals testified that what they saw in examinations was consistent with abuse. They testified that there were injuries present, yet it was possible that something looked like it was there that wasn't there. Yet all their findings were rejected by leading experts in child abuse. They testified to evidence of abuse that has since been refuted: 5 mm hymenal openings and crescent-shaped thinning hymens. They testified that even in the absence of physical evidence of abuse, histories and behaviors were proof that abuse occurred. They testified that the interviews were for medical and not mental health evaluations, yet protocols for techniques, such as questioning, and the use of anatomically correct dolls seemed to lean toward mental health evaluations. And did they follow protocols for use of the dolls?

The interviewers testified that they did not videotape, record, keep notes of, or recall critical evidence from interview sessions. They testified to relying on Heger and Woodling, whose recommended use of colposcopy has since been criticized and rejected by experts on protocols. They testified that histories provided by parents could weigh as much as 100 percent in determining if abuse had occurred without verifiable physical evidence to support those diagnoses. They testified to concurring with each other about their diagnoses of abuse, yet the three doctors did not use consistent techniques between them in conducting the physical examinations of the children.

Since this trial, the North Carolina Supreme Court, in *State v. Clark*, reaffirmed that the use of testimony that abuse has "in fact occurred" is impermissible expert opinion absent physical evidence supporting a diagnosis of sexual abuse.

Considering all of this, one must ask if the state created its own reality. Did they seek evidence that proved their decision? Did the CMEP doctors become pawns in the pursuit of conviction at all costs? And what would the impact have been had Robin's case gone to trial? She and the others would have faced the same accusers and accusations, the same lack of verifiable physical evidence, the same lack of eyewitness testimony, the same medical expert testimonies, the same prosecutors, and the same judge. Would she have experienced the same injustice? Bob Kelly was found guilty and sentenced to twelve consecutive life sentences based on no verifiable physical evidence and without any eyewitnesses. Dawn Wilson received a life sentence based on no verifiable physical evidence and without any eyewitness. Not one of the seven defendants ever confessed.

Due to errors in both Bob Kelly and Dawn Wilson's cases, the North Carolina Court of Appeals overturned their convictions and ordered new trials in 1996. The cases were later dismissed by then-District Attorney Frank Parrish, who had unseated H. P. Williams in a primary election in May 1994.

A Necessary Conversation

First, do no harm.
—Hippocrates

Nearly ten years after the first charges were brought against the Edenton Seven, Desmond Runyan, director of the CMEP program at UNC–Chapel Hill, wrote an article on the epidemiology of child abuse. In it, he expressed his belief that there exists a "clash of cultures between the medical and legal professions." He continued, "Medical diagnostic processes favor the initial inclusion of 'patients' with any possibility of [abuse]." Further, Runyan said, "There is no specific test for sexual abuse that can convincingly conclude that sexual abuse has not occurred. Children won't always tell, and a normal medical examination doesn't rule out the possibility of sexual abuse. And it is rare that medical examiners can be 'specific' and say 'no' abuse has occurred."[1]

Runyan also wrote that he believed "the medical exam" can actually "dwarf the original abuse" . . . and he wondered "how important is a medical examination to the prognosis for the child? Are there children for whom a medical examination should be contraindicated?"[2]

Therein lies a serious conundrum. Considering Runyan's statement, there is a clear conflict between what he believes about medical professionals attempting with "sensitivity" to diagnose abuse, and what the courts of law require to have "specificity." But the North Carolina Supreme Court reaffirmed that the use of testimony that abuse has "in fact occurred" is impermissible expert opinion absent physical evidence supporting a diagnosis of sexual abuse. This ruling makes convictions without physical evidence especially troubling, particularly when the defendant could go to prison, perhaps for the rest of their natural life.

Because Dr. Runyan was the director of CMEP, and because he took the stand as an expert witness for the prosecution, I reached out to him in 2023 to see if he would be willing to talk to me. Fortunately, he agreed. I then emailed several questions for him to consider before we talked:

Were there clearly defined legal, ethical, and moral guidelines then for questioning children in sexual abuse cases?

Was he able to see the transcripts from the interviews with the indictment children?

Was he able to see the transcripts from the interviews of the children who insisted nothing happened?

Did he see the interviews the state withheld from the defense team?

Were the questions used by the therapists within guidelines now accepted by his profession?

Was he concerned about the many months that lapsed between the alleged abuse and when he and his team examined the children?

Was he concerned about the apparent lack of verifiable physical evidence, or the bizarre and fantastical claims made by the children?

I wondered—would his diagnosis still be the same were he to testify in these cases today?

What was Runyan's response to those questions? He recalled that during the exams he talked with the kids, "just normal open-ended talk . . . asking them 'what happened' and trying to put them at ease."[3] He remembered some of the parents were present in the examinations. Runyan conceded that "the knowledge about evidence of abuse was relatively early" in 1990. But even now, 90 percent of all exams for sexual abuse are diagnosed based solely on history, making a diagnosis without physical evidence a daily experience in medicine."[4]

He compared it to diagnosing something like ulcers. We don't "open the abdomen of people" with those symptoms, he said. He also offered this medical insight: "People are malleable. They heal. Tissues can stretch under lots of different circumstances . . . lubricated condoms . . . they don't cause as much damage. The standard at the time was the presence of a 5mm or larger opening of the hymen . . . but [today] that is not gospel. . . . We were more taken in by the evidence then . . . and it's not as definitive now. We would not be as dogmatic now. The science has changed. However, we see children in our clinic all the time. We have a scale that is not definitive, but rather a 'concerning exam' scale using 5 points. The bottom score is no evidence, [to] concerning, and up to consistent with history. Most child abuse physical exams are normal. Conventional pediatric wisdom is that it was more likely than not that abuse had occurred."[5]

Is this an example of what Lee Coleman called the *tour de force* term: "consistent with"? The exams were concerning but not definitive. What about now? Runyan reiterated that the science has changed since the case. Still, the lack of verifiable physical evidence continues to haunt the Little Rascals case. Too many experts disagree with Runyan's assumptions and, instead, say that the "irregularities" he and his team identified as evidence of penetration were normal and that there was no "absolute" in how a hymen in a prepubescent girl should appear. Would his diagnosis still be the same were he to testify in these cases today? Based on 5 mm? Based on crescent-shaped hymens? He didn't answer that. And would the science of 1990 that led the CMEP doctors to use a Q-tip, a Polaroid photo, or a measuring tape convict someone today of first-degree sexual assault or rape?

In a follow-up email exchange, Runyan suggested, "We know that 97 percent of abused kids have normal exams."[6]

I found that statistic startling. Ninety-seven percent? If there is no verifiable evidence of physical penetration, how can such a sweeping assumption about confirmed abuse be made, and is that admissible in court?

To verify Runyan's assertion that 97 percent have normal exams, I located research from February 2019 by Stephanie Block, a psychologist, and Linda Williams, PhD. They wrote about the prosecution of child sexual abuse in a study funded by the National Institute of Justice. In it, they, too, suggested that "medical evidence is available in less than 5 percent of reported cases," and prosecution often relies on "testimonies of the child." Their report certainly corroborated Runyan's statement about the 97 percent; however, it must be noted that Runyan and Astrid Heger, from the McMartin Preschool case, were among the many sources Block and Williams used in their study. Their study was limited to only "case records" that contained "information deemed relevant by the prosecutors and other investigators," and was "limited to one period of time" in one region of the country.[7] Given that, was the study broad enough, and was it reliable enough to justify conviction without physical evidence?

In our conversation, Runyan suggested that the current system would only use "skilled interviewers . . . and in the case of so many victims, no single interviewer would have interviewed a large number of children."[8] But only Hadler and Berson from CMEP did the interviews of nearly fifty children. Was he acknowledging the system in 1990 was flawed? And after Hadler and Berson conducted those interviews, they shared them with the doctors, often before the physical exams. Would this have influenced the examination results? Runyan also said that "interviewers would be expected to conduct their interviews in a manner considered appropriate . . . with no leading questions . . . as part of the process."[9] But that left the question of what is appropriate. Was it appropriate to fail to video or audio tape the interviews? What were the ethical, moral, and legal guidelines for those interviews? Were their questions within the guidelines now accepted by his profession?

There was another inconsistency in Runyan's reflection. He said, "We would have been more insistent on repeating the interviews ourselves. In retrospect, it would have been good to hear from the children. We didn't know how the histories were obtained. For us to interview them again might not have been particularly harmful, but the kids had already been put through the wringer. We just didn't want to do them any more harm."[10] But did they know how many times the children had been interviewed? Did they know how many times they had been exposed to techniques like the anatomically correct dolls? Did they know how the histories were obtained? Regardless, the doctors' testimonies under oath revealed that they interviewed many of the children prior to the exams, took histories from the parents, and saw prior medical records. At a minimum, they knew ahead of time that the children had been in therapy for months.

His next recollection was staggering. Runyan added, "No child mentioned abuse by any of the women. Not once." During the interview, he made that same observation about the accusations against the women two different times, and he then went on to say he "still finds it problematic."[11] Did he testify to that? Did the state know that? If so, why didn't they immediately dismiss all the charges against the five women? The prosecution had Runyan, Smith, and Fredrickson's reports and testimonies. Was it because the state had parents' stories and therapists' reports that created a preferred version of the truth?

In what seemed to me to be an afterthought, Runyan said he still believes maybe "there were a few children who were sexually abused, but the fuss, poor interviewing, and hysteria that resulted in [the Little Rascals] kids being brought in for exams completely obscured what . . . happened. Ultimately, it made it impossible to sort it out."[12]

I asked again: Would the Edenton Seven be convicted in today's court of law? Based on that observation and the fact that only a handful of people investigated, interviewed, interrogated, or examined all the Little Rascals children, is it fair to say that the Edenton Seven would likely not be convicted under today's moral, ethical, and legal standards? What about the children who did not go to UNC to be examined by Runyan and his team? Where were the notes and findings from their examinations? Runyan might not know that, but the state did. Were the answers buried in the unsealed boxes that Jeff Miller and Mark Montgomery discovered?

In what appeared to be an effort to defend the prosecution, Runyan recalled running into "the social worker a bunch of years later who still believed it happened." He told him, "They had substantiated evidence against Kelly of abuse long before the Little Rascals case broke."[13] This was an interesting point for him to raise. I interviewed a few residents of Edenton who asked to remain anonymous for obvious reasons, and they also said many people still believe the abuse happened. The tension over this case is still thick. The "substantiated" accusation Runyan mentioned was the one Lamb charged Kelly with as soon as his case was overturned on appeal. The very day Kelly was released from jail, Lamb had him re-arrested (that case was dismissed almost immediately after he was charged). Was that more vindictive prosecution?

Runyan recalled meeting Nancy Lamb several times and believed her to be "reasonable," and it seemed to him "that she truly wanted to protect the children."[14] Perhaps. But that was more opinion. Based on the facts, did Lamb want to "protect the children"? If she had, would she have participated in and endorsed the months of devastating interrogations? Was the prosecution team ever rational about the accusations? Did they want the truth? Did they want to see justice served? Did Judge McLelland want to ensure justice was served? Or were they concerned only with conviction—at all costs?

Given that the legal standard for opinion testimony from experts in child abuse cases is clear about what is and is not permissible, I told Runyan that my legal resources said the law does not allow experts to assert opinions without verifiable physical evidence.

"That's not true," he said. "I give my opinion all the time in these cases." Later, he added, "They subpoena [us] and we give out medical diagnoses. Deciding that medical evaluations should ignore histories unless there are physical findings would make child abuse unique to all medical evidence submitted to courts."[15]

Runyan said he believed there are "true consequences for abuse" and has written extensively on the risk for adverse outcomes. He believes "longitudinal studies" are imperative and could help "protect children from further victimization from sexual abuse."[16]

I had to agree with his observation. Perhaps a longitudinal study of the Little Rascals children would have been appropriate to see how they had fared over thirty-five years. Moreover, what about the victimization of the children by a system that supported and endorsed what was highly likely all false? What about the therapists and prosecutors who went on to benefit professionally and financially from their roles in the prosecution of the Edenton Seven? What about victimization by the court system? If abuse *cannot* be ruled out by the tools they used, did experts go too far in their claims?

Chapter 28

Attorneys for the Defense

In all criminal prosecutions, the accused shall . . . have the
assistance of counsel for his defense.
—Sixth Amendment, the United States Constitution

In the process of writing this book, I encountered many people who were unfamiliar with the Little Rascals case, some because they were too young, some who were not from North Carolina, or some who just weren't paying attention. However, a significant number of people were familiar with the case, and they believed that the seven defendants were victims of a great miscarriage of justice. This made me realize that if I wanted people to understand how this had happened, it was critical to explore not only the medical experts' opinions but also the legal opinions of those close to the case—the defense attorneys. It was not difficult to persuade the attorneys to agree to talk with me.

Joe Cheshire is a nationally known criminal defense attorney, with a colorful reputation for some high-profile cases he has defended over the years. When I reached out to him, I was surprised to hear that he is taking his "shingle down" after fifty years of practicing law. I always thought lawyers never retired.

One of his most haunting cases was defending Betsy Kelly in the Little Rascals Day Care case. Like all the attorneys I talked with, he never doubted Betsy Kelly's innocence, and he believes to this day that her prosecution was a profound tragedy.

"I'm the fifth-generation lawyer in the Cheshire family," he said, and "this case is the one that haunts me the most. It was a massive injustice." He went on to say, "My family was originally from Edenton, but I was never able to go back there after that trial." He remembered going to his family's vacation cottage in Nags Head and running into people from Edenton whom he had known all his life. "They were awful to me. We just stopped going." Cheshire had strong feelings about the prosecution team and said, "The people that pushed that case and especially the people that brought it to trial should be ashamed at best and should have gone to jail at worst."[1]

Bo Simmons, Dawn Wilson's defense attorney, still practices in Edgecombe County. He admitted the case was devastating to his legal practice because it took such a long time to go to trial. But he has never regretted defending Dawn. He told me he continues to be troubled over the fact that there was "no evidence. It was all a fairy tale. Dawn Wilson, like Robin and the others, refused plea deal after plea deal right up to her trial. None of them were willing to plead guilty to something they didn't do." Simmons thought it was particularly ironic that the jury seemed to "really like Wilson and even sent her a slice of birthday cake during the trial."[2]

All I could think was, *Who does that and then sends that person to prison . . . for child abuse . . . for life?*

In an effort to fully grasp how dangerous this entire case was, I knew I needed to talk with both Mike Spivey and Jeff Miller, and I began with Spivey. I first met him in 1979 when he was hired as a young prosecutor. In January 2023 when we talked, I knew I was chatting with an old friend. He stays busy with appellate work, which is very demanding, so I promised not to consume his time, a promise I could not keep. I remember my husband saying about Spivey, "He is a brilliant attorney with a photographic memory," something every defense lawyer wishes they had. Now nearing seventy, Spivey is more seasoned and slowing down professionally, but he has never stopped thinking about the injustice of the Little Rascals case and was actually relieved to finally talk about it.

I wasted no time and began with the simple question: "How did you get involved in the case?" He said he was court appointed by Frank Brown, the Superior Court judge in Tarboro, North Carolina, right after Kelly's first attorney, Chris Bean, had not only withdrawn from the case but was also going to be part of the prosecution and would testify against his former client.

"Chris Bean sold Bob Kelly down the river," Spivey said. "It was disgusting and deeply troubling for him to turn on his own client . . . Bean could have fought the subpoena, but instead, he did it willingly. I was offended that he would do that and then later be appointed to the bench as a district court judge." Bean would go on to serve as the chief district court judge and president of his local Bar Association.

In 1990, Spivey was not practicing in the Chowan district, yet one Saturday morning, Judge Frank Brown called him at his home and said there was a "difficult and unusual case that needed an attorney from another district." Brown told him it would probably take three months to try and asked if he'd take the case. According to Spivey, it is pretty widely accepted among defense attorneys that when a lawyer is appointed to represent a defendant, "regardless of the charge, there is probably a [good] chance that the person did *something* wrong."

Spivey went to the jail and met with Bob Kelly that next week, thinking he was one of those "'probably-did-something' clients." After talking with Kelly, Spivey remembers feeling horrified as he walked away from the jail thinking, "Oh my God! This man hasn't done anything." He kept saying to himself, "Kelly is a truly innocent man, and I feared I wouldn't be able to do anything about it." It did not take him long to realize the depth of this tragic situation. These seven people had been sucked into a burning pit, and he especially remembers how young and terrified Robin was. Of all the defendants, he felt the worst for her. The deeper he got into the case, the more horrified he became, saying it was "stunning to me the mob mentality and mass hysteria. How could anyone get this many educated people to believe the ludicrous, irrational accusations?"

All the attorneys began to discuss how to mount a defense, especially because there were so many defendants and lots of lawyers. They did not know how the state would approach these cases, so they had to devise a strategy. They decided to plan a "comprehensive defense strategy," but it was extremely difficult because the state was making it nearly impossible for them to get any information to form a defense. Judge Tillery heard the arguments on the Motion for Joinder and was going to allow the cases to be tried together.

"The prosecution team fought Tillery all the way on this," Spivey said. "Tillery was so appalled by their conduct and what the prosecutors were saying that he felt he could no longer be fair to the state, and he withdrew from the case." That's when McLelland was appointed.

My recurring question was, "Who was the most to blame for the miscarriage of justice?" I mentioned that many people I spoke with blamed Jane Mabry as the instigator, but who committed the greatest sin against the seven defendants? Spivey admitted that while most people blamed Mabry as the trigger for the hysteria, he also believed much more was happening.

"The state was literally holding group meetings with the parents," he said. "The state was building a case. It was like a wildfire—and everyone just kept pouring gasoline into the flames. They even hired Roland Summit, a controversial psychiatrist whose theories had been completely rejected by most experts. They brought him in to speak to the parents and even sold tickets and hired guards to stand at the doors so non-believers could not get in."

"The greatest culpability was probably the prosecution team," he continued. "They should have handled the case in a more responsible and cautious way. They should have investigated more carefully, but instead, it was poorly done. They were driven by building a case. It was no longer about investigating the truth, but rather building that case. They funneled the children into a specified group of therapists who were recruited and paid by the state. Those therapists were filled with silly crackpot theories and spent hours and hours putting things into the heads of the children. One therapist would interview a child, and eventually, that child would say, 'This happened.' Then a week later, that same charge would show up in an interview with another child, who previously had never mentioned it. It seemed clear the therapists were talking and sharing information. And the state was gleaning 'evidence' from testimonies when the therapists hadn't even written the interviews down or recorded them in many cases. There were no recordings made available to us of what was being said to those children. Except one. In the courtroom, one recording was offered into evidence that was a statement by Betsy Kelly. When the state gave it to us, on side two it contained an audio of Toppin interviewing one of the children using anatomically correct dolls. In it, you could even hear Toppin tapping the genitals of the dolls."

He was dismayed when I told him I had found an interview with McLelland in the Greensboro *News & Record*. I told him it reported the "amused Judge McLelland" offering his opinions on the case while the jury was out deliberating Kelly's fate.

Spivey was silent, then said, "No, I didn't know about the interview. No judge should ever offer a personal opinion about a case before, during, or after. They should remain neutral and impartial. Most judges divorce themselves from the case, even after it is over."

Clearly, McLelland failed to adhere to that. Spivey also believed the state intentionally withheld the box of testimonies that Montgomery found later in the Pitt County clerk's office. Children as old as twelve years old were at that day care. Yet only the very young children's testimonies were used in the indictment, and they were the only children the defense team was allowed to cross-examine. Where were those interviews? Were they in that box? Was the *truth* in that box? The state blocked the defense lawyers' access to those interviews. Surely an older child might have seen something or "said something . . . about hamsters being killed in the hallways," Spivey said.

When the verdicts finally came down in April 1992, I asked Spivey whether he expected the guilty verdicts.

"No, I didn't expect the guilty verdict, but I was also not surprised," he said. "Not shocked. It was going to be next to impossible to get a not guilty verdict because of the nature of the charges."

But what about the jury's conduct? He said the "defense team asked the judge to set aside the verdict" because of the jury misconduct, and the court refused. He asked, "How bad must misconduct be? How much misconduct must you have before the state will address it?"

Did he know Betsy Kelly would plead no contest?

"Yes, I knew ahead of time that she was going to plead no contest. The odds were against her. She risked leaving her young child without a parent. It was painful for her to do this, but she knew she had to. We all knew."

We couldn't end our conversation without circling back to Robin. She had been so young back then.

"It was amazing that someone so young could have so much courage to face this," Spivey said. "She risked everything, and she stood her ground. The temptation, with all she had to risk, had to be incredible. The Millers took such good care of Robin and were what kept her going . . . they became her family. Not very many people have that amount of integrity and courage . . . and for someone so young. All of them, really . . . Bob Kelly was not going to admit to something he did not do. At one point, Kelly was offered a plea that could have ended it. Instead, he spent six years in jail . . . for nothing. Kelly said to me he would rather spend the rest of his life in jail than admit to a lie. I think the state thought if they indicted all these people, someone would make a deal."

"The fear on the streets in Edenton during that trial was palpable," Spivey continued. "You could feel it in the air. Everyone was terrified they might be next. Some twenty-eight to thirty people in town were also accused in one way or another, but none of them were ever charged. Really, there's no telling how many were accused because the defense didn't have access to those interviews."

I spent more than a year researching facts and interviewing people, and night after night, sleep eluded me as I tried desperately to understand what happened, how it happened, and why it happened. If this was the effect on me, more than three decades later, what must Robin and the others have experienced as they fought against these malevolent lies? The more I learned, the more humbled I was by Robin's strength and courage. Could I have withstood the pressure to tell the prosecutors what they wanted to hear? How could I piece all that I had learned into a coherent interfusion that did justice to Robin's story? I feared I would miss a link in Robin's chain of events, the paradox of coincidences that tethered us all together. Over the months, each person I talked to opened another door and raised another question, yet all the conversations ended with the same observation: "We were all scarred by this tragedy and miscarriage of justice."[3]

I always thought of storytelling as a sort of weaving of a tapestry with each past and future piece of the yarn linked together with a cohesive thread. In the final steps of weaving Robin's tapestry, I needed to give her the gift of healing. To do this, I knew I had to sit with her attorney, Jeff Miller, whom she said, and others confirmed, was the person who held her together and saved her. He and his wife, Rachel, were her family, part of that village that helped raise Robin, who was just a young girl at the time of her indictment. I reached out to Miller's office and talked with his paralegal, Sandra, who Robin mentioned had been a vital part of the team. Sandra arranged a meeting with Jeff Miller, and I made my way to Greenville, just a short drive from my old house on the river. I spent hours the night before our interview ensuring that I had written out every question I wanted to ask.

Miller met me at the door of his office, hand extended and dressed like a gentleman lawyer of his generation. I smiled when I noticed he wore Crocs with his suit, which gave him an easygoing, genuine aura. *Sweet,* I thought, as he guided me to where we would spend the next several hours.

His head was full of beautiful silver hair, and his black beard, an ever-present signature in the photos from the trials, was now snow white. It suited him. Behind his scholarly, rimless glasses were the eyes of a gentle, honest, sincere soul. I could sense his authenticity and kindness. Like the others before him, he was more than willing to talk to me and share Robin's story. It was as if I had always known him.

As we sat down, he just began talking—he did not need my lengthy list of questions. After all these years, Miller was ready to talk. He wondered out loud why someone had not written Robin's book before now. He stalled on his words, "It is hard . . . even now . . . to believe what they did to Robin. I've lost touch with her over the years." And there they were, those too-familiar words, "We were all scarred by what they did to her."

Remembering the first time he went home after meeting Robin in the jail in Edenton, he said he told his wife, "Rachel, our lives will never be the same." He credited Robin's mother, Lou, for raising Robin the right way and teaching her to be so honest and courageous. Lou was "an amazing mother. A good soul." He could "only imagine the pressure to give in to this kind of case" and is "convinced that they arrested Robin and kept her in jail thinking they could pressure her to deal, to give them the evidence they sought." But we all know she "insisted nothing happened, she saw nothing, she knew nothing, and she did nothing. Think about it. Seven people were charged with this kind of conspiracy, and not one person broke. In cases like this, some people would just lie and say anything to get out of it. Yet no one did. These were seven principled people from the very beginning."

At first, Miller apologized for his memory, saying it was "not so good at his age," and he was sure someone else could likely fill in more details than he could. That proved not to be true at all. Other than an occasional mental search for a name, he recalled the details quite well. In his opinion, the politics of the case were horrible. It seemed to him that some people in the case were influenced by malice, particularly the prosecutors. He recalled Bill Hart, the special prosecutor, as someone trapped in a "competitive enterprise. He was competitive in every single thing in his life, and this trial was part of his masculine agenda. He was filled with testosterone and [hyper] masculinity. Early on, when H. P. Williams was alone on the case before Hart joined the team and Chris Bean was still representing Bob Kelly, it was less threatening. The accusations had been made, and Williams just wanted it over. He wanted a conviction on something so that he could end it. He had no confession. No eyewitness. No inculpatory physical evidence. But during this time . . . in Edenton . . . it was a climate conducive to those allegations." Though Williams wanted the case resolved, the town had other ideas, and in the hands of a dangerously inadequate and incompetent investigator, the stories morphed.

"Why did Nancy Lamb fall so deeply into the conspiracy?" I asked.

Miller thought perhaps this was Lamb's back story. "Women [as mothers] were just easy targets with these kinds of allegations—perhaps it was the maternal instinct to protect the children." He was kinder to her than I expected. He went on to say he also believed "it gave Lamb a sense of recognition and feeling successful, both personally and professionally."

"Didn't she go on later to establish a non-profit in New Bern for children traumatized by child abuse?" I asked.

He nodded. "Nancy's House gave her a cause in her life." But this was a situation where it was about "child protection," and you just "can't be the bad guy in these cases," he said. In his opinion, Lamb was determined to prove malice, and curiously, it seemed many folks were filled with it.

Miller believes if they did not have "the knowledge or the truth, that vacuum was easily filled." Lamb was biased by the whole process because she believed she *knew* with certainty what the truth was. It all began with "bad Mr. Bob," but there was a problem. "How could this have occurred without anyone seeing anything?" he said. "How could it have occurred without the help of someone else, of others? So, they met the demand at the time and just kept adding people to the accusations until they got to Robin. They simply added layers to the story. Then Toppin and therapists wrote out the children's testimonies in their own words and in a very different narrative way because they needed the story to make sense. The whole story was built on Bob, then the more the kids talked, the more the state was building the narrative. They also knew they needed a pornography element, so Privott, a buddy of Kelly's, was an easy target. Robin, however, was the weak link in the conspiracy. They thought, 'She is going to tell us what we want to hear. What we want to know.' They offered her all sorts of proposals along the way for her to tell them their version of the truth, then she could plead to a misdemeanor, get out of jail, and go home. She never once thought about doing that. I never once suggested she do that."

Miller had already been appointed to Robin's case and was well-versed in the facts when he was appointed as co-counsel in Bob Kelly's case. He had done extensive research into medical and mental health experts. In preparing for Bob Kelly's trial, Spivey was responsible for the witnesses and the individual stories that were part of the case, and Miller was responsible for the medical and psychological experts for the case.

"First, there was no physical evidence at the scene anywhere," Miller said. "It came down to children's testimonies and medical witnesses, primarily from the examination of the vaginas and hymens of the little girls. . . . The [medical] experts were willing to testify that the female children had been abused based on photographs of the crescentic hymen and the suggested presence of 'synechia' in four little girls, which in their opinion was consistent with the evidence of abuse. Those doctors were willing to testify based on the evidence they collected using the colposcope, a high-powered camera that magnified the genitals rather than being intrusive. Then they would say, 'We have this photograph of a child, and the physical examination showed some kind of physical evidence consistent with abuse.' They were presenting it as objective evidence.

"In response, we presented medical experts that showed diametrically opposed opinions of the presence of abuse or trauma. The defense showed another photograph also taken using a colposcope." The photograph came from a "medical school treatise used to teach and presented a normal crescentic hymen." That photograph was nearly identical to the one used by the state. Miller said, "You could have put one of those pictures on top of the other and would not have been able to tell the difference between them. They were identical!"

"The political pressure to confirm the state's charges was profound," he continued. The experts for the defense would go on to testify, but they were under "immense professional pressure not to do so." Miller went first to his friend, Tom Irons, professor of pediatrics at East Carolina University's Brody School of Medicine. Irons was a well-regarded and respected pediatrician in his field and president of the American Association of Pediatric Physicians. When Miller talked with him, Irons said, "Gosh, I was thinking you might have a hard time defending your client against these charges . . . until I saw the photographs." Irons went on to affirm what Miller suspected to be true.

"Irons believed there was no basis, from anything he viewed, to conclude or form a medical opinion from those photographs that the children had been abused," Miller said. At first, Irons did not believe he could testify because of his position at ECU's medical school, but he agreed to help Miller find other experts who could. At some point, however, he did agree to testify about child sexual abuse procedures and medical terms. Of course, the prosecutors wanted to challenge him in a way that concerned Irons, so he testified more directly and forcefully that he had "reviewed the materials and found no evidence of sexual abuse from his review."

Eventually, Miller also secured the medical expertise of Dr. Bob Brayden, a postdoctoral fellow in general and behavioral pediatrics at Vanderbilt University School of Medicine. Miller thought it significant that "Brayden had testified for hundreds of prosecutions in Nashville, Tennessee, and this was the only testimony he had ever given for the defense."

Miller said Brayden looked at the photographs and "established that there was no objective evidence of any abuse, nor any evidence that the girls had been penetrated." According to Miller, Brayden also came under "enormous political pressure for taking a position that was in opposition to the state's opinions. As a result, he left his university position at Vanderbilt." Afterward, Brayden returned to Colorado to practice and teach at the University of Colorado School of Medicine. "It was the politics of it," Miller said. "You were either on their side, even if you disagreed, or you were a pariah. Many went against their personal and professional interests and then paid dearly for it."

Miller, like Spivey, was quite critical of Dr. Desmond Runyan. He believed Runyan created the form used at CMEP that he claimed gave doctors a backbone. However, in Miller's opinion, it was a form and checklist specifically designed to *prove* that the child had been abused. Miller laughed softly as he recalled preparing to cross-examine Runyan. They were in the courtroom, and he laid a series of documents with experts' statements on the floor. Lamb, Hart, and Williams were all standing with Runyan as he watched Miller lay out the statements. Runyan shouted, "I never said that!"

Miller looked him right in the eye and said, "I'll tell you what. I'll bet you $1,000 that I can prove you said it. If I can't, you get the $1,000. If I do prove it, I get the money." Miller said Runyan shut up immediately.

Miller mused about talking later with a colleague and professor of Runyan's from the University of Minnesota, where Runyan received his medical degree. Runyan's professor quipped about his former student, "That fella had no business testifying. He doesn't know what he is talking about." That professor also was threatened with losing his grant funding if he testified.

Moisy Shopper, William Kenner, Maggie Bruck, and others who studied the case were all extremely critical of the therapists, Miller said, especially of "Judy Abbott and the other therapists. Abbott lacked qualifications and academic credentials to be an expert therapist. She saw this as an opportunity for her own advancement."

Miller said there was a conflict at the time in North Carolina between "statutory rights for the defense to have access to witness statements and the constitutional rights of the defense to have those testimonies. And exculpatory evidence had a broad definition." At the time, if the "evidence could negate the case in any way, the defense was supposed to have access to those testimonies" conducted by the therapists and investigators. However, they were denied access to "any testimony until each one was introduced in court."

And then Miller confirmed something distressing that Spivey had also mentioned. The state "turned over a two-sided cassette tape with an interview between Brenda Toppin and Betsy Kelly. We serendipitously put the tape in on the wrong side . . . and there it was . . . an interview between Toppin and one of the child witnesses. She was very clearly doing what she had testified in court under oath that she did not do. We could hear the leading questions, the child's responses, and her *tap, tap, tapping* on what was clear to be one of the anatomically correct dolls, the ones that she specifically testified she was not trained to use."

In the end, because the therapists never testified, "We got the bulk of evidence that contained therapists' notes, police officers' notes, and parents' diaries that were not quotations," Miller said. "They were third-party statements summarizing what that person said, and that's all we got until the trials. We just got bits and pieces of what therapists wrote about what each child said. We didn't get what the prosecution had on each witness until after the witness had finished testifying. And we didn't get anything ahead of the next person to testify. And that cycle continued."

"During the trial, we were sitting there in the court, and Bill Hart had a huge collection of files." Miller silently measured the deep stack with a gesture of his hands and then said, "Hart handed them to us and began to walk away. I told the judge we needed several days to review the evidence. Hart got very upset and then complained that he wouldn't have given them to us if he had known that, so he objected, and McLelland allowed the objection. Hart took the files back. What followed was that we had no sense of the chain of events we would have had with those files. Instead, we had to wait to get each one, one testimony at a time, rendering it nearly impossible for us to mount a comprehensive defense."

Miller then recalled another phenomenon in Edenton. "It was 'the thing' to be one of the victims," he said. "Folks wanted to be part of it. Chris Bean's professional obligation was paramount. He never should have been co-opted to testify against his one-time client. If he believed his child was abused, he should have stepped aside and sat silently in the courtroom. I despised him for it and thought his actions were reprehensible." He went on, "We learned too late to help us that Bean and his young son were riding in a car together, returning from something, and his son said something like, *'You know, Dad, it's not true. It never happened.'*" That event was validated by the entry dated November 14, 1989, in Grace Bean's journal and then in Chris Bean's own testimony.

Inevitably, Miller and I cycled around to those recurring and ever-disturbing questions. Where was the physical evidence? Where were the eyewitnesses?

"There was no inculpatory physical evidence to prove guilt," Miller said. "However, these cases did foster a change in the law. Doctors can no longer testify that there was abuse unless there is verifiable physical evidence."[4]

Miller mentioned that there was only one person who alleged to be an eyewitness, a police officer whose name he could not recall. After Miller and I talked, I went back to Duke and found the officer's testimony.

Officer Wayne Forehand testified that he was spending a lot of time on his grandmother's front porch during this time and claimed to have a clear view of both the marina and Scott Privott's store. He further testified to have seen Kelly's van "on several occasions" and said that the doors "slide back so that you have full view of the inside of the vehicle." Forehand went on to testify that sometime in late August 1988, he was driving behind the van and said, "I saw a child wave to me out of the back window." As he remained on the witness stand, the defense submitted a picture of the truck. Did he perjure himself? The picture showed the door actually opened quite the opposite way from how the officer testified. Even more, the defense proved Forehand could not possibly have seen into the back of the truck . . . because there were no windows.[5]

Miller also believed Judge McLelland was especially vindictive. At the end of Kelly's trial, all the attorneys and experts had to submit time sheets to the judge to get paid. "We had spent hundreds of hours in pretrial preparations, interviews, and research, and then the trials," Miller said. "Mike Spivey had a partner to help him, but I was a solo practice. It was terribly stressful for all of us. McLelland awarded the CMEP experts for the state $400 per hour and allowed them to submit their time. However, when the judge received the time sheets from Shopper and the other defense experts, McLelland awarded them about one-third the amount that the state's experts received. He also tried to set our attorney fees at a ridiculously low fee, and he then tried to limit our reimbursement to a set fee, rather than by the hour. Rachel got her back up about that and wrote him a blistering letter saying he was being unfair!"

I asked, "Do you believe you would have won Robin's case? Could you have gotten a not guilty?"

He did not hesitate. "Yes," he said. Miller still believes they "could have won her case because her story was different from all the rest. She was so young. A little girl. She had no connection to the others. It was her first real job. She had just started working there. She was an unwitting victim and was astounded by where she found herself. But you know, it is mighty hard to prove your innocence when there's no evidence. It was the perfect storm of time, people, and place."

Suddenly, Miller chuckled, a beautiful teary-eyed chuckle, as he remembered getting her out on bond. "We finally got Robin's bond reduced. It was Herb Gardner, a gentle, strapping bail bondsman who drove a big, black Lincoln. He agreed to reduce his fee so Robin's family could bond her out. He showed up at the jail to bring her home. This was the first time Robin had been out of jail since they arrested her on the charges a year before. It still chokes me up . . ." He paused as his eyes filled with tears, and it took him several seconds to regain his composure. "It chokes me up what they did to that little girl. That was one of the few happy times. We were all so excited. We had planned a big surprise party for her at my office. Gardner picked her up, drove her to Greenville, and escorted her in, where she then saw all of us waiting for her. We even booked a room for her and Kevin at the Hilton Inn for that night." He and I laughed together as I told him how different her reflection was about the night at the hotel.

As we finished our conversation, Miller looked at me and said, "Things like this will never change until someone important is accused. It was a scary time. Scary business for us personally, too. We were godparents to our neighbor's little girl. We did everything together. Sometimes I had to take her to the bathroom." He paused. "But after this, everything changed considerably. You know what I mean?" I nodded as he finished by saying, "I never agreed to do that again . . . with little girls. You know? Yep, we were all scarred by it."[6]

Chapter 29

The Mirror Test

It is not conceivable that . . . the prosecutors responsible
for these latter-day Salem witch trials believed
a word of the charges responsible for ruining the
lives of so many people.
—Paul Roberts and Lawrence Stratton

It was April 8, 2023. The text message he sent to me read:

"We use flip phones and take forever to text—am fixing lunch can call you about three. Ok or not?"

"Yes, 3 is Perfect!" I replied.

And so began the final journey between stakeholders in the Little Rascals Day Care case. But where would I begin with Robert Fulton Kelly Jr., the person at the center of the witch hunt, the events that changed Robin's life? As with the others, I got his phone number from Lew Powell, and he was sure Bob would talk with me.

"You'll find him quite likable and easy to talk with," Powell said, and he was right.

I sent him a text message first, telling him I was writing a book about the Edenton Seven and that Powell had recommended I reach out to him. "Would you be willing to talk?" I asked in the message.

He was willing and replied with the text cited above.

"If you had the chance, what would you say to Nancy Lamb?" I asked him that afternoon.

"What would I say to her? Nothing. I'd say nothing," Kelly said. "Except

I do stand by what I said all along. They should all be in jail. Someone who has been raped or molested carries a tremendous emotional burden for their entire life. The prosecutors told people that I may have molested more than ninety children. Ninety children! And those children were raised to believe they had been molested and raped. We can't fault the kids. They trusted their parents. They trusted the grownups. They trusted everybody. Now they all carry the same emotional burdens as someone who really has been raped and molested. For life. They grew up believing what those therapists and Brenda Toppin and prosecutors convinced them happened."

Kelly wanted to talk about Betsy, Robin, Dawn, and Betty Ann Phillips, recalling, "It's sad. Betsy loved those children like her own. She loved all of them. They were mostly drop-ins, but we spent more time with them than their parents did. We fed them breakfast. We fed them lunch. We spent quality time with them."

He wondered aloud, "Why do I still care?" He knew why. "Because those children were family to Betsy. And because it was our name. Am I still angry? Yes. I'm still upset that the state has never admitted they were wrong."

I asked him the inevitable question. "What about Mabry?" And because no one knows better what happened, I asked him about the slap. He paused briefly to gather his thoughts.

"Mabry's child was a drop-in," he said. "The rule was at nap time they had to lie down. They didn't have to sleep, but they had to lie down and be quiet. Her son wouldn't do that. He wouldn't lie down. I was over by the phone. So, I got up and went to him, patted the mat, and said, 'Lie down.' He refused . . . so I popped him upside the head."

He remembered that Mabry picked up her son that afternoon and left before he could tell her what happened. But she called the day care after she got home.

"I told her then what happened, and she said, 'It's fine,'" Kelly recalled. "Then some days later, she called Betsy. I couldn't hear the conversation, but I heard Betsy say, 'Don't talk about child abuse.' I think that was at the end of September. We hadn't been in the new day care for very long. Anyway, sometime later, maybe even in January, her husband came to the day care. He said it was 'to give us one more chance.' I told him, 'I did apologize. The day it happened. I can't undo it. I did it, and I can't undo it.' He left. Within a few days, Toppin and DSS showed up at the day care. The rest is history."

Kelly was light-hearted, and he didn't really seem bitter, but there was a sort of soft anger beneath his words. "I'm sorry we had to go through all this, but hopefully, it made me a better person. My philosophy is one I developed in prison while I awaited my appeal. I don't take any day for granted. One day I will die, and I thank God every day for giving me the time I've had . . . the good, the bad, and the ugly."

His wish? He hoped his children have learned to stand up for what is right. "Do what you can live with," he said. "I tried to do what was right . . . what was best. People believe what they want to believe. If they believe I did something, did the things I was accused of, they can tell me, and then leave. I don't want to be around anyone who doesn't believe in me."

Reflecting on how he survived prison, Kelly believes in the 75/25 philosophy: "Take one hundred people, line 'em up, give each one $1 million, and send them home. Twenty-five of them will complain about the million. One group got all twenty-dollar bills. Another got theirs before you. Something will be wrong with the gift. The other seventy-five will be gracious and say, 'Thank you.' That's kind of what I saw in prison." He knew that "75 percent of the people at Central Prison believed" in him. One old-timer he met there said to him, "You know why nothing happened to you in here? Because we are all cons and murderers. We know it when we see it. And when there are two or more people involved in something, someone will snitch them out. Seven of you! Nobody snitched anyone else out."

Recently, Kelly was talking to his son, born to his current wife. The son asked if Kelly had any regrets. He replied, "If I had not gone to prison, you would not be alive. If we changed something, one thing, I would not have met Mattie, my wife. If you turn left and have an accident, what would have happened if you turned right?"

Even more, Kelly pondered on people who do not stand up for the right thing, those who "ride the fence" and don't take a stand. "I don't like people like that," he said. "Do what's right." What if Chris Bean had done the right thing? What if more of those parents had stood against the tidal wave? As I listened to him, I couldn't help but think about the line from Dante's *Divine Comedy*: "The hottest places in hell are reserved for those who in times of great moral crisis maintain their neutrality."

But then, in Bob Kelly's philosophy, if the trial had never happened, he would not be where he is today. After he got out of prison, he and Betsy divorced, and eventually, he reconnected with someone he had dated before marrying Betsy. A condition of his release on bond was that he not go into District 1, which included Elizabeth City, Mattie's hometown. He said, "Basically, I couldn't go across the Chowan River Bridge," so he courted Mattie by phone. Twenty-five years later, they are still together. He and his wife live in quiet obscurity, much like Robin, and he believes his life is good. He's happy. He's content. He loves to cook. He thinks overall, people have forgotten about the case. But then he said, "I've aged, and they probably don't recognize me."

He recalled how young Robin was at the time of his trial. He hadn't seen her in more than thirty years. She was so vulnerable, and the state used her to get him. He and I both believe she was the pawn. Get a conviction by charging the youngest, the most defenseless. After all, what young, new mother would not confess to save herself? But Robin wouldn't. Robin didn't. He hoped that she was happy and has been able to "enjoy life." When I told him about her precious grandkids, his response was immediate. "What? She's not old enough to be a grandmother." I assured him she was but reminded him that she started having children very young. It occurred to me that Robin and the others must be sort of frozen in time for him. That happens to all of us.

Kelly asked about Betty Ann Phillips. He especially wondered about her because "she was so strong" and remembered that Williams threatened her by warning her "to watch what she said in public." All these years later, he remembered those words.

And even though Betsy Kelly told him many years ago she didn't want him to be part of her life anymore, he wished her well. He knew they were all victims of this witch hunt. "I hope Betsy's happy. She deserves to be happy. They all do." Occasionally the daughter he shares with Betsy comes to visit him, to eat his home cooking, and to pick some tomatoes during the summer. Was she damaged by the case? He said that of course she had been.

I had to think about all this. I suggested to him that at the end of the day, we all hope we can "pass the mirror test." *Can I live with myself, with my actions, and the choices I've made?*

Kelly said, "Yeah. I can. And I want to pass good things along to my children, grandchildren, and great-grandchildren. My first forty-five years set me up for the last thirty years of my life, and I'm happy."

Chapter 30

A Lunch to Remember

It was like being a mule caught in a Texas hailstorm. You
can't run. You can't hide. And you can't make it stop.
—President Lyndon B. Johnson

Two women—Robin Byrum and Betsy Kelly—trapped in a cesspool
of lies, their fates and that of the others all colliding in a single cruel
confrontation in time and space, in what became a modern-day witch
hunt. Perhaps, as they believe, the concurrence of events was somehow
prearranged in ways they cannot fully understand. None of us can.

The many coincidences in the Little Rascals timeline and sphere were
too many to ignore, and I understood each event was an essential part
of a larger puzzle, each one necessary for this day to take place. Without
each, I would not be where I am in Robin's life. That Lou would become
Robin's mother. That Lou would accept a job in Edenton, of all places.
That Betsy Kelly would become unlikely friends with Jane Mabry.
That Robin would so quickly accept a job at Kelly's day care. That two
irrational mothers would cry "abuse," submerging them and the entire
town into the abyss. That miles away, I would watch their stories unfold,
never expecting to meet them, let alone know them or write about them.
Even that Betsy Kelly and I share a first name. That I would meet Robin
in a most unlikely place so many years after her pain, which would lead
me to Lew Powell, to Nancy Smith, and ultimately to her sister, Betsy
Kelly. Through that chance meeting with Robin in my husband's office, I
was given the opportunity to delve into their shared tragedy.

Chance. Yes, I took a chance. On a "possibility," I reached out by email to Nancy, knowing it was unlikely that she would even read my email, let alone respond to it. Why would she? I was far into researching the book when I wrote to her, "I am a friend of Lew Powell . . . he thought you and perhaps Betsy might be willing to talk with me. Would this be possible?"

Several days later, Nancy answered. "Maybe . . . I'll be in touch." Another email arrived many more days later. She and her sister had mulled over my request as they walked along the streets of Edenton, the same streets they had paraded down with the Little Rascals Day Care children, hand-in-hand, on so many sweet field trips to the drugstore, the library, and back to school. Locals would stop, smile, and pat the children, talking with them and high-fiving them. Giggles abounded. Those were the same streets my husband and I cycled through, lined by the same haunting, massive trees, sentries still standing guard over the past. There Betsy and Nancy lingered in downtown Edenton . . . "something [Betsy] had not done since being released," Nancy said. It had changed very little in more than thirty years. Was it time to face the past? The sisters decided together to take the chance. Yes, it was time.

So off I went to Edenton, in the middle of winter on what was predicted to be a rainy Friday. On the drive, my mind raced nervously through "what ifs." *What if Betsy decides not to come? What if Robin changes her mind? What if no one talks? What if the pain is just too vast, too deep, too postponed? What if the risk is simply too great?* Driving into Edenton was different from the many times I had visited there in the past, mostly because I was no longer an observer from afar. I was now part of this complex story.

As I arrived at Nancy's home, the clouds and drizzle disappeared, and the day blossomed into a beautiful, warm, spring-like day, as if Mother Nature had opened her doors to let the healing in. Apprehensively, I knocked on the front door and was greeted by a smiling, bubbly woman with a buttery Southern drawl.

"I'm Nancy . . . and you're family," she said. "Family always comes to the side door. Come on." She wrapped her arms around me in a sisterly embrace, and we made our way inside.

Then Betsy arrived—naturally, she already knew to go to the side door. I thought, *She is so delicate, so serious*, and I felt the energy change. It was as if a whisper had just entered the room behind her. No introductions were necessary. We each knew who the other woman was. We just hugged sweetly, in the "nice to meet you" way that Southern ladies do. We chatted comfortably as we waited for Robin to arrive. The sisters told me about their parents, about losing their beloved father eleven years before, about their ninety-seven-year-old stoic but angry mother, still bitter after all these years, and about what it was like to still live in Edenton.

At one point, Betsy asked her sister about the angels lining the shelves around the room.

"They are from the children's auction," Nancy said. "At church. These were the ones no one bid on . . . and I just couldn't let them stay . . . so I bid on them." The sisters both understood why it mattered that Nancy couldn't leave them behind. Of course, they needed "angels to watch over them."

As I was explaining about the book and about how I came to meet Robin, Betsy stopped me, collected herself, and through tears said, "There is no one else in this world I would do this for but Robin."

Yes, I knew that. It was at that moment I fully realized how deeply these women were connected. They are family. I looked up, and there she was, standing at the side door. I noted Robin's pause as if she were gathering herself before walking in. Then Betsy and Nancy saw her and rushed over to her, and the years melted away, and the tears erupted from both Betsy and Robin. I stood back, an observer, an intruder in this tear-filled embrace so long overdue. Robin—no longer the timid, insecure nineteen-year-old who walked into Little Rascals Day Care all those many years ago—was back in the love and care of Betsy, who helped her survive that year in prison. The room was filled with sunshine and good energy, and a few angels as well.

As they quickly settled into sharing stories, the "what ifs" that haunted me on my drive began to dissolve. This was an important gathering of long-lost girlfriends, chattering about their children, their grandchildren, and the missed years. Robin chattered happily about her family, the one she always wanted. The one she almost did not have. With that, the inevitable happened. We all knew why we were there, and in our hearts, we knew that it was necessary.

The conversation turned to darker memories. Nancy made an observation about what all of them had been through. She asked me if I had ever heard the expression about being "trapped in a Texas hailstorm, where you can't run, you can't hide, and you can't make it stop."

Laughing heartily, I said, "No, I have not!" I jotted it down, realizing the utter truth in that quote. Yes, Nancy was right. Robin, Betsy, and the others knew they could not run away from all that happened around them, nor could they hide from it. And worse, no matter how hard anyone tried, nothing they could do would make it stop. Sadly, the only ones who could do that had refused to do the right thing.

The women each talked about the shared fear of being recognized out in public. One day, not long after her release, Betsy had settled into a new life and was shopping as anonymously as she could. She glanced down over the railing to the first floor of the shopping mall, and there stood Chris and Grace Bean. Needless to say, she wanted to scream, "This is my home. Not here. Go away!" Even today, decades later, Robin and Betsy constantly "scope" the landscape of their daily lives to see who might be nearby and who might recognize them. They still fear who might attack them as villains of what was a made-up story.

"What about those Edenton accusers? Do you see them?" I asked.

In one of only a few times that day, I saw Nancy's underlying resentment. "Yes, we see them," she said. "They cross the street, avoid contact—they just ignore us."

When I asked about why she stayed in Edenton, she was quick to respond. "My mother is here. We grew up here." That was enough. And in truth, many people in Edenton supported them and still believe in their innocence to this day. As Robin talked about recently discovering her box of letters of support, Betsy recalled the hundreds and hundreds of letters of support she received from all over the world. Never once did any of the letters condemn them, charge them, or accuse them. The world saw the truth. Why didn't the people of Edenton?

The most painful moment of the day came in an exchange as Betsy turned to Robin, chin quivering, and said quietly, "I'm sorry. I'm sorry I haven't been in touch in such a long time. It was just . . . I was afraid to bring back memories for you. I felt like you had suffered the worst of all of us . . . a young mother with a young baby at home." Through that long-withheld apology, she uttered the unnecessary burden she carried for so many years: "I felt like I was to blame for what happened to you. If I . . ." Her words trailed off, but the "what if" hung in the air.

"No," Robin lovingly assured her. "You were not to blame. You were never to blame. The parents were to blame."

Gradually, their remembering moved to their time spent at Central Prison. Of all the shared memories, the ones from that period were what they believed to be the most important. Why? Betsy reflected on the incredible kindness and strength they experienced there, saying, "They were the kindest people I've ever met." Earlier, Robin had made that same observation to me. She made friends there too. Many women took them under their wings and protected them, prisoners and guards alike. They remembered many of them. Names. Events. People. They remembered the horror of breakfast duty, of serving trays at 6:00 a.m. to prisoners angry at the early-morning intrusions. They remembered being locked in a cell with an inmate who really had killed her baby in a microwave. They remembered the fear of bunking above a murderer, agonizing over the irony that, unlike their cellmates, they had done none of the horrible crimes they were accused of committing. But in time, they learned those women in prison with them were human, people in trauma, in trouble. They especially recalled the women who loved and protected them . . .

Rey, Maggie, and the guard who was like Betsy's mama—sadly, she could no longer remember her name—and they both wondered where those women were now.

A few memories brought unreserved laughter into the room. The roaches! The giant, grotesque, creeping, crawling cockroaches had been everywhere. Robin recalled the "terror at the hundreds running all over the place." Betsy remembered that for entertainment, she and some other inmates spent hours "rolling peanut M&Ms across the floor and under the cell doors to watch the giant cockroaches snatch them up and carry the sweet surprises away." They giggled about passing notes to one another through the cell doors, secrets of survival, prison cell gossip, and private fears.

Our conversation drifted back to the artifacts and leftovers of the case. Curiously, Betsy admitted to Robin that she had gradually burned most remnants of that time. On each trip to visit Nancy or her mother, she would bring more—more sheets, more papers, more documents—and together, they would burn them ceremoniously in a purging funeral pyre. And each time, she laid to rest more of the remnants of their nightmare. Unlike Robin, who kept everything, Betsy kept almost nothing. In one more coincidental moment, she said, "I kept only one small box," and she fingered the size and shape for us, smiling when she recalled that it contained "silly relics—a few receipts and notes." She was not sure why, but she had not been able to let go of that last reminder.

It was clear to me why Betsy, like Jeff Miller, meant so much to Robin. They were all her family. Betsy likes to refer to those years as the time when she was "enjoying the hospitality of the governor." How does one create a positive metaphor for years unfairly spent imprisoned? Yet these two women found goodness and even humor in their shared experience in prison, in spite of what the State of North Carolina did to them. And on this day, reunited at long last, they spent hours shedding tears and guilt, but more, sharing love. I was so grateful to be there.

Chapter 31

Robin's Story—Bloom Where You're Planted

There is mud, and there is the lotus that grows out of the
mud. We need the mud in order to grow the lotus.
—Thich Nhat Hanh

Afterward, to truly find myself and to begin to heal, I needed to find answers.

Momma was always honest with me about being adopted, and like others, I was curious about my birth mother. So, in 2002, with the encouragement of my husband, I started the search. I signed on to the adoption registry, but I didn't do DNA testing until 2019, and it was through the DNA tests that I finally found my birth family. Certainly, I was hoping to find them sooner than I did, and it was an emotional and complicated search, but a worthy one. Only seven days after Lindy, my "search angel," connected my DNA, that discovery led me to Georgia, to my biological mother, Millie, and then to my brother Matt. I was overjoyed!

There were parallels between Lou, my adoptive mother, and Millie, my birth mother, which were confusing and unbelievable, even for me. Both mothers were nurses. Both mothers had marriages that lasted only seven years. Both mothers had babies they put up for adoption. Millie was told she could never have children, so in 1968 she adopted Matt from her sister, Sue, an unwed mother. But Millie did get pregnant, and she gave birth to me and then put me up for adoption. Lou, a single mother, had a son in 1960, put him up for adoption, and then adopted me in 1970. As an adult, I learned that I'm not an only child, and instead,

I have two brothers, but neither brother is my full biological brother. God's plan!

Curiously, Millie was always honest with Matt too. Maybe that's why we were so close. We were both raised by a single mother and as an only child, so it was compelling once we finally found each other. He said he always knew I was somewhere out there. Initially, Matt and I just talked by phone and got to know each other before meeting face-to-face. I was unsure about Millie. Was her health okay? Or would she even want to meet me? But Matt assured me she was anxious to meet me. We talked for hours on the phone at first . . . about everything—our lives, our ups, our downs, our children. We all had so many questions. I had so many questions. Did she plan to give me up? Did she ever hold me? No, but I know she heard my first cry, and she knew I was a girl. Did she tell her parents, my grandparents, or my father? I really wanted to know about my father because I never had one. With all that, I assured Millie she "did the right thing. I had a wonderful Momma and a big family that loved me very much."

Hanging in the air between us, though, was Little Rascals Day Care, a rancid, decomposing memory. I knew eventually I would have to tell them, but did they need to know this? It was such a huge part of my life, and I felt that if we were going to be close, they needed to know. I told Matt first. Then he told Millie, but how much he told her, I don't know. I only gave him an abbreviated version of the case . . . falsely accused, imprisoned for a year, trials, appeals, cases dismissed. That was about it. Yet, once I told them, they never brought it up again, just like everyone else in my life who knows. However, not one person in my current husband's family knows, except an ex-brother-in-law, who was floored when he learned about it, but then never mentioned it again.

For months, Millie, Matt, and I spent a slow, southern Georgia time getting to know each other, discovering all our connections, and recovering lost time. Matt and I talked on the phone every single day, talking about his failed marriage, his life, and his beautiful daughters.

But something was amiss with Matt. I recognized a melancholy in him, those all-too-familiar waves that crashed in on him. The waves I also felt in the days after the accusations, the indictment, and the prison cell. It was hard for me not to give in to those waves. But Matt was a lost soul, trapped by some inner darkness, and he knew the waves would finally consume him. He lost his struggle with depression on August 10, 2020, in the house he shared with my biological mother —his adoptive mother. There, he gave in to despair and ended his life by his own hands.

In my life, phone calls seem to bring monumental, occasionally wonderful news, but sometimes painful, devastating news. Long ago, one call came, the one that informed me that all the charges against me were dismissed. Then, that August afternoon, another phone call came, the one when a friend of the family called to tell me about my brother. That call told me my brother was dead, that he could not hold on, only fifteen months after he came into my life. I couldn't breathe. His death utterly devastated me. I wasn't able to talk with any of them until I arrived in Georgia on August 13. On that day, we consoled each other the best we could, and we tried to have only good thoughts of Matt, but his girls had to focus on his funeral, and I had to focus on other problems. I knew Uncle Scotty was sick, and I had to get to Kentucky to see him and Aunt Penny. But I didn't make it. On my way to Georgia, I received the call from my cousin that my larger-than-life Uncle Scotty had died.

I felt like my world was falling apart. My mother was in a nursing home, alone and isolated because of COVID-19. My daughter-in-law miscarried her second baby. I then lost Momma, the mother who raised me. That was too much. It was true that Millie gave me life. For that, I'm grateful. When she made her decision to let me go, she gave the woman I would call Momma a gift and the chance to love and surround me with my big, wonderful Kentucky family. From the day she took me into her arms that day in 1970 in that Florida hospital, Momma assured me I was enough, and she taught me to be the strong woman I am today. When she met my new adored husband, she knew I was finally living my love story, the one she always believed I deserved, and she wanted so much for me.

At Christmas, Momma was diagnosed with COVID and moved to the hospital. Once she recovered, she went back to the nursing home, and then in late January, I got the phone call that she was declining. At the time, I was working in the healthcare field, and I had to get the vaccination. Once I was vaccinated, I drove ten hours straight to be by her bedside.

The nursing home bent the rules and allowed Aunt Penny, Aunt Sue, and me in to be with Momma. The fact that the nursing home allowed us in to see her—perhaps because she had a privately paid room—was stunning, but we were so grateful! We were her only visitors from March 2020 to January 2021. By this time, they had tight regulations for visiting. We had to sign in and out every few hours and put on new gowns/masks/gloves/shoe protectors every time. Also, the sheets of plastic and trying to maneuver down the hall reminded me of that movie *Outbreak*.

When I finally arrived at her room, the same one I had visited numerous times before, it was evident this time was different. She wasn't waiting anxiously for me to enter the room. She wasn't sitting up in her chair watching TV. Instead, she was lying in bed, sleeping. She didn't wake up the entire three days I was there. I talked to her and held her hand, telling her stories of her great-grandkids, which she never met because of COVID and because of time. After nine months of isolation, Momma finally had visitors, but she was unresponsive, not eating, not talking, not even opening her eyes. We made the awful decision to bring in hospice.

I sat by her bed for days, but when it came time to go back to North Carolina, to my family and job, I knew I would never see her alive again. Ironically, she lingered for six more months with my aunts visiting her every day, feeding her, talking to her, and loving her. She passed away on the morning of July 19, 2021, with no one there as she took her last breath. My biggest regret in life was not being by her side when she took her last breath. She died alone, and my heart was broken.

Now her grandsons are grown men. They know my story, but they don't fully realize they are the reason I survived it all. I kept praying everything would work out, that it would all be okay, right up until I was finally released, and charges were dropped. My inner strength came from my son, from knowing I had to be back with them, even if it meant going back to Kevin, to the abuse, the threats, and the neglect. After all, I survived prison.

By 2000, Kevin and I were done. I was tired of his cruelty, the injuries, the pain, and what I went through cured me of him. But Kevin always knew how to hurt me the most, so in 2000, he, his mother, and his girlfriend conspired against me and went to DSS to charge me with the worst thing he could think of: child abuse. My boys. MY BOYS! He knew, because of Little Rascals, it was a way to get back at me in a dangerous way. Fortunately, the court saw through it, issued a restraining order against him, and finally, we were done.

After divorcing him, I found my Prince Charming. That was twenty-two years ago, and yet it seems like yesterday. And now I am living the fairy tale I always wanted. I understand too well how time can crawl, on all fours, as slowly as the tectonic plates at the beginning of time. Those days in Central Prison, those days and months waiting for justice, moved inch by inch, moment by moment, day by day, sometimes feeling as if time had completely stopped dead in its tracks. But the suffering, the wait, brought me a new love, so I moved on.

Together, he and I have raised "our" boys into fine young men. Both have their own families, and all are my purpose for being. Yes, both our boys live within a few miles of us. It reminds me of my days in Kentucky when I had a village to raise me. How lucky are we? How lucky are my children and grandchildren? As I hope is true for all grandparents, there is just nothing in this life like having grandkids. Because people believed in me—Jeff and Rachel, Momma, Pap-pa and Mam-ma, Aunt Penny and Uncle Scotty, Aunt Sue, my friends, and even strangers—I breathe the taste of freedom every day, and I can enjoy every moment with my own family.

In gratitude, I think back to Pap-pa and Mam-ma and how much they loved me. Like them, to me each of my grandchildren is special and loved. Our first grandchild is six years old and has the biggest heart and personality anyone could ever meet, and our princess is three years old, strong-willed, and independent. After having two of my own boys and a grandson, I was ready to make pigtails, play dress up, and spoil a little girl. She is full of her great-grandmother's sass and is a bundle of energy that will make her a force to reckon with. And then there's "M." He's seven. He's technically a step-grandson, but I understand more than anyone how important Momma and Grandma are. So, he is our own . . . because he is our own. After all, biology doesn't make someone family. He will never think there is a difference because there isn't. And finally, there's the latest, another baby grandson. We were so excited to welcome him into our universe, and I'm beaming to have another baby in our family. But more, I am overjoyed that I have so many reasons to let go of my past.

After everything I have lived through, I chose to retire early and enjoy my life . . . I mean really enjoy what life is about. It doesn't take much to make me happy. We have ten acres, where I can garden to my heart's content. I spend lots of time in the soil, burying my hands in the earth that gives life to everything. It's a special kind of fun to see the inquisitive looks on my grandkids' faces when we plant a seed. I help them understand how they are like the little plants. We all need sun and water . . . and a little love and attention . . . and soon children and plants will grow, and as my momma said, "bloom where they are planted." None of us know how life will turn out, and no matter what happens, we survive because we have faith, maybe a few angels looking out for us, and a belief that everything will work out and be okay. It may not be according to our timing, but in the end, there will be sunshine.

I can't help but question the path that started it all in August 1988 when I innocently chose to go to work at Little Rascals Day Care. I question the path that I was forced down by Officer Toppin, Agent McGinnis, the DSS, the parents, H. P. Williams, Nancy Lamb, Bill Hart, the State of North Carolina, and the many others who were complicit in this absolute miscarriage of justice. I will always believe they picked me because they thought I would give them what they wanted. I was swept up in the firestorm so that I would turn on the others. I often wonder about the children of Little Rascals Day Care. Who are they now? Where are they now? I never understood what the adults did to those children, what they did to me, what they did to all seven of us. How could they have gone down that treacherous rabbit hole that ruined so many lives? I said it then, and I still believe it: "The parents did this to the children. I didn't do anything." When it was obvious that parents lied or refused to consider the absurdity of the accusations, and many of them grabbed onto those lies and pushed them as truth, there were also people who knew the facts. People knew I was innocent. People knew we were all innocent.

The people who know me and watched what I went through often say how courageous and strong I was. I thank them, but I also know I had no choice. What was the alternative? To lie? To sign my name to a lie and live with that for the rest of my life? No. That was not an option. Probably because I am by nature an optimist, I was able to make the best of the cards I was dealt and the good things in my life, like my family. My moral and emotional foundation was fixed in the soil of Kentucky where I was raised, reinforced by Momma, Mam-ma, Pap-pa, Aunt Penny, Uncle Scotty, and Aunt Sue, all who loved me so deeply.

My outrage against the lies and the people who spread them gave me a relentless drive to refuse to sign to the lie. My courage to step out into life, to put my past behind me, to heal from the damage of Little Rascals, and to free myself once and for all from Kevin and the fear he inflicted on me, all came mostly from my precious husband. These people were my motivation to survive the charges, the prison, the hate, and the lies that surrounded me. They were my reasons to move past it all, to find and make a new life, and to heal.

This book is my chance. I still want to ask the people who hurt me and lied against me, "How do you live with yourselves now?" I pray that no one else will ever have to endure the unnecessary pain, the heartache, the tragedy, and the lie that was the Little Rascals Day Care "witch hunt" in Edenton, North Carolina.

Tragically, before we could finish Robin's story, her other brother, John Edward "Eddie" Sparks Jr., passed away on March 9, 2023, after a long, courageous battle with cancer. She reflected, "I am grateful for the time I had with him. He was one hell of a character! I'm sure he's cracking jokes in Heaven already."

Epilogue

The Other Accused

Mary Wolcott claimed she saw Goody Easty's apparition
come and pinch and choke her: and it terrified her
much . . . and she saw Easty above Mercy Lewis,
choking her and pressing upon her breast, and putting a
chain around Mercy's neck, saying she would
kill her that night if she could.
—Deposition of Mary Wolcott, Salem Witchcraft papers,
University of Virginia

Like Robin, I was always curious about my own ancestry. Unlike Robin, I have always known who my parents, brothers, and grandparents were, but beyond that, I wondered, *Who came before us?* The answers varied depending on which person I asked. My favorite family storyteller was my wonderful, bespectacled great-uncle, Bill Babbitt. To me, he was the wisest man in the world, challenging my curiosity with words like "discombobulate" and "copacetic," daring me to do my own research to learn the definitions. Most of all, I remember his adorable chuckle and stories about the Babbitt family dating back to the first settlers of New England.

In 2019, I retired from teaching, and within months, COVID-19 struck. Rather than fretting about what to do with my time, I chose the inevitable. I bought an ancestry package and started my own search. Of course, all the while, my husband was still whispering in my ears, "Write the book" during our long hours of confinement. The ancestry search seemed a healthy way to pass the hours, days, weeks, and months waiting for life to return to normal, but little did I know where it would lead. I would get profoundly bored after hours of the same task. So I gave up one thing for another to break the endless monotony, putting aside genealogy in favor of painting watercolors, cleaning closets, or riding bicycles. But then, when I met Robin in April 2022, my teacher-brain returned, and I became obsessed with research about the Little Rascals case. The more I learned, the more consumed I became. I had to escape at times, so my brain-breaks took me back to ancestry for an hour or so, and then I'd return again to the Little Rascals research.

Then something happened. Slowly, my ancestry search evolved. It was like peeling away layers of an onion, with each name marking a fresh discovery, and each generation revealing the next. My fourth great-grandmother was another Betsey—Betsey Faye—born in 1775 during the Revolutionary War. As far as I know, she was the only other Betsy in my family, ever. More layers . . . five, six, seven, eight, nine generations. What my uncle had told me was true: my ancestors had settled in Massachusetts, and there, my search narrowed even more. I found them in Essex County . . . in Ipswich, Topsfield . . . in Salem!

The thrill set my brain afire. This was the village made famous in Arthur Miller's *The Crucible*, the very play I taught to high school students for twenty-three years. I knew every character as if they were my blood relatives. One of the most notable was Rebecca Towne Nurse, known in Salem as the picture of goodness. In the play, people were astounded when she was accused of causing the unnatural deaths of the Putnam babies.

My passion for teaching this play was always a bit otherworldly, and I'm sure my students would confirm that. Several years back, on a cycling trip along the coastline of Massachusetts, my husband and I visited the historical sites in Salem. As I walked through a small graveyard dedicated to the victims, I rubbed my hands across the gravestones of those hanged as witches and felt a strange, ghostly connection. I could not wait to tell my students when I returned.

I never was able to ignore my visceral reaction to Miller's play. And then—right there in my own family search—I uncovered a name all too familiar: Mary Towne Easty, one of the many women who fell victim to the witchcraft delusion of 1692. Mary, her sisters Rebecca Towne Nurse and Sarah Towne Cloyce, along with their mother, Joanna Towne, were all accused of witchcraft. The genealogy records confirmed that Mary Towne Easty was my ninth great-grandmother.

In 1628, a small group of Puritans left England aboard ships bound for the colonies and what they hoped was religious freedom. William Towne was one of many men awarded land grants from King Charles I to establish Salem, Massachusetts. William, his wife Joanna Blessing Towne, and their six children boarded one of many ships from Norfolk bound for Massachusetts around 1635. Their daughter, Mary Towne, was born and baptized on August 24, 1634, in Norfolk, England, just months before they left for the new world. Once in Salem, William purchased his first twenty acres of land, went on to increase his landholdings, and had two more children. William died in 1673, leaving his land and holdings first to Joanna. By 1692, Joanna was dead, and the children owned the land.

In 1655, Mary Towne married Isaac Easty, a land surveyor by trade, and between them, they had nine children. According to both *Isaac of Topsfield and Some of His Descendents [sic]* and *The New York Genealogical and Biographical Registry: Registration of Pedigree*, Mary was "a most worthy woman" and respected for her "sound judgment and exalted character." She and Isaac were "members in full communion" of their church.[1] Little else is known about her. I am descended from her second child, Joseph, born in Topsfield on February 5, 1657.

The reason Mary was accused of witchcraft was because of "bad blood" between the Towne and Easty families and Thomas Putnam, the man believed to be behind much of the naming in Topsfield and Salem. The conflict first originated over the selection of a minister in Topsfield about whom Joanna Towne was very outspoken, not a good thing in Puritan New England. Then Mary's husband and her brothers, John Towne Jr. and Joseph Towne Jr., all testified against Thomas Putnam's father for harvesting timber on land that belonged collectively to the Easty and Towne families. Though Thomas Putnam and his wife publicly accused Rebecca Towne Nurse of killing the unborn Putnam children, some historical evidence suggests land grab was behind the naming. Putnam wanted their land, and if they were condemned as witches, he could challenge the will and seize their land.[2] Was it fear or vengeance at work?

Soon, Mary was named for sending her spirit on Ann Putnam. She was arrested on April 21, 1692, and appeared in court to face the charges. At her pretrial hearing before Judge Hathorne, the magistrate, the young girls who accused her of witchcraft looked on and "behaved in a troubling manner,"[3] throwing themselves back in their chairs, moaning, and copying Mary's every gesture in front of the court, reminiscent of Act III in *The Crucible*. As Hathorne asked her what she had done to torment these children, she refused to accuse herself. He demanded, "Confess if you be guilty."[4] She refused again.

She was eventually released, but days later, Mercy Lewis told the court that Mary continued to send her shape on the girls. John Putnam Jr. and Benjamin Hutchinson also accused her of flying naked into their rooms at night and forcing herself on them. Subsequently, Judge Hathorne issued a second warrant charging her with "witchcraft" on May 20, 1692. Mary was arrested again and taken to the Salem jail, where she was placed in chains and lingered through the summer. While there, her older sister, Rebecca, refused to confess, was tried, condemned, and hanged as a witch on July 19, 1692. At Rebecca's hanging, Rev. Noyes begged her and the others to confess "so that they could die with truth on their lips."[5] Even then, she refused.

At Mary's trial in September, the spectral evidence that convicted her came from the stories told by seven children, the same ones responsible for the naming of Rebecca, as well as everyone charged and all twenty convicted and hanged in Salem Village in 1692. All the accused and condemned were tried based on spectral evidence that "could not be proved."[6]

While in jail, Mary petitioned the court on behalf of the accused, who had "belied themselves" and confessed to being witches because she believed the confessions were "wrung from suspects by torture." Mary knew she could not save her own life at that point, yet she continued to refuse to give them a confession. She asked only for mercy for the others and for the hangings to stop so that "no more innocent blood would be shed."[7]

Nearly to the day, 296 years before "the slap" at Little Rascals, on September 22, 1692, Mary Easty was "packed in a cart," and the seven condemned women and one man were taken to "Gallows Hill." There "she took her last farewell of her Husband, Children and Friends . . . drawing Tears from the Eyes of almost all present. Hands and feet tied, one by one, they were turned off the ladder, and one by one, they died with the usual painful, messy contortions. And there was nothing left . . . but the corpses . . . bodies swaying at the ropes end . . . firebrands of hell hanging there" from an oak tree. Isaac Easty recognized his "duty to his martyred wife" and vowed to "do all that in his power to rescue her name from reproach and her children from disgrace."[8]

Mary Easty was one of the last of the accused witches to be condemned. Salem finally sickened of the hangings and began to question the children's inflictions and demand an end to the deaths. Many players in the delusion, like Judge Samuel Sewall, publicly confessed error and guilt, admitting that the trials had been a miscarriage of justice. On January 14, 1697, the general court ordered a day of fasting and soul-searching for the tragedy of Salem. Sadly, some magistrates who participated in the trials, convictions, and executions never admitted they were wrong and went to their graves believing the delusion.

By 1702, the court declared the trials unlawful, and in 1706,

Ann Putnam, then twenty-six years old, was one of the last to admit the delusion was a lie. She went before the church to make a "public confession . . . asking a pardon for those that hanged . . . and asking the families of Mary Towne Easty and the others to forgive her." It took twenty years and a considerable number of petitions to clear Mary's name. In 1711, Isaac Easty's "petitions were recognized and the verdict annulled." The Massachusetts Colony restored the rights and good names of those accused and granted Isaac Easty twenty pounds restitution for the loss of his beloved Mary, "acknowledging the injustice" committed against her.[9]

History will not forget them. Instead, it will forever remember them as martyrs of the first great delusion. In 1945, Massachusetts introduced a bill to clear some of the names. Then in 1957, 265 years after the hangings, Massachusetts formally apologized for the events of 1692. In 2001, the Massachusetts Legislature passed a formal resolution exonerating five women not mentioned in the legislation of 1957. One woman left off the 2001 Resolution, 22-year-old Elizabeth Johnson, was "officially exonerated" in 2022, 330 years too late.

Sadly, this was not the end of America's obsession with conspiracy and delusion. And now we ask . . .

Will it take three hundred years to vindicate the Edenton Seven?

A Call to Action
By Lew Powell

I had been only somewhat aware of the Little Rascals Day Care case until 1993 when I happened onto the first installment of Ofra Bikel's "Innocence Lost" trilogy on PBS's long-running *Frontline* series. I watched, appalled, as Bikel, an accomplished documentarian, dispassionately and meticulously exposed historic Edenton, North Carolina, as a petri dish of groundless "satanic ritual abuse" allegations about the town's most respected day care.

In the beginning, in 1989, more than ninety children at the Little Rascals Day Care Center accused twenty adults of 429 instances of sexual abuse over a three-year period. It may have all begun with one parent's complaint about the punishment given to her child. Among the alleged perpetrators? The sheriff and mayor. But prosecutors would charge only Robin Byrum, Darlene Harris, Elizabeth "Betsy" Kelly, Robert "Bob" Kelly, Willard Scott Privott, Shelley Stone, and Dawn Wilson—the Edenton Seven.

Along with charges of sodomy and beatings, allegations also included a baby killed with a handgun, a child being hung upside down from a tree and being set on fire, and countless other fantastic incidents involving spaceships, hot-air balloons, pirate ships, and trained sharks.

By the time prosecutors dropped the last charges almost a decade later in 1997, Little Rascals had become North Carolina's longest and most costly criminal trial. Prosecutors kept defendants jailed in hopes that at least one would turn against their supposed co-conspirators. Remarkably, none did. Another shameful record: five defendants had to wait longer to face their accusers in court than anyone else in North Carolina history.

Between 1991 and 1997, Bikel produced four extraordinary episodes on the case for *Frontline.* While the spotlight of the national TV show did not deter prosecutors, it exposed their tactics and fostered nationwide skepticism and dismay.

With each passing year, the absurdity of the Little Rascals charges has become more obvious. The North Carolina Court of Appeals resoundingly overturned the convictions of Bob Kelly and Dawn Wilson, but only after they had served, respectively, six and three years in prison. No admission of error has ever come from prosecutors, police, interviewers, or parents. When Nancy Lamb bitterly dropped the last charges against Bob Kelly—timed to compete for news media attention with an oncoming hurricane—she claimed it was only to protect the child witnesses from another trial.

When the initial episode of "Innocence Lost" aired, I was approaching the middle of my thirty-four years as a journalist at the *Charlotte Observer.* I wasn't then—and never would be—among the newsroom's acclaimed investigative reporters. It wasn't until I left the paper in 2009 that my interest in prying loose some belated justice for the Edenton Seven took shape, however modestly.

First, my former colleague Steve Johnston created the website littlerascalsdaycarecase.org, then later a Facebook page. Attention came slowly. But allies turned up. The Duke Law School library agreed to house the only surviving transcript from Bob Kelly's trial. The law school hosted a panel on the Little Rascals case that included Bob Kelly and his brilliant appellate lawyer, Mark Montgomery. Allen Frances, professor emeritus of psychiatry at Duke Medical School and head of the DSM-IV task force, bravely acknowledged his failure to push hard enough against the "satanic ritual abuse" contingent.

The *News & Observer* published my column on the case. I took wildly disproportionate pleasure in obtaining from the DMV an EDENTON Seven license plate and from the Edenton Historical Society a publicly displayed commemorative brick naming the defendants.

Among my many failures: Former District Attorney H. P. Williams hung up on me rather than reconsider Little Rascals. Half a dozen editors of professional journals refused to retract their articles supporting claims of "satanic ritual abuse." Ten former child witnesses ignored my letters. The State of North Carolina turned down my request for a historical marker at the former day care center. Governors Pat McCrory and Bev Perdue did not respond to my appeals for the exoneration of the defendants. The state bar association rejected a continuing legal education course on Little Rascals.

More positively, littlerascalsdaycarecase.org was the first to make available Bikel's epic "Innocence Lost," which had been shockingly absent from the *Frontline* site because of a failure to renew rights. It was also the first to digitize "Justice Abused: A 1980s Witch Hunt," a 1980s series in the Memphis *Commercial Appeal* that first linked the "satanic ritual abuse" cases springing up across the country.

But few moments gave me such excitement as when I heard from Betsy Hester, a retired IB English teacher with a deep knowledge of Arthur Miller's *The Crucible*, an account of the Salem witch trials that foreshadowed Little Rascals, the McMartin Preschool, and so many other prosecutions of the "satanic ritual abuse" day care panic of the 1980s and early '90s. Betsy Hester's chance encounter with the youngest defendant, by now a grandmother, inspired her to recount Robin Byrum's excruciating, nightmarish, but ultimately uplifting journey.

Betsy quickly became an invaluable ally in seeking renewed attention for the plight of the Edenton Seven. This book takes a bold step toward the full public exoneration of the true victims of the Little Rascals prosecution—most ambitiously, a "Statement of Innocence from the State of North Carolina."

We invite you to visit the website and view the *Frontline* documentary series. And, please, help us in our efforts by writing to the governor and the attorney general of North Carolina, urging them to exonerate the Edenton Seven.

ACKNOWLEDGMENTS

This book began as an act of love but quickly became a crusade for justice. In the hundreds of hours of research, interviews, reading, and discovery, I encountered extraordinary courage, profound cowardice, unimpeachable integrity, and unbelievable deceit. I saw justice at work and revenge at play. This very book exists today because of what the Edenton Seven endured. I wish it didn't. However, I am filled with gratitude and deep respect for each of the defendants and for their attorneys, who fought so hard to see that justice was served. What the Edenton Seven lived through is beyond what I personally could imagine having to endure.

This project could only have happened with Robin Couto. When I asked her "to just write," we were unsure where this would take us, but she was ready, and so was I. She put pen to paper, and as her story grew, so did my own. Robin, you personify courage, perseverance, patience, and love. You came out on the other side of this tragedy with a smile and heart as big as any I have ever witnessed. I am in awe of you now and always.

Thank you, Betsy Kelly and Bob Kelly. I know how difficult it was to revisit this case, and like Robin, it took great courage to bring the past back so that I could write this book. Betsy, you said you would not do this for anyone else in the world but Robin. And thank you, Nancy Smith, the sister-protector whose tenacity, courage, and southern charm won my heart. I hope I have done it justice.

Thank you, Lew Powell. Your contribution to this book is endless. Because of you, we all know the truth. You saw the injustice from the beginning and made certain that many thousands of pages of documents are safely stored at Duke Law Library. It was all there, and all because of you. You have dedicated more than three decades to keeping the story of the Edenton Seven alive in hopes of getting the exoneration they all deserve.

Thank you, Peter Ornstein. I am beyond grateful that you took a risk on me, a never-before published author. Over the months, you became my mentor, sharing your knowledge and resources to help me understand and use the research on how children's memories are formed and how those memories are potentially impacted by mother-child conversations. Even more, you willingly gave up precious time out of your recent, well-earned retirement to encourage me, to read the manuscript, to advise me on my sources, and finally, to write the Foreword.

Thank you to my precious family. To my husband, Joe, the love of my life and the most brilliant attorney I have ever known. You encouraged and guided me through the entire project, beginning with pushing me for thirty-four years to "write this book." You suffered through my incessant questions, ceaseless reading aloud, and angry outbursts at the injustice. Your incredible legal mind was my greatest resource. I would not have written this were it not for you. And to my precious children. To Maggie for seeing "the box!" And to Bryan for the title. And to Joey and Kennan for putting up with my endless chatter about my book. Forgive my prolonged absences. To Bryson and Charlie, Nana is back now. I love you all to infinity.

Thank you to my sweet and cherished friend and proofreader, Sue Kammers, who supported my effort early on, willingly reading, re-reading, re-re-reading many versions of this manuscript. You guarded the story to keep from spoiling it for others, and you listened to my rantings and shared in my horror and rage as I uncovered more and more. I love you, Sue. And thank you for telling me, "It is so good!" Because without that, I might have given up months ago.

Thank you, Jeff Miller, Mike Spivey, and the many defense attorneys who fought hard for the truth and to see justice served. I know this case took a tremendous toll on each of you in ways we do not fully understand, but you never quit. You believed in the innocence of the Edenton Seven. Thank you for being willing to revisit this case so I could write this book.

Thank you to my editor, Betsy Thorpe, who put the draft into motion, and to Kathy Brown, my copyeditor, who rocks! She literally sifted through the manuscript letter by letter, word by word, sentence by sentence. You were both more than an investment in my manuscript. You were the eyes I needed to find the flaws I could no longer see. And to Diana Wade, my graphic designer, and my friend Jim Adams, who added his artwork to the cover, and who both made it look like a real book.

Finally, thank you to Robin's village: her mother, Lou, and her Aunt Penny, Uncle Scotty, Aunt Sue, Pap-pa, and Mam-ma. They are the remarkable people who devoted their lives to supporting her and raising Robin to be the strong, resilient, optimistic, and grateful person I have come to know and love.

Rest in peace, Lou Boles. You raised an incredible daughter.

Notes

A striking parallel exists between the Little Rascals case and the Salem witch trials of 1692, and ironically, researchers wrote extensively about that parallel in most of the works I referenced. The information about the Little Rascals case, the charges against the Edenton Seven, and the moral panic and hysteria of this case are taken directly from hundreds of trial artifacts—court documents, letters, summaries of therapy and interview sessions—and more than 20,000 pages of trial transcripts, as well as outside research on the malleability and suggestibility of children's memories, and the reliability of their testimony. It also comes from research suggesting there was a failure of the justice system to seek the truth and to see that the defendants received a fair trial. Last—and most importantly—it came from personal conversations and interviews with individuals directly involved in the Little Rascals Day Care case, both on the side of the defense and the side of the prosecution, as well as some of the children whose names are withheld to protect them as much as is possible since this was a very public trial and all the documents from this case are public record.

Chapters with no sources referenced were narratives created from the conversations, notes, and journaling by Robin.

All the conversations are reconstructed as closely as possible, but for clarity and ease of reading, the conversations are sometimes combined, and all sources are listed in the order in which they appear in each chapter.

Chapter 4: Strange Behaviors and Invisible Evidence

1. Joseph Klaits, *Servants of Satan* (Bloomington: Indiana Univ. Press, 1985), 51-52.

2. Klaits, *Servants*, 52.

3. Tom Peete Cross, "Witchcraft in North Carolina," Studies in Philology. Vol. XVI, no. 3 (July 1919), 217–287, https://www.jstor.org/stable/pdf/23297991.pdf.

4. Cross, "Witchcraft in North Carolina," 217–287.

5. B. L. Robinson, "The Doctors John Brickell," *Rhodora*, Vol. 18, no. 215 (Nov. 1916), 7, https://www.jstor.org/stable/pdf/23297991.pdf.

6. Robinson, "The Doctors," 7.

7. Elizabeth Loftus, PhD, and Katherine Ketcham, *The Myth of Repressed Memory: False Memories and Allegations of Sexual Abuse* (New York: St. Martin's Griffin, 1994), 155.

8. Klaits, *Servants of Satan*, 121.

9. Marilynne Roach, *Six Women of Salem, The Untold Story of the Accused and Their Accusers in the Salem Witch Trials* (New York: Hachette Books, 2013), 89.

10. Roach, *Six Women of Salem*, 93, 94.

11. Marion L. Starkey, *The Devil in Massachusetts, A Modern Enquiry into the Salem Witch Trials* (New York: Anchor Books, 1949), 42–45.

12. Starkey, *The Devil in Massachusetts*, 42–45.

13. Roach, *Six Women of Salem*, 101–105.

14. Starkey, *The Devil in Massachusetts*, 48.

15. Richard Gardner, MD, *Sex Abuse Hysteria. Salem Witch Trials Revisited* (Cresskill: Creative Therapeutics, 1991), Intro.

Chapter 5: A Quiet Tranquility

1. Ofra Bikel, *Frontline*, "Innocence Lost." Originally aired on PBS 1991–1996. Accessed on YouTube, April 2022.

Chapter 7: The Slap

1. State of North Carolina v. Robert Fulton Kelly Jr., Defendant-Appellant Brief. Appendix 1, "Statement of Facts," 1992, North Carolina Court of Appeals. No. 933SC676.

2. Betsy Kelly, interview with author, 2023.

3. Robin Couto, interview and correspondence with author, 2022–2023.

4. *State v. Kelly*, Defendant-Appellant Brief (NC Court of Appeals April 1995), 3.

5. Lisa Scheer and Edward Cone, "*The DEMONS of Edenton*," https://www.ncdcr.gov/blog/2015/04/14/hysteria-over-day-care-in-edenton 2016.

6. Betsy Kelly, interview with author, 2023.

7. *State v. Kelly*, Defendant-Appellant Brief, 6.

8. Ofra Bikel, *Frontline*, "Innocence Lost."

9. Bikel, "Innocence Lost."

10. Bikel, "Innocence Lost."

11. Bikel, "Innocence Lost."

12. *State v. Kelly*, Defendant-Appellant Brief, 3–6.

13. *State v. Kelly*, "July 22, 1991 Transcripts," Little Rascals Daycare Papers, State v. Kelly Trial Transcripts, J. Michael Goodson Law Library, Duke School of Law, volumes 11–97, vol. 56.

14. *State v. Kelly*. Defendant-Appellant Brief, 5–6.

15. *State v. Kelly*, Parent Journals, Box 14.

16. *State v. Kelly*, Parent Journals, Box 14

17. *State v. Kelly*, July 22, 1991, Transcripts, vol. 14.

18. *State v. Kelly*, Defendant-Appellant Brief, Excerpt w/Toppin, 8–17.

Chapter 8: Collective Hysteria

1. Ofra Bikel, "Innocence Lost," accessed April 2022.

2. Lisa Scheer and Edward Cone, "*The DEMONS of Edenton*," http://www.ncdcr.gov/blog/2015/04/14/hysteria-over-day-care-in-

edenton 2016.

3. Bikel, "Innocence Lost."

4. *State v. Byrum*, NC General Court of Justice. *State of NC v. Robin Byrum*, Superior Court Division, April 20, 1990. Lynne Layton's testimony at Robin's first bond hearing, 39–40.

5. Stephen J. Ceci and Maggie Bruck, *Jeopardy in the Courtroom* (Washington, DC: American Psychological Association, 1995), 120, 159, 240.

Chapter 9: Accused

1. *State v. Kelly*, Defendant-Appellant Brief.

2. *State v. Kelly*, "Bateman Testimony," Little Rascals Daycare Papers, J. Michael Goodson Law Library, Duke School of Law, vol. 13.

3. *State v. Kelly*, "Ambrose Testimony," vol. 13.

4. *State v. Kelly*, "Bateman Testimony," vol. 31.

5. *State v. Kelly*, Defendant-Appellant Brief.

6. *State v. Kelly*, Defendant-Appellant Brief.

7. *State v. Kelly*, Defendant-Appellant Brief.

Chapter 11: Conspiracy and Panic

1. Starkey, *The Devil in Massachusetts*, 64–65.

2. Starkey, *The Devil in Massachusetts*, 53.

3. Nathan Dorn, "Sir Matthew Hale and Evidence of Witchcraft," *Library of Congress Blogs*, October 30, 2021, https://blogs.loc.gov/law/2021/10/sir-matthew-hale-and-evidence-of-witchcraft/.

4. Alan Yuhas, "It's Time to Revisit the Satanic Panic," *The New York Times*, March 31, 2021, https://www.nytimes.com/2021/03/31/us/satanic-panic.html.

5. *State v. Kelly*, Defendant-Appellant Brief.

6. Yuhas, "It's Time to Revisit the Satanic Panic."

7. Gretchen Passantino, "Innocence Lost in Landmark Child Abuse Case," Cornerstone Magazine, Cultwatch, 1995, 2.

8. Loftus and Ketcham, *The Myth of Repressed Memory*, 56.

9. Bikel, "Innocence Lost."

10. Bikel, "Innocence Lost."

11. Bikel, "Innocence Lost."

12. Yuhas, "It's Time to Revisit the Satanic Panic."

13. Thomas Russell Freure, "A Modern American Conservative: How Ronald Reagan Legitimized the Religious Right and Helped Shape the American Zeitgeist" (thesis, University of Waterloo, 2021), https://uwspace.uwaterloo.ca/bitstream/handle/10012/16879/Freure_Russell.pdf.

14. Richard Beck, *We Believe the Children: A Moral Panic* in the 1990s (New York: Public Affairs, 2015), 64.

15. Beck, *We Believe the Children*, 24.

16. Michelle Smith and Lawrence Pazder, *Michelle Remembers* (New York: Pocket Books, 1980), 109, 120, 138, 158.

17. Beck, *We Believe the Children*, 64.

18. Loftus and Ketcham, *The Myth of Repressed Memory*, 53.

19. Ethan Watters, "The Forgotten Lessons of the Recovered Memory Movement," *The New York Times*, Sept. 22, 2022, https://www.nytimes.com/2022/09/27/opinion/recovered-memory-therapy-mental-health.html.

20. Watters, "Forgotten Lessons."

21. Jeffrey L. Miller and W. Michael Spivey, "Through the Looking Glass: Unraveling Issues in Child Custody Cases," presentation to the North Carolina Bar Association Family Law Section, CLE Seminar, November 12–14, 1992.

22. Miller and Spivey, "Through the Looking Glass."

23. Martyn Kendrick, *The Anatomy of a Nightmare. The Failure of Society in Dealing with Child Sexual Abuse* (Toronto: Macmillan, 1988), 1–27, 35.

24. Coleman and Clancy, *Has A Child Been Molested?*, 13, 14.

25. Coleman and Clancy, *Has A Child Been Molested?*, 13, 14.

26. Roland Summit, "*The Child Sexual Abuse Accommodation*

Syndrome," Child Abuse and Neglect, 1983, https://capc.sccgov.org/
sites/g/files/exjcpb1061/files/document/Child%20Sexual%20
Abuse%20Accommodation%20Syndrome%20copy.pdf.

27. Beck, *We Believe the Children*, 58–59.

28. Coleman and Clancy, *Has A Child Been Molested?*, 13, 14.

29. Jerri Williams and Kenneth Lanning, "Satanic Ritual Abuse,
    Confirmation Bias," May 8, 2019, in *Retired FBI Case
    File Review*, podcast, Episode 165, 1:40:54,
    https://podcasts.apple.com/gb/podcast/ken-lan-
    ning-satanic-ritual-child-abuse-confirmation-bias/
    id1082012464?i=1000437565026.

30. Williams, *Retired FBI*.

31. Williams, *Retired FBI*.

32. Williams, *Retired FBI*.

33. Kenneth V. Lanning, *Love, Bombs, and Molesters: An FBI Agent's
    Journey* (self-published by Lanning, 2018), 90.

34. Beck, *We Believe the Children*, 35–37.

35. Beck, *We Believe the Children*, 35–36.

36. Mary DeYoung, "The Devil Goes to Day Care: McMartin and
    the Making of a Moral Panic," June 4, 2004, *Journal of American
    Culture*, vol. 20, issue 1, https://onlinelibrary.wiley.com/doi/
    abs/10.1111/j.1542-734X.1997.00019.x

37. Beck, *We Believe the Children*, 44–45.

38. Coleman and Clancy, *Has A Child Been Molested?*, 20, 21, 39.

38. Coleman and Clancy, *Has A Child Been Molested?*, 62–63.

40. Coleman and Clancy, *Has A Child Been Molested?*, 20.

41. Coleman and Clancy, *Has A Child Been Molested?*, 21, 16.

42. Greg Henderson, "Supreme Court Allows Suit by Target of
    McMartin Preschool Probe," UPI Archives, November 30, 1992,
    https://www.upi.com/Archives/1992/11/30/Supreme-Court-allows-
    suit-by-target-of-McMartin-Preschool-probe/6498723099600/.

Chapter 12: Constructed Memories

1. Maria S. Zaragoza, Robert F. Belli, and Kristie E. Payment, "Misinformation Effects and the Suggestibility of Eyewitness Memory," in *Do Justice and Let the Sky Fall: Elizabeth Loftus and Her Contributions to Science, Law, and Academic Freedom*, ed. Maryanne Garry and Harlene Hayne (London: Routledge, 2007), 47–48.

2. Kaitlin Luna, "How Memory Can Be Manipulated, with Elizabeth Loftus, PhD," October 2019, in *Speaking of Psychology: How Memory Can Be Manipulated*, podcast of the American Psychological Association, Episode 91, https://www.apa.org/news/podcasts/speaking-of-psychology/ memory-manipulated.

3. Loftus and Ketcham, *The Myth of Repressed Memory*, 104.

4. David E. Mapes, PhD, *Child Eyewitness Testimony in Sexual Abuse Investigations* (Hoboken: John Wiley & Sons, 2003), 11.

5. Judith K. Adams, PhD, "Investigation and Interviews in Cases of Child Sexual [Abuse]: A Look at the Scientific Evidence," *Institute for Psychological Theories*, vol. 8, 1996, http://www.ipt-forensics. com/journal/volume8/j8_3_1.htm.

6. Mapes, *Child Eyewitness Testimony*, 13.

7. Loftus and Ketcham, *The Myth of Repressed Memory*, 3, 56, 40, 38.

8. Loftus and Ketcham, *The Myth of Repressed Memory*, 38–39.

9. Williams, *Retired FBI Case File Review* podcast with Kenneth Lanning.

10. Lanning, *Love, Bombs, and Molesters*, 63.

11. Miller and Spivey, "Through the Looking Glass," 2–11.

12. Miller and Spivey, "Through the Looking Glass," 2–11.

13. *State v. Kelly*, vol. 14, 3,413–3,415.

14. *State v. Kelly*, Vol. 14, 3,413–3,415.

15. Miller and Spivey, "Through the Looking Glass."

16. Ceci and Bruck, *Jeopardy in the Courtroom*, 240.

17. Peter A. Ornstein and Taylor E. Thomas, "A Constructed Perspective on Mother-Child Conversations, and Children's Eyewitness Memory," *Journal of Applied Research in Memory and Cognition*, American Psychological Association, vol. 11, no. 3, 2022.

18. Anonymous parent interview with author, May 2023.

19. Interview with anonymous child #3, March 2023.

20. Scheer and Cone, "DEMONS."

21. Ceci and Bruck, *Jeopardy in the Courtoom*, 240.

Chapter 13: *The State v. Byrum*

1. Jeffrey Miller, JD, "Letters and Court Documents," 1990.

2. Miller, "Letters," 1990.

3. Miller, "Letters," 1990.

4. *State v. Byrum*, NC General Court of Justice. *State of NC v. Robin Byrum*, Superior Court Division, "Motion to Joinder," 1990.

5. Miller, "Letters," 1990.

6. Miller, "Letters and Court Documents."

7. Miller, "Letters and Court Documents."

8. *State v. ALL*, NC General Court of Justice. *State of NC v Robin Byrum*, Superior Court Division, "Motion to Joinder," 1990.

9. Miller, "Letters and Court Documents."

10. *State v. Kelly*, Defendant-Appellant Brief.

Chapter 17: The Box of Evidence

1. Paul Roberts and Lawrence Stratton, *The Tyranny of Good Intentions*. (New York: Three Rivers Press, 2000), 190–91.

2. Roberts and Stratton, *The Tyranny of Good Intentions*, 190.

3. *State v. Kelly*, Defendant-Appellant Brief.

4. Mark Montgomery, JD, interview with the author through correspondence, 2022.

5. *State v. Kelly*, Defendant-Appellant Brief.

6. Perry Parks and Anne Saita, "Children Getting Little Rascals Payments: Injuries and Treatment Costs Will Help Determine Payments," *The Virginian-Pilot*, B1, August 6, 1994.

7. Parks and Saita, "Children Getting Little Rascals Payments."

8. *State v. Kelly*, Defendant-Appellant Brief.

9. *State v. Wilson*, 456 S.E.2nd 870 (1995), 118 N.C. App. 616, *State of North Carolina v. Kathryn Dawn Wilson*. No. 931SC1277. Court of Appeals of North Carolina, May 2, 1995.

10. *State v. Kelly*, Defendant-Appellant Brief.

11. Mark Montgomery, email message to the author, 2022.

12. *State v. Kelly*, Little Rascals Daycare Case. Robertson, Betty, Therapy Session Notes with Children named in Indictments, J. Michael Goodson Law Library, Duke University School of Law, Box 14.

13. *State v. Kelly*, Robertson Therapy Notes, Box 14.

14. *State v. Kelly*, Robertson Therapy Notes, Box 14.

15. Roberts and Stratton, *The Tyranny of Good Intentions*, 190.

Chapter 18: The Court of Public Opinion

1. Mark Montgomery, email to the author.

2. Roberts and Stratton, *Tyranny*, 190–91.

3. Bikel, "Innocence Lost."

4. Charlie Rose, "Edenton Abuse Scandal: Innocence Lost," *Charlie Rose: The Power of Questions*, July 20,1993, https://charlierose.com/videos/25031.

5. Rose, "Edenton Abuse Scandal."

6. Bikel, "Innocence Lost."

7. Rose, "Edenton Abuse Scandal."

8. Rose, "Edenton Abuse Scandal."

9. Associated Press, "FATHER: TODDLER SCREAMS WHEN HIS CLOTHES ARE REMOVED," *Greensboro News & Record*, Sept. 5, 1991, https://greensboro.com/father-toddler-screamed-

when-his-clothes-were-removed/Article
_08f7fb19-228a-5912-a023-794b9f505420.html.

10. Associated Press, "Ex-Day-Care Worker Says She Was Intimidated," *Greensboro News & Record*, Feb. 3, 1992, http://greensboro.com/ex-day-care-worker-says-she-was-intimidated/article_6e0ea67f-e448-5d82-bd53–4c7746df97b6.html.

11. Associated Press, "Ex-Day-Care Worker."

12. Sean Bailey, "Rascals Prosecutor Romance Questioned," *News & Observer*, Dec.19, 1991.

13. Lorraine Ahearn, "Little Rascals Judge Says Trial Too Long," *Greensboro News & Record*, March 31, 1992, https://greensboro.com/little-rascals-judge-says-trial-too-long/article_87ddb932-dd2a-585f-b2c0-201e4b342830.html.

14. Ahearn, "Little Rascals Judge."

15. Megan Rosenfeld, "The Small Town with a Puzzle Too Big to Resolve," *The Washington Post*, May 10, 1991, https://www.washingtonpost.com/archive/lifestyle/1991/05/10/the-small-town-with-a-puzzle-too-big-to-solve/55738a22-3712-404b-9648-d9aa0ea2dbc3/.

16. Ronald Smothers, "Big Molestation Trial Nears Its Close," *The New York Times*, March 23, 1992, https://www.nytimes.com/1992/03/23/us/big-molestation-trial-nears-its-close.html.

17. Ronald Smothers, "Closing Arguments in Child-Abuse Trial," *The New York Times*, March 24, 1992, https://timesmachine.nytimes.com/timesmachine/1992/03/24/112792.html.

18. Rose, "Edenton Abuse Scandal."

19. Lew Powell, "Little Rascals Day Care Case" (website), https://www.littlerascalsdaycarecase.org/, accessed May 2022.

20. Duke Law Innocence Project, "The Little Rascals Case Unfolded," February 28, 2019. Accessed on YouTube July 2022, https://www.youtube.com/watch?v=uOdZ9TXcdaE.

21. Powell, "Little Rascals Day Care Case."

22. David Loomis, "Witch Hunts: How Media Have Mishandled

Ritual Child-Sex-Abuse Scandals, (thesis, UNC–Chapel Hill, 1997), 1, 6, 7, 9, 38, 37, 21, 22.

23. Loomis, "Witch Hunts."

24. Loomis, "Witch Hunts."

25. Associated Press, "A Little Rascals Speaks Out 7 Years of Waiting
in Child Sex Abuse Case is Long Enough," *Virginian-Pilot*,
Sept. 24, 1996, https://scholar.lib.vt.edu/VA-news/VA-Pilot/issues/1996/vp960924/09240270.htm.

26. Associated Press, "A Little Rascals Speaks Out."

27. Rose, "Edenton Abuse Scandal."

Chapter 19: Trial by Ambush

1. *State v. Kelly*, Court of Appeals of North Carolina.

2. Roland Summit, "The Child Sexual Abuse Accommodation Syndrome," *Child Abuse and Neglect*, 1983, https://capc.sccgov.org/sites/g/files/exjcpb1061/files/document/Child%20Sexual%20Abuse%20Accommodation%20Syndrome%20copy.pdf.

3. Adams, "Investigations and Interviews."

4. Rose, "Edenton Abuse Scandal."

5. Miller, "Letters and Court Documents," Shopper.

6. Moisy Shopper, MD, "What I Learned from the Edenton 'Little Rascals' Sex Abuse Trial, *Psychoanalytic Inquiry*, 29:6, (Nov. 10, 2009): 513–527, https://doi.org/10.1080/07351690903014031.

7. Shopper, "What I Learned from the Edenton Trial."

8. Shopper, "What I Learned from the Edenton Trial."

9. Shopper, "What I Learned from the Edenton Trial."

10. Shopper, "What I Learned from the Edenton Trial."

11. Shopper, "What I Learned from the Edenton Trial."

12. Shopper, "What I Learned from the Edenton Trial."

13. Shopper, "What I Learned from the Edenton Trial."

14. William Kenner, MD, "Letter to the Editor," *The Journal of the American Academy of Child and Adolescent Psychiatry*, September 1988.

15. Kenner, "Letter to the Editor."

16. Kenner, "Letter to the Editor."

17. Kenner, "Letter to the Editor."

18. Kenner, "Letter to the Editor."

19. Klaits, *Servants of Satan*, 25.

20. Duke Law Innocence Project, "The Little Rascals Case Unfolded."

21. Anna Twiddy, "The Little Rascals Case: A Case for Regulating Children's Testimony," *The People, Ideas, and Things Journal*, Cycle 7, 2016,https://pitjournal.unc.edu/2023/01/05/the-little-rascals-case-a-case-for-regulating-childrens-testimony/.

22. Shopper, What I learned from the Edenton Trial.

23. Shopper, What I learned from the Edenton Trial.

Chapter 21: Twenty-One Boxes

1. *State v. Robin Byrum*, "MEMORANDUM IN SUPPORT OF DISCLOSURE OF INFORMATION SUBJECT TO QUALIFIED PRIVILEGE," North Carolina Chowan County. *State of North Carolina v. Robin Byrum*, 90 CRSA 81-93, 141. 12/17/1990. p. 2, pp. 6–9.

2. *State v. Byrum*, "MEMORANDUM IN SUPPORT OF DISCLOSURE."

3. *State v. Kelly*, Box 14, Children's Statements and Honorable Mention.

Chapter 22: "I Don't Remember"

1. Powell, "Little Rascals Daycare Case."

2. Child #1 (anonymous), interview and correspondence with author, 2023.

3. Child #2 (anonymous), interview and correspondence with author, 2022/2023.

4. Child #2, interview.

5. Child #3, author interview with parents (anonymous), May 2023.

6. Child #3, author interview with parents (anonymous).

7. Gabrielle Principe and Erica Schindewolf, "Natural Conversations as a Source of False Memories in Children: Implications for the Testimony of Young Witnesses," *Developmental Review*, Elsevier, vol. 32, issue 3, Sept. 2012, https://www.sciencedirect.com/science/article/abs/pii/S027322971200024X?via%3Dihub

8. Principe and Schindewolf, "Natural Conversations."

9. *State v. Kelly*, Archives, Box 14, Documents.

10. *State v. Kelly*, Trial Transcripts, vol. 14.

11. Adams, "Investigation and Interviews," 2.

12. Mason Peters, "Little Rascals Pain Reaches Prosecutor, Sex-Abuse Case Spurs Change in System," The *Virginian-Pilot*, Jan. 22, 1995, https://scholar.lib.vt.edu/VA-news/VA-Pilot/issues/1995/vp950122/01230191.htm.

13. Principe and Schindewolf, "Natural Conversations."

14. *State v. Kelly*, Archives, Box 14, Parent Journal Transcript—Stever.

15. *State v. Kelly*, Archives, Box 14, Parent Journal Transcript—Bean.

16. *State v. Kelly*, Parent Journal Transcript—Bean.

17. *State v. Kelly*, Parent Journal Transcript—Bean.

18. *State v. Kelly*, Court of Appeals of NC, Justice Arnold, NC Court of Appeals Ruling.

19. *State v. Kelly*, Parent Journal Transcript—Bean.

20. *State v. Kelly*, Parent Journal Transcript—Bean.

21. *State v. Kelly*, Parent Journal Transcript—Bean.

22. *State v. Kelly*, Archives, Box 14, Mother's Journal Transcript (names withheld to protect the children).

23. *State v. Kelly*, Parent Journal Transcript.

24. *State v. Kelly*, Parent Journal Transcript.

25. *State v. Kelly*, "Trial Transcripts," vol. 42.

26. Bikel, "Innocence Lost."

27. Child #3, author interview with parents (anonymous).

Chapter 23: Christopher Bean for the Prosecution

1. Roberts and Stratton, *The Tyranny*, 145–46.
2. *State v. Kelly*, Court of Appeals of North Carolina, NC Rule of Evidence 403.
3. *State v. Kelly*, Archives, vol. 43.
4. *State v. Kelly*, Court of Appeals of North Carolina, Justice Arnold, NC Court of Appeals Ruling.

Chapter 24: The Medical Experts

1. Desmond K. Runyan, MD, PhD, interview with the author via email, February 25, 2023.
2. Runyan, interview with author.
3. Runyan, interview with author.
4. Runyan, interview with author.
5. Runyan, interview with author.
6. Runyan, interview with author.
7. *State v. Kelly*, Archives, vol. 58, Runyan testimony.
8. *State v. Kelly*, Archives, vol. 58, Runyan.
9. Runyan, interview with the author, March 1, 2023.
10. *State v. Kelly*, vol. 58, Jean Smith testimony.
11. *State v. Kelly*, Archives, Box 6.
12. Runyan, interview with author, March 1, 2023.
13. Runyan, interview with author, March 1, 2023.
14. *State v. Kelly*, Archives, vol. 57, Smith.
15. *State v. Kelly*, Archives, vol. 58, Runyan.
16. *State v. Kelly*, Archives, vol. 58, Smith.
17. *State v. Kelly*, Archives, vol. 58, Smith.
18. *State v. Kelly*, Archives, vol. 58, Smith.
19. *State v. Kelly*, Archives, vol. 58, Smith.
20. *State v. Kelly*, Archives, vol. 58, Smith.
21. *State v. Kelly*, Archives, vol. 58, Smith.
22. *State v. Kelly*, Archives, vol. 58, Smith.

23. Coleman and Clancy, *Has A Child Been Molested?*, 65.

24. *State v. Kelly*, Archives, vol. 58, Doren Fredrickson testimony.

25. *State v. Kelly*, Archives, vol. 57, Smith.

26. *State v. Kelly*, Archives, vol. 58, Fredrickson.

27. *State v. Kelly*, Archives, vol. 58, Runyan.

28. *State v. Kelly*, Archives, vol. 58, Fredrickson.

29. *State v. Kelly*, Archives, vol. 58, Fredrickson.

30. *State v. Kelly*, Archives, vol. 58, Smith.

31. *State v. Kelly*, Archives, vol. 58, Smith.

32. *State v. Kelly*, Archives, vol. 58, Fredrickson.

33. *State v. Kelly*, Archives, vol. 58, Fredrickson.

34. *State v. Kelly*, Archives, vol. 58, Runyan.

35. *State v. Kelly*, Archives, vol. 58, Runyan.

36. *State v. Kelly*, Archives, vol. 58, Runyan.

37. *State v. Kelly*, Archives, vol. 58, Runyan.

38. *State v. Kelly*, Archives, vol. 58, Runyan.

39. *State v. Kelly*, Archives, vol. 58, Runyan.

40. *State v. Kelly*, Archives, vol. 58, Runyan.

41. *State v. Kelly*, Archives, vol. 58, Runyan.

42. *State v. Kelly*, Archives, vol. 58, Runyan.

Chapter 25: The Dolls!

1. *State v. Kelly*, Archives, vol. 40, Janet Hadler testimony.

2. *State v. Kelly*, Archives, vol. 40, Hadler.

3. *State v. Kelly*, Archives, vol. 40, Hadler.

4. *State v. Kelly*, Archives, vol. 40, Hadler.

5. *State v. Kelly*, Archives, vol. 40, Hadler.

6. *State v. Kelly*, Archives, vol. 40, Hadler.

7. *State v. Kelly*, Archives, vol. 40, Hadler.

8. *State v. Kelly*, Archives, vol. 40, Hadler.

9. *State v. Kelly*, Archives, vol. 40, Hadler.

10. *State v. Kelly*, Archives, vol. 40, Hadler.

11. *State v. Kelly*, Archives, vol. 58, Runyan.

12. *State v. Kelly*, Archives, Box 21.

13. *State v. Kelly*, Archives, vol. 58, Runyan.

14. *State v. Kelly*, Archives, vol. 58, Runyan.

15. *State v. Kelly*, Archives, Box 2.

16. *State v. Kelly*, Archives, Box 21.

17. *State v. Kelly*, Archives, Box 21.

18. *State v. Kelly*, Archives, vol. 40, Hadler.

Chapter 26: The State Rests

1. *State v. Kelly*, Archives, vol. 63, Thomas Irons testimony.

2. *State v. Kelly*, Archives, vol. 63, Irons.

3. *State v. Kelly*, Archives, vol. 63, Irons.

4. *State v. Kelly*, Archives, vol. 63, Robert Brayden testimony.

5. *State v. Kelly*, Archives, vol. 63, Brayden.

6. *State v. Kelly*, Archives, vol. 63, Brayden.

7. *State v. Kelly*, Archives, vol. 63, Brayden.

8. *State v. Kelly*, Archives, vol. 63, Brayden.

9. *State v. Kelly*, Archives, vol. 63, Brayden.

10. *State v. Kelly*, Archives, vol. 63, Brayden.

11. *State v. Kelly*, Archives, vol. 63, Brayden.

12. *State v. Kelly*, Archives, vol. 63, Brayden.

13. *State v. Kelly*, Archives, vol. 63, Brayden.

14. *State v. Kelly*, Archives, vol. 63, Brayden.

15. *State v. Kelly*, Archives, vol. 63, Brayden.

16. *State v. Kelly*, Archives, vol. 63, Leibert Devine testimony.

17. *State v. Kelly*, Archives, vol. 63, Devine.

18. *State v. Kelly*, Archives, vol. 63, Robert E. Lane testimony.

Chapter 27: A Necessary Conversation

1. Desmond Runyan, MD, PhD, "Prevalence, Risk, Sensitivity, and Specificity: A Commentary on the Epidemiology of Child Sexual Abuse and the Development of a Research Agenda,"

Departments of Social Medicine and Pediatrics, The University of North Carolina at Chapel Hill School of Medicine, *Child Abuse and Neglect*, vol. 22, no. 6 (1998): 493–498.

2. Runyan, interview with author via email, February 11, 2023.

3. Runyan, email interview.

4. Runyan, email interview.

5. Runyan, email interview.

6. Runyan, email interview.

7. Stephanie Block, PhD, and Line M. Williams, PhD, "The Prosecution of Child Sexual Abuse: A Partnership to Improve Outcomes," National Criminal Justice Reference, Office of Justice Programs, Document 252768 (March 2019): 1, 4, 5, 28.

8. Runyan, email interview with author, February 25, 2023.

9. Runyan, email interview with author, March 1, 2023.

10. Runyan, email interview.

11. Runyan, email interview.

12. Runyan, email interview.

13. Runyan, email interview.

14. Runyan, email interview.

15. Runyan, email interview with author, March 1, 2023.

16. Runyan, email interview.

Chapter 28: The Defense

1. Joseph B Cheshire V, JD, interview via email with the author, January 23, 2023.

2. Edward B. "Bo" Simmons, JD, phone interview with the author, March 1, 2023.

3. Michael Spivey, JD, interview and correspondence with the author, March–September 2023.

4. Jeffrey Miller, JD, interview and correspondence with the author, March–September 2023.

5. *State v. Kelly*, Wayne Forehand Testimony, vol. 31.

6. Miller, interview and correspondence.

Chapter 29: The Mirror Test

    1. Robert F. Kelly Jr. interview by phone with the author, April 2023.

Chapter 30: A Lunch to Remember

    1. Nancy Smith, interview with the author, February 2023.

    2. Betsy Kelly, interview with the author, February 2023.

    3. Robin Couto, interview with the author, February 2023.

Epilogue: The Other Accused

    1. *Isaac of Topsfield and Some of His Descendents*, Augustine Family Tree, Ancestry.com, 2022, and *The New York Genealogical and Biographical Registry: Registration of Pedigree*, Augustine Family Tree, Ancestry.com.

    2. David Saville Muzzey, "New England Settlements," *Legends of America*, 1920, edited 2023, https://www.legendsofamerica.com/ah-newenglandsettlements/.

    3. Rebecca Brooks, "The Witchcraft Trial of Mary Easty," *History of Massachusetts Blog*, https://historyofmassachusetts.org/mary-easty-salem/.

    4. Rebecca Brooks, "History of the Salem Witch Trials," *History of Massachusetts Blog*, https://historyofmassachusetts.org/the-salem-witch-trials/.

    5. Bill O'Reilly and Martin Dugard, *Killing the Witches: The Horror of Salem, Massachusetts* (New York: St. Martin's Press, 2023), 80.

    6. "Salem Witchcraft Papers from the Essex County Courthouse," *Salem Witchtrials* Documentary Archives and Transcripts, vol. 1, no. 163, no. 276, and nos. 280–286, https://salem.lib.virginia.edu/archives/ecca.html.

    7. Ancestry.com, *New England, Salem Witches, and Others Tried for Witchcraft 1647*, 1997. Original information from surviving legal records from the towns and villages in question and appearing in Richard Godbeer's comp. *The Devil's Dominion:*

Magic and Religion Early New England [information taken from Boyer and Nissenbaum, *The Salem Witchcraft Papers: Verbatim transcripts of the Legal Documents of the Salem Witchcraft Outbreak* (New York: Cambridge University Press, 1992)]. Augustine Family Tree. Ancestry.com, 2021–2023.

8. Starkey, *The Devil in Massachusetts*, 206–208.

9. Starkey, *The Devil in Massachusetts*, 258–260.

Additional Sources and Documents for Ancestry Search

- Ancestry.com, genealogical and family history of western New York Vol III, Front Matter, p. 1394, and Essex County Massachusetts Biographies, biographical review, Ancestry.com, 406, accessed 2023.

- Gay Etsy Bangs, "Isaac Esty and Some of his Descendants," Accessed 2023, https://www.ancestry.com/imageviewer/collections/29938/images/dvm_GenMono008534-00002-0?ssrc=&backlabel=Return&pId=2000000000.

- "Etsey Lineage," *The New York Genealogical and Biographical Record. Registration of Pedigree* (1918) Volume XLIX, p. 90, www.ancestry.com.

- Fionnuala Boyle, "Ann Glover—The Irish Laundress Who Was the Last Hanged 'Witch' in Boston," *The Boston Star*, accessed July 2023, https://www.irishstar.com/news/boston-news/ann-glover-irish-laundress-who-30355479.

- "A Husband and Father's Duty," *Essex Institute Historical Collections*, Essex Institute, Peabody Essex Museum, vol. 36, p. 134, www.ancestry.com.

- Jess Blumberg, "A Brief History of the Salem Witch Trials," *Smithsonian Magazine*, October 23, 2007, https://www.smithsonianmag.com/history/a-brief-history-of-the-salem-witch-trials-175162489/.

Betsy Hester lives in Washington, North Carolina. *TWENTY-ONE BOXES*, her first book, is based on a subject she taught to high school English students for more than two decades. She holds a bachelor's in English Education from East Carolina University, has an advanced degree in "Mindfulness for Educators" from Antioch University, and is a nationally board certified educator. Betsy has been honored with numerous teaching awards and taught literature, writing, drama, research, and critical thinking to hundreds of students in Rocky Mount, North Carolina. Now retired, she lives and writes from the home she shares with her husband of forty-two years, Joe, an attorney and the love of her life. They love spending time with their children and grandchildren, riding bicycles, gardening, and doing their part to save the environment.

www.ingramcontent.com/pod-product-compliance
Lightning Source LLC
Chambersburg PA
CBHW032003150726
47990CB00005B/1819